THE
UNPREDICTABLE
CERTAINTY

INFORMATION INFRASTRUCTURE
THROUGH 2000

NII 2000 Steering Committee

Computer Science and Telecommunications Board

Commission on Physical Sciences, Mathematics, and Applications

National Research Council

National Academy Press
Washington, D.C. 1996

Support for this project was provided by the National Science Foundation, the Advanced Projects Research Agency, and the National Institute of Standards and Technology under grant number IRI-9421465. That support does not constitute an endorsement of the views expressed in the report.

Library of Congress Catalog Card Number 96-67383
International Standard Book Number 0-309-05432-X

Additional copies of this report are available from:

National Academy Press
2101 Constitution Avenue, NW
Box 285
Washington, DC 20055
800-624-6242
202-334-3313 (in the Washington Metropolitan Area)
B-728

An electronic version and information about the publication can be found at the NRC World Wide Web site http://www.nas.edu.

NII 2000 STEERING COMMITTEE

LEWIS M. BRANSCOMB, Harvard University, *Chair*
CYNTHIA H. BRADDON, The McGraw Hill Companies
JAMES A. CHIDDIX, Time Warner Cable
DAVID D. CLARK, Massachusetts Institute of Technology
JOSEPH A. FLAHERTY, CBS Incorporated
PAUL E. GREEN, JR., IBM T.J. Watson Research Center
IRENE GREIF, Lotus Development Corporation
RICHARD T. LIEBHABER, MCI Communications (retired)
ROBERT W. LUCKY, Bell Communications Research
LLOYD N. MORRISETT, John and Mary Markle Foundation
DONALD W. SIMBORG, KnowMed Systems
LESLIE L. VADASZ, Intel Corporation

Staff

MARJORY S. BLUMENTHAL, Director
LOUISE A. ARNHEIM, Senior Staff Officer (through August 1995)
JOHN M. GODFREY, Research Associate
LESLIE M. WADE, Research Assistant
GLORIA P. BEMAH, Administrative Assistant

The National Academy of Sciences is a private, nonprofit, self-perpetuating society of distinguished scholars engaged in scientific and engineering research, dedicated to the furtherance of science and technology and to their use for the general welfare. Upon the authority of the charter granted to it by Congress in 1863, the Academy has a mandate that requires it to advise the federal government on scientific and technical matters. Dr. Bruce Alberts is president of the National Academy of Sciences.

The National Academy of Engineering was established in 1964, under the charter of the National Academy of Sciences, as a parallel organization of outstanding engineers. It is autonomous in its administration and in the selection of its members, sharing with the National Academy of Sciences the responsibility for advising the federal government. The National Academy of Engineering also sponsors engineering programs aimed at meeting national needs, encourages education and research, and recognizes the superior achievements of engineers. Dr. Harold Liebowitz is president of the National Academy of Engineering.

The Institute of Medicine was established in 1970 by the National Academy of Sciences to secure the services of eminent members of appropriate professions in the examination of policy matters pertaining to the health of the public. The Institute acts under the responsibility given to the National Academy of Sciences by its congressional charter to be an adviser to the federal government and, upon its own initiative, to identify issues of medical care, research, and education. Dr. Kenneth I. Shine is president of the Institute of Medicine.

The National Research Council was organized by the National Academy of Sciences in 1916 to associate the broad community of science and technology with the Academy's purposes of furthering knowledge and advising the federal government. Functioning in accordance with general policies determined by the Academy, the Council has become the principal operating agency of both the National Academy of Sciences and the National Academy of Engineering in providing services to the government, the public, and the scientific and engineering communities. The Council is administered jointly by both Academies and the Institute of Medicine. Dr. Bruce Alberts and Dr. Harold Liebowitz are chairman and vice chairman, respectively, of the National Research Council.

Preface

In October 1994, the Computer Science and Telecommunications Board convened, at the request of the Technology Policy Working Group (TPWG) of the Information Infrastructure Task Force, a steering committee to assess medium-term deployment of facilities and services to advance the nation's information infrastructure. The project was designated NII 2000 by the steering committee, and its tasks were the following:

- To reach out to a broad range of industries with a stake in the future of U.S. information infrastructure—those industries expected to be major market drivers as well as those expected to be major service providers—to explore their expectations and motivations for technology deployment in the next 5 to 7 years;
- To infer from this exploration the extent to which there is a shared vision of the importance of common features of system architecture, such as interoperability or open system interfaces, and the alternative likelihood that major parts of the system will develop along proprietary, incompatible lines; and
- To conclude with suggestions to the U.S. government on public policy choices that might serve both the rapid, orderly, and successful development of information infrastructure and its satisfaction of important public interests.

To achieve these goals, the steering committee was asked by the TPWG to undertake a specific series of activities: convene a workshop of professionals and scholars to discuss and identify key issues related to technology deployment, call for white papers to gain further information on these issues, organize a forum to discuss the white papers and other key ideas, and write a synthesis report of its findings. As a preliminary step, the steering committee solicited inputs and suggestions via liaisons (listed in Appendix E) from trade, professional, and advocacy organizations, as well as government agencies, beginning in late 1994.

The workshop, which was held in Washington, D.C., on January 17-18, 1995, brought together invited members from business, industry, and interest groups as well as federal government representatives. Panels during the 2-day proceedings focused on technology deployment, end-user hardware and software issues, domain-specific applications, the Internet as a national information infrastructure (NII) model, and what different industries meant when they used certain terms and concepts. For example, "architecture," "programming," "service," and "network" are among the many fundamental terms (see Box 1.2 in Chapter 1 for a longer list) that are defined differently by different industries. See Appendix A for the workshop agenda and a list of participants.

Following the workshop, the steering committee released a call for white papers (Appendix C) on issues related to architecture and facilities, enabling technologies, recovery of costs, middleware technologies and capabilities, applications, equitable access and public service obligations, and research and development. The call was distributed through various media (the Internet, press advisories, direct mail, and so on) to producers of communications, computer, and software systems goods and services; Internet access and other network-based service providers; scholars specializing in relevant technical, economic, and public policy research and analysis; and project liaisons and other representatives of industries and sectors believed likely to become major users of advanced information infrastructure (such as the arts, banking and finance, education, health care, government agencies, libraries, manufacturing, and transportation). The white papers (see Appendix D for a list of papers received and their authors) were distributed to participants at the spring forum and to interested federal agencies. Their content, representing a broad spectrum of views from knowledgeable participants in the evolution of information infrastructure, was a major component in the development of the steering committee's report, which quotes from and refers specifically to several of them. The white papers will be made available in a forthcoming companion volume.

Shortly after the call for papers was issued, the steering committee received a letter (Appendix F) from Vice President Albert Gore underscoring the high-level interest in the project's potential to generate "an objective assessment of the capabilities of different residential broadband architectures (e.g., hybrid fiber coaxial cable, fiber to the curb, and wireless alternatives) being deployed by the private sector." Explained the Vice President, "We would like to see an NII that allows individuals to be producers as well as consumers of information, that enables 'many to many' communication, and that provides a 'general purpose' infrastructure capable of supporting a wide range of services."

The Vice President's letter contributed to the steering committee's preparations for the spring 1995 forum, which was structured to assess the difficulties inherent in developing a nationwide information infrastructure built largely with private resources, but having the capacity to further social and economic goals as well. (See Appendix B for the forum agenda and a list of participants). Like the evolving NII itself, the forum embraced a range of models that provided different perspectives on the possible roles of infrastructure: one-to-many distribution of large quantities of preselected video, combinations of television and telephony to support interactive programming, one-to-one voice telephony augmented by a variety of conveniences, many-to-many explorations over computer networks, most notably the Internet, and many-to-one interactions between consumers and information sources over the World Wide Web, in particular.

This synthesis report represents the collective view of 12 experts who monitored and participated in a unique public policy undertaking. The NII 2000 project was an experiment of sorts, an attempt to hold other issues constant by focusing attention on technological and business models. Although each of the following elements is part of the overall NII "story," this report is not a description of an optimistic vision of future possibilities and benefits for various business and nonprofit entities, for the purpose of motivating interest in the NII; an analysis of legal and regulatory barriers to competition; or an attempt to resolve broad policy concerns such as universal access or the democratization of cyberspace. Nevertheless, comments from many contributors to the project convey the message that a complete assessment of NII deployment, and the role of government as well as industry in its evolution, must take these issues into consideration to at least some degree.

Finally, it is also important to state that the NII 2000 Steering Committee's synthesis report is a technology deployment "road map" only in the most metaphorical sense. Participants described many roads, or in some cases territory through which roads might be constructed, but most of these roads have unknown, indeed unknowable, destinations. As the TPWG's Howard Frank observed at the January 1995 workshop:

The government is not doing a road map that says how do we get from here to there. . . . If you look at the United States, and look at the interstate highway road map, or look at the road map of all of the roads in the United States, you can see that no path is dictated; there are a variety of ways of moving, as opposed to a specific formula. What we are trying to do is identify those capabilities and metrics of an NII, and the barriers associated with those various roads, [so that] we could speed the creation of the NII and eliminate some of the barriers.

The NII 2000 Steering Committee shares this view. Like Howard Frank, we do not know where "there" is, and we observe many forks in the roads we can see. We do believe, however, that the future offers many very attractive options for U.S. society and its many business communities, if government and private interests collaborate in understanding how to enable that future to emerge in a way that best satisfies each other's needs, concerns, and expectations.

This report is an effort to explore the limits of consensus on a broad array of fast-changing issues. As a result, it benefits from the work of many individuals, among them the participants in the January 1995 workshop and the May 1995 forum, and the authors of the white papers. We are grateful to them for the level and range of expertise they brought to the project. The steering committee gratefully acknowledges the assistance of several individuals and organizations, including Rupert Stow, who provided numerous suggestions for enhancing the discussion of broadcasting; Stewart Personick, who provided insights into technical and business perspectives from telephony; Duane Adams and Howard Frank, whose vision motivated and guided the establishment of the project; Y.T. Chien, John Hestenes, and Michael Papillo, whose ongoing questioning and suggestions on behalf of the TPWG provided regular encouragement and feedback; the liaisons, particularly Michael Roberts of EDUCOM, Suzanne Tichenor of the Council on Competitiveness, and Charles Brownstein of the Corporation for National Research Initiatives' Cross-Industry Working Team; and of course the anonymous reviewers, whose criticisms, reflections, and suggestions were essential to the strengthening of this final report.

The members of the steering committee devoted much of their time for about a year to formulating the project and guiding its conduct. But more importantly, each member brought a level of professional knowledge and competence from many areas of technology, allowing the project to be authoritative in its coverage. I am particularly grateful to one member of the steering committee, David Clark of MIT, who gave much more than his share of devotion to this project, frequently filling in for the chairman. But the most especial thanks from all the steering committee members is due to Marjory Blumenthal, leader of a fine team from the

CSTB and now a recognized authority on public policy issues related to information technology. Among all of us, she should be considered the principal author of this work. Other members of the CSTB team to whom our appreciation is owed are John Godfrey, who amassed and analyzed considerable amounts of technology and industry data; Gloria Bemah, who tracked the large number of participants and documents associated with the project; Pamela Rodgers, who orchestrated the logistics for the spring forum; Leslie Wade, who transformed the draft into a fully documented and appropriately formatted final report; and Susan Maurizi, whose editorial assistance helped make this report more readable.

Lewis Branscomb, *Chair*
NII 2000 Steering Committee

Contents

THE
UNPREDICTABLE
CERTAINTY

INFORMATION INFRASTRUCTURE
THROUGH 2000

Wanderer, your footsteps are
the road, and nothing more;
wanderer, there is no road,
the road is made by walking.

Selected Poems by Antonio Machado,
translated by Betty Jean Craige
Louisiana State University Press, Baton Rouge, 1978

1

Introduction and Summary

DEFINING THE NATIONAL INFORMATION INFRASTRUCTURE

Are there any dominant trends in the evolution of a global or national information infrastructure (NII) for which there is no specification, no overall plan, and no institutional mechanism for reaching consensus about what it is or what it should be? That question motivated the NII 2000 project, which sought to characterize the technology deployment, market expectations, and proposed activities of communications and information facilities and service providers over the next 5 to 7 years. Perspectives provided directly by these suppliers—drawn from multiple industries—were complemented by inputs from a cross section of users in industry, private nonprofit organizations, and the public sector. The diverse inputs on deployment plans and prospects revealed that there are as many visions of the information future as there are sectors of the economy helping to create them.

Today, the range of players, starting positions, and strategies underscores the fact that the information infrastructure is not static; it is evolving in ways that reflect its initial components as well as ambitions for its growth. It is nearly impossible to overstate the implications of the combination of powerful low-cost microprocessors, high-capacity multistream digital servers, low-cost memory and digital storage media, and broadband connections to and from homes and businesses. Each of these capabilities is advancing quite rapidly, and the combination of them makes possible an enormous number of applications, some clearly seen and some as yet unimagined. There will be missteps and failures, along with full and partial successes, but the technology and its uses will advance steadily.

History tells us that systems as complex as a nation's information infrastructure evolve incrementally, driven by private investment in the pursuit of unrealized opportunities, consensus-based public needs, and countless entrepreneurs testing the system for natural niches, for unique sources of customer value. Given that future plans are marked by diversity of vision and action, is the NII itself a paradigm that is losing its lustre? Perhaps, if it is interpreted to refer to conformance with a grand plan, which appears increasingly unrealistic.

Given a future only partly seen, how shall we characterize the NII? The steering committee for the NII 2000 project sees no choice but to define the NII broadly and inclusively:

> The national information infrastructure (NII) is the collection of all public and private information services—both facilities- and content-based—operating as a complex, dynamic system. It exists today but is and always will be in a state of flux.

Since more and more devices, systems, and processes will contain computing elements and be interconnected in some way, it is important that the NII be defined early on as being inclusive. Of course, the global information infrastructure of which it is a part extends the notion of inclusiveness geographically, technologically, and economically.

Rather than a single coherent technical framework, the NII is a concept to focus thinking about a very important set of resources whose value to society depends on their connectivity, accessibility, and functionality for many important purposes.[1] This view of the NII admits to different perspectives, as expressed by various readers of an early draft of this report. Box 1.1 gives two examples. In particular, perspectives differ significantly across industries. Approaches to testing new markets are as different as conducting market trials for integrated multiservice packages and making new applications available on the Internet. But the difference between the personal computer (PC) vision and the set-top box vision is not about the detailed technical choices to be made; it concerns instead a choice about the role of infrastructure—should infrastructure deliver a particular service (e.g., telephony or television), or should it enable the creation of entirely new services via general-purpose (e.g., Internet) services?—and differences in the funding model (identify a specific "killer app," or assume that the aggregate of the demand will come from millions of customer uses, none of which is important by itself). Symptomatic of the many differences among industries are semantic disagreements

BOX 1.1
The NII: What Is in a Name? A Range of Reactions

"NII," in my thinking, is a rallying phrase, not to be confused with or perceived as a tangible definable entity. It is not a predetermined universal architecture or even an orchestrated collection of interworking architectures to be furthered by some form of consensus, even at the highest level. NII . . . is the sum of countless U.S. and global initiatives, driven by continuous intellectual discovery, and by conceptualization, development, and implementation of a wide variety of applications and services. "NII" is founded in scientific curiosity, social need, historic experience, national character and goals, standard-of-living expectations, the needs of individual users and of corporations and organizations, security requirements, profit motives, current and future national economy considerations, global policies, and so on. The list is very lengthy. . . .

—Thomas Plevyak, Bell Atlantic

[Beware falling] victim to the tendency in Washington to add coats to every available coat hook. The NII cannot possibly be the sum of all of our expectations for a better society based on improved communications and electronic information. Even if someone were capable of articulating a vision of that scope, none of the rest of us would grant him or her the power to execute it. What we can have, what is doable, what we can build reasonable consensus around, is a "system of electronic communications and information resources based on computing technology." Despite efforts by many to promote ideological visions of what the system can do for society, the system is fundamentally amoral. Much of its development has been, and will continue to be, based on technological Darwinism. . . . I have two suggestions. Don't refer to the NII as an "it." At best, the NII is a complex system of systems spanning a variety of new and older technologies and consequently never embodying the holy grail of developers—a "single system image." Secondly, be cautious in using terms that have been captured by social and political visionaries and already have emotional baggage attached.

—Michael Roberts, EDUCOM

that confound public debate and private sector interactions. Box 1.2 lists terms that are fundamental to information infrastructure but subject to differing definitions and usage among industries.

Does a broadly encompassing definition of the NII preclude any expectation of effective interoperation of the parts of the NII? To what extent will a more or less integrated nationwide system of computer network services be able to attract users and capital investment? Had these questions been posed, say, 5 years ago, the answers would have been more divergent. Today, the answers reflect the extraordinary impact of the Internet, which has become increasingly attractive for commercial activities over the past 2 years.[2] The Internet is a critical component of many of the business plans of industrial contributors to this project. Ad-

---

BOX 1.2
Vocabulary Test: Key Terms on Which Many Differ

ABSTRACT	INTERACTIVE/INTERACTIVITY
ACCESS	INTERFACE
ACCESS CIRCUIT/SUBSCRIBER	INTEROPERABILITY
LOOP/DROP	LOCAL/RESIDENTIAL/PERSONAL
ARCHITECTURE	MARKET FORCES
ATM	MODALITIES
BACK-CHANNEL/UPSTREAM/	MULTICAST
RETURN PATH/UPCHANNEL	MULTIMEDIA
BROADBAND	NETWORK
BUNDLING/UNBUNDLING	OPEN
COMPETITION/COMPETITIVE	PROGRAMMING
CONSUMER	SCALABLE
COST	SEAMLESS
DOMAIN	SERVICE
FLEXIBLE	SOFTWARE
FULL-SERVICE NETWORK	TECHNOLOGY
GATEWAY	UNIVERSAL (ACCESS, SERVICE)
GENERAL	USER

---

ditionally, the steering committee notes an increasing recognition in all sectors of industry that interconnection and interoperation are a powerful stimulus to content creation, ubiquitous communication, and the opening of new markets. Thus, despite multiple visions and definitions, the steering committee concluded that there is a good chance of attaining a "seamless web" with interoperable facilities and services that compose a *subset* of the larger NII,[3] as broadly defined above. The Internet protocols will help to achieve this outcome. Other components will probably remain disconnected, proprietary, vertically integrated business "towers."

This chapter provides an overview of the key issues and findings covered in the NII 2000 project. Like the rest of the report, it draws on inputs gathered via a workshop, forum, white papers, and a variety of consultations and secondary source materials. It relates technological capabilities to evolving plans for business strategy, competition, and structure, characterizing private sector views and stated plans to illuminate opportunities for the public sector. It explains why the Internet and also federally supported research and development came to play a greater role in the project and in the steering committee's assessment than originally anticipated.

DRIVING DEPLOYMENT:
BUSINESS TRANSITIONS, BUSINESS MODELS

The opportunities presented by the evolving information infrastructure are as speculative as they are rich: enormous technical, business, and public policy uncertainties about the future face investors, the public, and policy makers. The communications and information marketplaces are changing as technologies converge and the production processes of different industries overlap increasingly.

Today, the most widely used information systems—telephones, television (cable and broadcast), and, to a lesser extent, hard-copy publication (e.g., print, videocassettes, compact disks)—are mature services resting on many billions of dollars of installed equipment. Their viability depends on the continuing provision of services to established consumers and business users at profit-making prices; they attract investment because growth in profit is anticipated. As a result, the business plans of many established communications and information service suppliers appear to center on extending existing high-revenue business offerings such as telephony and video delivery, upgrading the underlying facilities, and hoping to be properly positioned if and when new applications mature. (De)regulation permitting, cable TV will be able to deliver interactive services and voice telephony. Telephone companies will offer video delivery. Cellular services will become digital, as they already are in many other countries around the world, and will evolve to personal communication services. Digital broadcast satellites will eventually acquire practical uplinks and offer interactivity.

It is not surprising, considering the magnitude of the capital investments anticipated for new infrastructure, that telephone and cable TV companies are each viewing the other's business as attractive, since these are mature businesses generating billions of dollars in revenues, representing major sources of capital for expanding the NII (although there is no evidence that the revenue pool will grow in proportion to the number of providers). Nor is it surprising that both sectors are planning on initial growth in applications that constitute modest and incremental extensions of current lines of business (TV on demand, games, home shopping, passive access to information).

New information infrastructure markets are characterized by a large number of small players, who divide the total (initially limited) revenues. Will the information infrastructure market follow the pattern seen in PC software, in which a large pool of providers shrinks to a few dominant players after only 3 to 4 years? The prospects for competitive losses, combined with economies of scale and scope, immature applications, and a skeptical public, suggest that, as is often the case with maturing markets, a shakeout among information infrastructure providers will eventually result.

Many sectors of the information industry (notably print publishing and broadcast television) will find the new environment highly disruptive—even threatening—as well as filled with potential for new activities. Others whose businesses bring together consumers with goods and services produced by others may also be challenged. When customers themselves have direct access (of the type envisioned via the NII), the previous intermediary either is eliminated or becomes a facilitator rather than a dispenser of knowledge.

In agreement with most of the industry experts contributing to this project, the steering committee believes that the future information infrastructure will provide more than just basic telephony and entertainment: a wide range of applications will combine to form the economic base of the NII (see Box 1.3). This broader vision implies that existing facilities will be used in fundamentally transformed ways. In particular, termination of the network in affordable but powerful computing devices will create an inherently more general-purpose communication environment. At the same time, new physical facilities will have to be built to provide expanded interactive bandwidth to more users.

Virtually all industries and public institutions will use the NII to do their work better, often in quite industry-specific ways that will implicitly increase demand for information infrastructure. Examples from contemporary experience include pharmaceutical companies incorporating communications facilities and services into delivery of drug information to physicians and hospitals, and banks incorporating communications into on-line retail banking, bill paying, and investing. The business models associated with such embedded service delivery ultimately may bring far greater resources to the NII than will the direct user fees that support the current infrastructure. But that supposition is difficult to quantify, given the difficulties various industry sectors experience in characterizing their future infrastructure service requirements.

Facilities providers contemplating major investments to create the next generation of networks want to ensure that there will be reasonable ways to recover their costs. Some are creating and testing new applications that they hope will be broad enough to adapt to new markets. Still others are holding back until the crystal ball becomes considerably less cloudy. Market trials have attempted to probe the attractiveness (as well as the performance and cost-effectiveness of delivery technologies) of new forms of network-based entertainment and shopping as well as educational and other "public interest" services. But results reported are not encouraging—the trials are bounded by the lack of genuine novelty in the former and a lack of substance in the latter.[4]

BOX 1.3
Tenets of the Information Society

If NII technology deployment will be driven by multiple applications, what might we expect to see? The steering committee collected many inputs that echo or amplify frequently cited tenets of the "information society":

• Customers for goods, services, and information in every sphere of everyday life will want to be able to influence the form and makeup of some of the information they consume, while continuing to be passive recipients of other, prepackaged information products. They will also use more avenues to send out more kinds of information to others. For example, it will become routine to generate and transmit video for personal (business and pleasure) as well as job- or education-related purposes.

• Personalization of information and communication services will be a key consequence of the availability of computer intelligence to almost every individual through a variety of devices. An important impetus will be significant changes in available wireless systems, from two-way paging to wireless links for text or video communications.

• The distinctions among the workplace, home, and schools will continue to erode as part of a broader blurring of the association between activities and locations and the broader penetration of computing and communications in all manner of jobs and activities. Public data networks will provide a key mechanism to (1) integrate widely separated work locations into collaborative institutions, (2) allow the office or business transaction to extend to the home and to many other off-site locations (nomadic computing), and (3) allow the home to become the base for a wide variety of entrepreneurial work (and public service) activities. When coupled with rapidly expanding wireless capabilities, the end result will be a truly anywhere, anytime workplace.

• Professional activities and services will increasingly be supported—and perhaps transformed—by information networks, merging education and professional service delivery, improving efficiency and enhancing the quality of work undertaken by a wide range of paraprofessionals, and increasing the consumer's ability to obtain desired information directly. Similar phenomena will transform citizen participation in the political process in ways that are hard to foresee.

Facilities providers are stymied by the prospect of financing an infrastructure that will be characterized increasingly by low marginal costs for use but large fixed costs for facilities deployment, a problem that regulatory reform will not solve.[5,6] The difficulties with justifying investment are most serious for providers of access circuits to individual residences and small businesses. Given that almost all the wireline options for access technology cost the same to within 20 or 30 percent, it is possible to form a rough guess as to the monthly fee needed to recover these costs. All current forms of wireline residential access technology, if installed new, cost about $1,000 per home passed, which seems to imply a monthly fee near $30. The only alternative that might give a lower price under some circumstances is wireless, which has the advantage that it involves less major investment up front and thus could support emerging markets with lower initial penetration.

It was further noted in the project's workshop, forum, and white papers that an important role for research and development in this context is to explore network and information access technologies that would alter costs and capabilities over the long term. Reducing per-home access costs by a factor of two, a cost reduction that (for constant function) occurs in the computer industry at intervals of less than 2 years, would change completely the prospects for rapid deployment of advanced broadband services to the home. However, the cost structure of the access circuit appears to be driven by factors other than those that help to reduce computer costs, and has indeed remained stubbornly constant for some time.

The consequence of uncertainty about future network and information requirements and the potential for profitability is hesitation in planning for future infrastructure investments. In this respect, there has been a marked change over the last 5 years, at least in public posture. What was, a few years ago, the vision of a rewired America, to be accomplished as a single planned reengineering over a fairly small number of years, has become a much more incremental plan for experimentation and upgrades. This more incremental approach to investment, which is discussed in Chapter 3, is probably more realistic than the earlier visions (and indeed those earlier plans may never have been as concrete as some of the media discussions suggested).[7] It has the advantage that instead of a single massive upgrade to some chosen new technology, which then becomes obsolete over time, it involves smaller staged investments that bring in a series of new technologies. This incremental process could establish a pattern of continuous technology upgrade as justified by proven market demand. However, it will almost certainly lead to a slower and more measured pace of investment and deployment. One of the steering committee's conclusions is that timing, as much as direction, is the major uncertainty in the current planning for the NII.

The divergence of opinion concerning the relative need for one-way communication, primarily for entertainment, and two-way communication, for various sorts of interactive uses, was a major theme of the workshop and the forum. A basic uncertainty is the rate at which upstream capacity (from the user into the network) will be required to support emerging two-way applications such as provision of information by individuals and interactive "telework" support. The concern is whether sufficient two-way bandwidth can be made available at affordable rates and whether lack of bandwidth will stifle the emergence of important new applications, especially those involving sharing of images and video. Perceptions of the true market demand will influence deployment decisions and will thus shape the ways in which end users in homes and independent offices can participate in a society that will depend increasingly on interactive electronic communications.

Reflecting the prominence of such concerns, one area where experimentation is notable and where multiple approaches may coexist for the foreseeable future is cost recovery. At least five different but overlapping economic models, representing different ways to allocate cost, are evident in the information infrastructure at large and in the Internet in particular: (1) usage-based fees (e.g., metered telephone service; consumer pays by the minute); (2) access subscription (e.g., cable or flat-rate telephone subscription; consumer pays by the month); (3) broadcast (e.g., TV and radio; advertiser pays by the minute, consumer does not pay for service per se); (4) end-user device-centered (e.g., PC-owning consumer pays for unlimited use of a device, including use that is independent of network-based services); and (5) embedded (cost is hidden in some other, possibly domain-specific, service; consumer leases set-top box in conjunction with purchased TV). The fates of these models may help to determine which businesses and industries endure or advance in the information infrastructure marketplace and, given their different capacities for generating returns on investment, how quickly underlying facilities are enhanced.

THE SIGNIFICANCE OF THE INTERNET

Much of the current excitement about information infrastructure and the convergence of many communications and information technologies to a digital basis has been catalyzed by the Internet. Thus, understanding the Internet may be key to understanding many of the opportunities in the NII.

Is the Internet a model for a commercially dominated interoperable infrastructure, or is it a remarkable but transitory development from the world of research and education? The steering committee concluded that the Internet is indeed a prototype for much of the emerging information infrastructure, despite its roots in experimentation and its current (but not necessarily enduring) limitations. Its future is evolution, not replacement.

What is the Internet? It is a network of many kinds of networks. But to understand its importance it is better to think of it as a capability for internetworking, allowing any user to find, touch, and if desired connect to a large variety of networks and the sources of information, users, and computational resources that each makes available.

As a Barometer of Potential

The number of Internet access service firms has been growing very rapidly, as has Internet access activity (e.g., acquisition of Internet addresses), although no one knows for sure how much of this growth is driven by faddism as opposed to enduring demand for access and associated goods and services. The most frequently cited illustration of the economic (and deployment) impact of the Internet is its role as the underpinning for the World Wide Web (Web), which has made the Internet easier to use and more broadly meaningful. The Web appears to provide what PC owners have always wanted: the capability to point, click, and get what they want no matter where it is. Whereas earlier manifestations of the information revolution bypassed many people who were uncomfortable with computing technology, it appears that the Web is now attracting a large cross section of people, making the universality of information infrastructure a more realistic prospect. If the Web is a first wave (or a second, if the Internet alone is a first), it is likely that further advances in utility and application will follow. Once people are comfortable finding information on the Internet, they will discover that they want much more: they will want help in locating reliable, useful information; they will want to discuss it with others, build communities around it, generate it, and so on. These activities will create demand for more applications and for different kinds of interactivity, formats, media, and so on. Box 1.3 suggests how technology and changing approaches to work, education, and recreation in the "information society" can continue to coevolve.

A powerful appeal of the Internet as a prototype for the new information environment is that innovators can take relatively small risks while still accessing a huge potential market. The economics of telecommunications facilities deployment contrasts markedly with that of the Internet, whose current state reflects a unique set of economic conditions: tremendous market access has been achievable with a very small initial investment, an advantage that has led to a wide range of experimentation and innovation. Combining low barriers to entry with unusually high potential for growth in usage volume, the Internet has been an extraordinary platform for innovation, one that is perhaps unique in human history.

However, a central conundrum at the present is that the Internet, with its very low cost of entry, must operate on top of expensive physical communications infrastructure. As discussed above, very large investments are required up front to achieve any substantial upgrade in U.S.

communications facilities, and without this investment the Internet itself, and the other possibilities for exploitation of the infrastructure, cannot flourish.

As a Laboratory for Development of Workable Standards

The Internet also demonstrates the remarkable potential (although perhaps the outer limits) for evolutionary standards development and implementation in concert with rapid technological change. In particular, many of the important Internet standards were not adopted until they worked in a real-life environment and passed the test of performance and scaling. Those standards processes and the associated architectural principles embodied in the Internet derive from the long-term involvement of a relatively small community of computer scientists, funded largely by the federal government, who saw the Internet as a collaborative enterprise in which they served as designers, developers, and users. They understood that the large number of alternative paths for technological evolution meant that standards must be open to technological change, anticipate future innovations, and either accommodate them or minimize the cost of accommodating them later.[8]

The current Internet standards development process is subject to a number of stresses that are a source of concern. Although there is no clear case for intervention, the process should be monitored. Because computer scientists are no longer representative users of the Internet, the technologists most active in Internet standards setting may be somewhat removed from the needs and preferences of diverse users. Conversely, the users who need standards are no longer mostly computer or other kinds of scientists, and their increasing involvement in the Internet Engineering Task Force standards process has led to a much balkier and more balkanized process. At the same time, increasing commercial interest in the Internet is creating pressures for alternatives to standards that are proprietary or that are defined by dominant industry players.

As a Basis for Critical Flexibility

Although to many people the Internet is synonymous with its applications, such as public or open electronic messaging or the World Wide Web, the power and utility of the Internet actually derive from its internal organization, the way the protocols and functions are designed and organized. The basis of its flexibility is that it defines a simple service interface that any application can use to request network service from whatever network technology is in use. Since this interface is independent of underlying technology details, and also independent of specific applications, it allows new applications to be devised and deployed, thus stimulating innovation in network technology. The 1994 Computer Science and Telecommunications Board report *Realizing the Information Future* (RTIF; CSTB, 1994b) advocated an open interface with these characteristics to support innovation of new network applications. The report called this interface the technology-independent bearer service and called the network that would result from providing this interface the Open Data Network, or ODN. The Internet features an ODN architecture, with a form of the bearer service in its Internet protocol.

In the course of the NII 2000 project, the steering committee heard repeatedly that the Internet standards are the basis on which new applications are being crafted. The current volume of deployed devices using the Internet standards, together with the observed level of investment in Internet-related products and services, constitutes a unique foundation, one for which there is no alternative now or in the next decade. The steering committee has concluded, based on its assessment of industry trends, that the call for an open, technology-independent bearer service as a basis for emerging applications, as voiced in RTIF, was correct. Now, moreover, a more concrete conclusion is justified: the Internet standards are in fact being widely used for this purpose and are regarded by a great majority of commercial players as the only viable option for an open, application-independent set of service interfaces at this time. Thus the Internet and the protocols on which it is based are critical components of the evolving NII.

As a Vehicle for New Market Structures

The Internet is but one example of the transformation now occuring in the marketplace, a transition arising from the ability of new service providers as well as existing infrastructure providers to make new services available by layering them on top of existing communications infrastructure. Innovation in services layered over physical (and virtual) facilities and offered by the same or different providers will flourish, reflecting the increasing dependence on software as a service-creating technology, as well as increasing ability to reap value from information.[9]

It is unclear at this stage how the various players—service and facility providers—will align, integrate, or interoperate.[10] Marginal costs and prices for communications services can be expected to fall as the use of digital technology and (assuming deregulation) competition increase. Communications firms may attempt to integrate vertically to take advantage of the higher profit margins possible in providing proprietary content, or they may choose to purvey the content of others but seek to control their market through proprietary access to their customers. Such business structures may not be conducive to open, interoperable arrangements and meaningful competition.

While business pressures may motivate attempts at vertical integration, there are countervailing forces for open competitive service interfaces. For the first time in the history of the computer industry, virtually all computers speak according to the same set of protocols, and content providers can write their applications to get their information to their users using a set of standards that are independent of the underlying media. The content provider (e.g., the publisher and editor or broker or repackager) seeking to reach the maximum number of subscribers will pressure the telecommunications providers to interoperate with their competitors if need be. The telecommunications providers, if they want to play, have to support these protocols—and they are doing so. Hence, interoperability may be a natural competitive outcome of stratification of content and conduit providers.

These pressures will play out as the various components of the NII evolve over the next decade. The Internet is an example of open interfaces providing a structure for a set of business sectors—facilities, Internet service, and applications. The availability of standard interfaces permitting interoperability will define the structure of the industries providing information infrastructure as much as any technology-based process can, but it is also the case that the structure of the businesses will define the interfaces, and therefore the degree of openness for the infrastructure over time.

Whither the Internet?

If the Internet is to continue to meet user requirements over the next decade, it must evolve in a number of ways. Some of these involve aspects of the current structure that are inadequate and need to be fixed (for instance, current Internet protocol addresses are too short); some involve the need to add new features for which possible approaches are well understood (for instance, end-to-end security); and some require major advances (for instance, a capability for intellectual property rights protection). The need for these various sorts of advances suggests the importance both of continued R&D and of a vigorous standards-development process.

The widespread call for better security on the Internet covers needs ranging from protection against system penetration to trustworthy transfer of information and protection of intellectual property. Although security is a concern for all information infrastructure, the open nature of the Internet in general as well as specific features of its evolving technology underscore the challenges to security in the Internet context. It is not yet clear how the necessary protections will be provided, especially given the importance of transnational communications, but advances are being made. Despite such concerns, lack of better security has not actually halted the expansion of the Internet; while efforts are being made to increase security, individuals and organizations are tailoring their use to the level and kind of protections available.

The transition of the Internet to a competitively provided commercial service has raised many questions about models, options, and expectations. Some, including long-time Internet players monitoring changes in network performance, have expressed fears about the prospect of unstable service, due to issues such as incoherent routing and other technical or business concerns. As commercial providers begin to keep operating statistics secret, it has become much more difficult to gather overall information on usage, such as the growth rates and usage patterns of different applications, which would facilitate long-term planning by all parties.

In terms of the broader operating environment, it appears to some that the community of shared interests represented a very valuable, but rare, historical opportunity, and we must now figure out how to develop shared, interoperable infrastructures without that type of user-developer community. Private and public actions should recognize how the Internet development process has factored into U.S. competitiveness in key markets. For example, leadership in creating and implementing key NII standards relates to leadership in the hardware and software that the United States exports.[11] This value is implicit in federal support of Internet standards setting.

REALIZING THE NII'S POTENTIAL—THE USER PERSPECTIVE

Enthusiasm about the NII is tempered by concerns about the difficulty of realizing its promised benefits in large application domains such as health care or education, let alone in the more diffuse context of individual citizens seeking access from their homes. After hearing several presentations by infrastructure facilities providers, emergency response expert Lois Clark McCoy observed: "I didn't hear the word 'user,' and I didn't hear, 'What does the user want?' I heard, 'This is what we're going to give you,' as well as a great deal of discussion about the tools, such as fiber optics and cellular, and about how the service was going to be provided." These observations point out a tendency for public debates to focus generally on the supply side, as well as the considerable and differing challenges in adopting new infrastructure within individual application domains. Industry sectors that may become big users of the NII—as represented by manufacturing, health care, education, and emergency response, for example—see barriers to progress that leave them with a sense of frustration.

New applications may well come from specific user communities or domains, but their development is snared in a "catch 22." Large-scale implementation and associated acceptance in the market await not only strategies for overcoming the constraints of traditional processes linked to legacy systems, but also the development of standards for data (for elements ranging from terminology to presentation), codes of practice, sector-specific institutional and market structures, and the removal of legal and/or institutional barriers within individual domains. Thus information services can improve health care delivery and lower its trillion-dollar cost, but only if they become integral to the processes associated with delivering health care. A similar situation exists for educational computing and communications, which already show the considerable influence of the emerging information infrastructure.

Providers of NII facilities do not appear to see as their concern the removal of domain-specific barriers to adoption of network-based applications; such matters go far beyond supplying networking facilities and services. Yet inputs from professionals from several specific communities eyeing the NII evolution suggested that the lack of apparent interest from infrastructure providers has compounded already slow progress in resolving cultural, content presentation, legal, and other barriers to use.

For example, sector-specific and broad-based standards and approaches must go hand in hand. There are hundreds, perhaps thousands, of niche information markets specialized by subject matter, corresponding to every industry sector and to every professional and skill category. They have specialized needs for data standards and sector-specific approaches, but with rare exceptions, each requires access to general information and information from neighboring niches or the larger sector or domain in which it fits, as well as specialized material. Consequently, even niche markets need communication access to other parts of the economy, and niche market providers will probably use general-purpose network capabilities and standards for achieving that access. Thus, infrastructure providers may have a greater interest in domain-specific circumstances than may appear obvious.

Although the steering committee heard considerable frustration and concern from key business domains about the current difficulties of utilizing the NII, this perspective should be viewed in the context of the current large business market for telecommunications. For example, business customers account for about 60 percent of carrier revenues (see U.S. Bureau of the Census, 1995). Large companies in particular are already purchasing bit transport services at wholesale, and they frequently invest in their own facilities. Large businesses thus clearly have access to the current information infrastructure and are starting to take advantage of it.

In contrast, one of the key concerns voiced at the forum and workshop was whether (or when) the reach of high-bandwidth networks and advanced services would extend to the home and small business, which are important locations for many of the business domains that voiced frustration with access and utility, such as health care and education. As regards this reality, the spokespersons for the various business domains, the infrastructure providers, and the visionaries on behalf of a new consumer were all equally frustrated.

DEPLOYMENT OF INFRASTRUCTURE TECHNOLOGY

In 10 to 15 years cheaper and more powerful microprocessor-based devices, broadband connections to and from homes and businesses, and other enhancements to the fundamental technology infrastructure of the economy will be widely available for a great variety of uses. If anything has been oversold, it is timing. While emerging infrastructure is relatively simple to grasp conceptually, in implementation it is quite complex and software-intensive. Notwithstanding appropriate public policy concerns about implications of the NII for society, attempts to constrain the fundamental technologies or to push the market for them in arbitrarily conceived directions will not succeed.

Several key technology issues are driven by the gap between requirements arising as a result of what users increasingly seem to do and want and the capabilities present or imminent from providers.

Access

A majority of the concerns and uncertainties uncovered in the NII 2000 project centered on the issue of future connections to homes and small businesses—the access circuits that will permit the end user to connect to the information infrastructure and take advantage of its promise. The discussions of access circuits revealed the great potential for technological advances, but also great uncertainty about the extent to which business realities would constrain rapid exploitation of that potential. Other technology areas discussed, such as backbone capacity and access for large businesses, were much less the focus of concern.

Access to the information infrastructure today is provided by proven and relatively mature technologies—the copper wire pairs of the telephone companies, the coaxial cable of the cable industry, and terrestrial broadcast television and radio. Newer technologies include cellular telephony and direct satellite broadcast of television. The future will bring an expanding range of technology options, including much higher band-widths over both copper pairs and coaxial cable alike, and several new forms of wireless communication. Increased transmission capacity to the home will be provided by the growing use of fiber-optic cables. Even if these fibers initially reach only part of the way to the home, they can provide much increased capacity to the system as a whole. Partial enhancement of current systems with fiber is the basis for upgrading both the copper pairs and coaxial systems.

Different industry sectors appear to be responding to these circumstances in different ways. The cable television industry, with its current base of coaxial cable, seems primarily to be planning a technology upgrade of that infrastructure to a configuration called hybrid fiber coaxial cable (hybrid fiber coax; HFC), which uses fiber optics to deliver signals part of the way to the residence and uses the existing coaxial cable for the final part of the path. In contrast, the telephone industry is exploring a number of different technology paths. Some reuse the copper pairs to provide higher bandwidth (the various digital subscriber line approaches), others involve new systems similar to advanced cable television infrastructure, and still others use wireless for advanced services. These various technologies are explained and evaluated in Chapter 4.

Flexibility and Interoperability

The steering committee focused on the extent and nature of actual technology limits, given that major investment in infrastructure cannot easily be repeated. If the infrastructure has the flexibility to adapt if and when there is proven market demand, then it is less necessary to be able to predict now exactly what the future will be. Different technologies involve different fundamental limits to two-way capacity. The further fiber-optic cable reaches toward the home, the more likely it seems that two-way bandwidth can be configured as needed. In this respect, the HFC technology received considerable discussion because it is being deployed widely by essentially all of the cable companies and at least some of the telephone companies, and compared to some other options, it is somewhat more limited in its ability to support large up-channel capacity. While project participants did not agree totally on this point, the steering committee concluded that HFC technology has sufficient capacity to support exploration of the emerging market and allow new applications to be launched. It may or may not have enough capacity to sustain a fully mature market with high penetration of advanced two-way services, depending on details of the application and the way the HFC system is installed. However, the steering committee believes that if the potential of the market is once proven, investment for upgrades will be made if necessary. It is the first steps that are the most tenuous, and HFC is adequate for that.

Ideally, hardware investments will incorporate the necessary flexibility and interoperability required to support a highly functional, evolving set of NII uses. The need for flexibility is a consequence of two expectations: regulatory change and the opening up of existing markets to competition, which implies the need to reuse existing infrastructure for other services (e.g., cable infrastructure for telephony). The steering committee noted that increased flexibility in reuse of infrastructure for different services is an important trend in most communications technology today, fueled by important factors such as the increasingly digital, as opposed to analog, transmission of information. Most of the presentations from industry acknowledged this need for flexibility, but expressed also concerns about the costs of major infrastructure upgrades.

Interoperable systems allow content providers to achieve wide dissemination without having to repackage their material for each different distribution system, and they enable end users to communicate using common standards and data representations. However, the need for interoperation does not imply that open and interoperable systems must be mandated as a part of new technology deployment. If the underlying physical infrastructure at the level of circuits and switches is engineered to support adaptability in a flexible manner, and if protocols and software can themselves evolve as markets mature, then the degree of service interoperability achieved at any given time need not be a major concern, because it can be changed later as the market requires.[12]

Additional Technology Concerns

Beyond the issues of access—including adequacy of bandwidth, especially in the up-channel—and interoperability, the following were other significant technological concerns identified in the project:

- The ability to give users the sense that they are always connected, as opposed to their having to undertake a time-consuming connection process before using a remote application;
- The ability to enable users to connect to a number of remote points on the network at the same time;
- The ability to support mobile users;
- The ability to provide for adequate security in the network; and
- The ability to mix different media types, in particular real-time traffic and traditional computer data.

User Interaction with Networked Infrastructure

Paralleling the importance of technology choices for network facilities—the access wires and wireless links, the cables and fibers in the ground—are the technology choices affecting how users are connected to the network, the means for humans or for computers to interact and communicate in a useful fashion.

Today, the obvious devices that are connected to the network in volume are the telephone, the television, and the personal computer. The importance of the television is its ubiquity and familiarity. Its drawbacks are its limited functionality, with low screen resolution, no useful input modes, and no computing power. The PC is more powerful and general but costs more ($2,000 is a persistent price point for current full-featured products). However, as has been pointed out numerous times, 30 percent of U.S. households have a PC today, and substantial additional penetration into the consumer space is predicted in a very few years. Essentially all new PCs will have a modem, and so a broad base of consumers will have the ability to go "on line" in some form. The PC is thus an important and growing consumer interface to the information infrastructure. Less change, in technology or use, appears to be anticipated for telephones.

How will the TV and the PC evolve over the next 5 to 7 years? Contributors to the project from the industries that supply these devices indicated that all would like to see their device evolve into a more general form capable of supporting a broader range of applications. The steering committee sees as unrealistic the suggestion that they will converge to a single multipurpose device. The differences in cost, resolution, viewing distance, and so on suggest that each will continue to play a distinct role. But there is no doubt that each will evolve so that it can to some extent play the role of the other.[13]

To broaden the base of access to more consumers, including those less able to bear the costs, several project participants raised the prospect of breaking the $2,000 price barrier for a home PC and producing a cheaper device (at $500 to $1,000) that can be used for limited PC applications and as an interface to on-line services and the Internet. Some of these attempts involve using the TV as a display, whereas others use a low-cost computer display or eliminate data storage or other features. Although in late 1995 this idea was translated into a variety of new-product announcements, cheaper PCs have been tried before, without much success, and there is skepticism as well as hope about the current undertakings. This area of innovation is an important one to watch during the next few years, because its success or failure could influence the options for consumer access to the network, and also because reducing the cost of access might be accomplished by an alternate approach, that is, pushing functions back into the network, which would change the performance and cost expectations for that part of the infrastructure.

Another point discussed at the forum was how the various networks entering the home would interconnect to the various end-user devices. Today, there is no single, common point of interconnection: telephone wires connect directly to a telephone or modem, and the cable feed connects directly to a TV, set-top box, or (in the future) a data modem. Numerous proposals for making this multiplicity of connections less complex and less costly involve providing a single point of attachment for wires entering the home, and for the networks distributing information within the home. Interconnection could be accomplished through some form of enhanced set-top box or through a network interface at the side of the house. What is perhaps most important is not the name or location of the physical box, but rather which particular functions are performed in which box, and who provides and controls these various functions. No one network provider should control the consumer's access to other networks, and so any single point of entry and cross-connection should not belong to any one of the network providers. The alternative would be for the consumer to purchase and control the device.[14]

PUBLIC VERSUS PRIVATE OBJECTIVES

The competitive drive of private industry will dominate the process by which the NII evolves. Private firms will build it; their business plans must justify the investments; and competition and the desire for new markets, not pursuit of abstract visions or societal goals, will define and shape it. This reality provides the impetus that will make it happen, and at the same time triggers many fears and concerns. In this context, opinions differ considerably on whether there is an appropriate government role in advancing the NII and, if so, what it is.

Most people can agree that an ideal information infrastructure should have such qualities as extended interoperability, broad accessibility, and support for broad participation. It should allow multiple channels for many-to-many communications and information sharing as well as one-to-one (familiar today through telephony), and also one-to-many (familiar through broadcast and cable television). Progress toward that ideal is more likely if the government can set an example with its own services and help enable a consensus on a vision of the future by removing barriers to its realization. The steering committee believes that rapid progress toward a harmonious national environment of interrelated information services and capabilities would be valuable to the nation. It does not believe that a rational set of public and private services is likely to emerge from the action of market forces alone. However, the government's role is as a partner and participant with the private sector, exercising its regulatory authority with restraint.

If private industry is to build the NII, how can the government ensure that the evolving NII meets critical societal goals, such as equitable access? This problem was not a focus of the project, but it came up on many occasions.[15] There was repeated concern about citizen access to those services that emerge as important to full participation in democratic processes and about equitable access to public services.[16] From this perspective, it is important to note that although consumers may in general be citizens, citizens are not all consumers, and public policy must consider the circumstances of the larger citizenry. Governmental units will play a role in helping to define what appropriate access really means and in establishing the means to assure that it is achieved.

Project contributors provided much encouragement for government to serve as a model promoter and user of NII. Success in these endeavors may not come easily; the public sector is not known as a model of efficiency in using information systems in its delivery of services. Nevertheless, many of its activities relating to information infrastructure have been widely acknowledged as constructive (CSTB, 1994b). One-third of economic activity in the United States is in the public sector, and for this and other reasons public services will represent a substantial fraction of the development, deployment, and operating costs of the NII. The federal government, in particular, also has a valuable tool in the form of support for fundamental and applied research and development, an area of activities that may range from university laboratory research to testbeds that can explore new technologies in the context of various user domains. Research and development (R&D) can enable more capabilities, greater ease of use, and lower cost for different components of the information infrastructure. The steering committee concluded that support of R&D is one of the most effective mechanisms available to the federal government.

Through the funding of network and applications research, its own visionary use of NII capabilities to better serve the public, encouragement of public-private partnerships in specific NII development and use situations, and the convening of the involved parties to discuss the importance of keeping technological options open, the government can favorably influence the coherence of physical information infrastructure and associated services. In the eyes of many from industry, practical government leadership will involve new ways of doing business as well as pursuing such proven models as those represented by the fostering of the Internet and related technologies.

Although it drew comparatively little discussion at the 1995 forum, the international nature of communications implies that enhancements to the NII will be deployed and used in the context of an evolving global information infrastructure. Governments have special responsibilities in the arena of international negotiations, which can affect interconnection arrangements, standards setting, markets for content, and other dimensions of the NII marketplace. Public policy decisions in the United States will affect primarily the growth of U.S. information infrastructure, but in a context where mistakes can shift the opportunity to European and Asian companies and markets.

Despite the many challenges confronting the private and public sectors in advancing the information infrastructure, it is important to remember that the problems discussed in this report are problems of success, not of failure.

ORGANIZATION OF THIS REPORT

This report is divided into chapters that present inputs collected from the NII 2000 project's many contributors. It serves partly to report what those inputs were—emphasizing, as requested, the views of contributors from a variety of industries. It also provides interpretation and commentary, including observations on what the steering committee did not hear and conclusions drawn by the steering committee from its deliberations.

The chapters complement each other, but they also present some similar material from different perspectives. Chapter 2 focuses on user problems and needs, addressing both organized users (e.g., users within different industries or application domains) and more independent users operating out of households or small businesses. Chapter 3 considers determinants of infrastructure supply, examining influences on the nature and rate of investment and alternatives for cost recovery or revenue generation. Chapters 4 and 5 examine key technologies being deployed: Chapter 4 describes different kinds of technologies, while Chapter 5 is a compilation of information generated through this project and published sources on actual deployment levels and forecasts. Chapter 5 is the closest the steering committee could come to providing the elusive "road map." Chapter 6 examines the role of government in shaping deployment; it is not a comprehensive discussion of information infrastructure policy making, but rather a consideration of the interaction between public and private actions intended to foster and shape the information infrastructure.

The chapters are complemented by seven appendixes with information relating to the information collection and synthesis processes that shaped the report. A forthcoming second volume will contain the white papers that are the basis of much of this report and that are quoted from and referred to throughout.

NOTES

1. In addition to the NII itself, the steering committee recognizes that there is a second tier of institutions and resources without which the NII cannot be effective. While not a part of the NII itself, these institutions require policy and market environments and sources of new technology, which are to a large extent influenced by public policy. Among such institutions and resources are the following:

- The industries that provide the machines and tools from which the NII is constructed;
- The schools and universities that train the human resources;
- The engineers and scientists who are exploring and developing information technologies and are learning about the cognitive and social dimensions of information;
- The state and federal agencies that make policy, provide resources, and set requirements for information services; and
- The business, trade, and professional associations whose stake in the NII is based on their dependence on the information provided through it.

2. Commercialization has in part reflected changes in government policy (e.g., with respect to acceptableness and users) associated with the National Research and Education Network).

3. The administration's Agenda for Action (IITF, 1993) describes a "seamless web" of universally accessible information services and interactive capabilities as its vision of the NII.

4. As constructed, they point to a limited willingness to pay more than current levels of expenditure for communications, entertainment, and other services offered through the trials. In other contexts—purchases of consumer electronics, cellular telephony—however, spending has been rising.

5. In addition, when there is radical technology change, it is rare for the new markets enabled by the technology to build up to volumes comparable with those of established markets in less than one to three decades—even though the new markets eventually outstrip and displace the old.

6. Although at issue are business decisions, there is a notable unevenness in the underlying economic conceptualization. In some cases the market model is relatively easy to understand, but we just do not know which technologies will win. The combination of high levels of infrastructure investment, low marginal costs for use, and competing suppliers is one for which economic theory provides only limited and ambiguous insight, which is one reason that predicting the future is difficult. Besides not being able to know in advance the technological winners, we also do not know how the market will behave, whatever the winning technologies. These issues are examined in Chapter 3.

7. See CSTB (1995c).

8. Although the collaborative aspects of Internet standards setting may receive the most attention, many associated standards, including those defining tools such as Gopher and the Web, were developed by a few people and spread spontaneously because the community liked them. This process is much more

like the de facto standards development that prevails in most of the rest of the computer industry; it can occur rapidly, and it fosters competition.

9.   These innovations will increase demand for bandwidth, possibly at a rate faster than it can be made available, especially for local access. On the other hand, facilities owners are making and acting on plans to incrementally expand available bandwidth. Reflecting their interdependence with pure service providers, their investments are due at least partially to orders by smaller service providers that are reselling the services, committing the sales and marketing resources in small niche markets, and/or adding content to the service (e.g., America Online on top of SprintNet).

10.   An interesting indicator is the relatively high incidence of carrier partnerships or initiatives to deliver information.

11.   Today Cisco Systems exports almost all of the routers for the Internet worldwide, and most of the supporting software for TCP/IP comes from the United States.

12.   However, changes in software should not be viewed as trivial. An important goal is reducing users' costs associated with adopting new software, since the cost in time, money, and discomfort of user retraining to new software systems can be a major barrier to adoption of alternatives, even if they are inherently superior. Note, however, that there have been relatively rapid changes in PC software user interfaces: Windows has effectively replaced DOS as a PC operating system; in word processing, Microsoft's Word is leading WordPerfect, both having replaced Wordstar.

13.   New products coming on the market today allow one to connect a PC to a cable TV network and to watch on the PC screen both TV pictures and information (in the form of Web pages) about the material being seen. Network interfaces for TVs are being developed that will enable TVs to be used for playing interactive games over the Internet, and (to some extent, limited by screen resolution) for searching and attaching to the Web.

14.   If, however, custom network interfaces for the different networks that enter the home have to be attached to such a device, then its final form, if it matures, will be in two parts, with the basic unit belonging to the consumer, and featuring attachment sockets or slots into which different network interfaces can be inserted. Such an architecture has not been developed or accepted for a consumer network interface yet, although it has been discussed. However, it bears some resemblance to a PC, which has a bus or external interface into which network cards are traditionally inserted. This raises the possibility that a PC could become a consumer network cross-connection device, a proposal that generates both interest and skepticism, depending on which industry sector is speaking. See Chapter 2.

15.   See CSTB (1994b and 1995b) and their references for fuller consideration. Anderson et al. (1995) provide a thoughtful examination of electronic mail as an initial focus for universal access.

16.   There are areas of application, in health, education, transportation, and library services, for example, where government has functional responsibilities that could be better served by full use of information and communications services.

2

Making Technology Work: Individual and Organized End Users

This chapter focuses on end users and the technology foundations they need in order to gain the benefits of the national information infrastructure (NII) in their everyday lives. Additionally, it describes how the absence of definitive information regarding end-user preferences is a major source of uncertainty that infrastructure providers must factor into their deployment decisions. As a starting point for analysis, it addresses these questions: How is demand for access evolving? How does the end user access what he or she wants? What equipment and systems compose the end user's means of access? How does private industry translate what it knows about the above into decisions regarding technology deployment generally?

WHO IS THE END USER?

The end user of the NII is potentially every man, woman, and child. The end user may be the person at work using a networked computer environment; the person at home doing on-line shopping, sharing ideas with fellow hobbyists, or collaborating on a work project with remotely located colleagues; a child accessing material in a library, sending homework to a teacher, or playing a game; a traveler changing an airline reservation; the household that has an energy conservation system; or the realtor who relays facts, pictures, and bid and contract details for a house to prospective buyers. Box 2.1 lists some of the categories of usage. User applications range from the critical to the trivial. As the January work-

BOX 2.1
What Do Information Infrastructure End Users Do?

As a general observation and as documented increasingly in the news media, individuals and organizations are using information technology in a number of endeavors:

- *Work:* In an increasing number of occupations, work involves some type of networked computing. Within the corporate environment, about 80 percent of computers are connected to networks (IDC, 1995f). Electronic mail has become a popular way to communicate, and complex design collaborations can be carried out effectively in networked environments. Further, telecommuting and other forms of distributed work involve individuals working on line from home or while traveling.

- *Learning:* Networked access to information, be it reference material, training material, or ideas arising through discussion, is becoming an important tool in the workplace and in schools, both of which involve important training opportunities for users. Experience with using information technology at work and in school carries over into more informal, unstructured learning opportunities enabled by broad access to networks for communications and information retrieval from the home, libraries, and other places not normally associated with training.

- *Financial and commercial transactions:* Many financial transactions are conducted by the banking industry in a networked environment, and consumers spend billions of dollars buying goods through shopping networks on cable television. On-line purchase transactions (plus on-line browsing, price comparison, and customer-service queries) using a PC are becoming increasingly common.

- *Entertainment and socializing:* The average U.S. household has a television set on for more than 40 hours a week (Veronis, Suhler, 1995). Television and radio provide entertainment, news, and other information. In addition to such broadcast services, discretionary user capabilities (e.g., pay per view, video on demand) are part of the future offerings that service providers expect to develop as more advanced network technologies are deployed. Games and on-line services also provide entertainment, as does socializing or communicating generally. From simple telephone calls to video and data conferencing, messaging, and collaborative work, end users communicate more frequently and in more ways via networks.

- *Religion:* Devout people are sharing faith on line. They hold religious services, complete with sermons and at times including music. There are on-line support groups for every creed.

- *Others:* The above categorization is quite broad and does not do justice to many critical areas in which technology deployment can and does have a major positive impact. For example, endeavors that rely on rapid response, such as civilian or military crisis management, already depend heavily on the networked environment, be it landline or wireless, voice or data communications.

shop and May forum made clear, there is no consensus on precisely how or to what extent end users will make use of evolving information technology capabilities—no consensus on demand. Nor, in the absence of expressed demand, is there a consensus on how large a fraction of U.S. households currently can access desired levels of services. Ross Glatzer, past president of Prodigy, noted that experience with on-line services emphasizes the role of communications as the foundation for how services are used, with information offerings and on-line transactions tightly integrated. He cautioned against overemphasizing any one type of activity or assuming that delivery of information and content will dominate.

While this view projects a continuum of uses for the NII, one particular issue shapes many of the specific considerations in this report—the distinction between the worker in the corporate setting or large institution and the end user in the small business or in the home. This distinction seems to have polarized the planning of many business sectors, including that of some of the facilities providers. In the near term, there will continue to be differences in the equipment and support available to different broad sets of users: large and small business users in the office or home will use computers and telephones, not television sets; they may use laptops or other computer equipment purchased by their employer, as well as business software or specialized systems to support remote work.[1] As discussed below, they have very different needs for their communications infrastructure, requiring such features as more accessible bandwidth to and especially from the home, continuous access with multiple ongoing connections at once, and different sorts of communications security. Over the long term, the distinction between home and small business users and users in large businesses and institutions will disappear as people work increasingly from the home. The trend toward self-employment, typically home-based, is strong, and the very small business and the home are similar in terms of expertise, purchasing power, space, and other attributes.[2]

In some instances, there are signs of overlapping uses of information technology for business purposes across home and office. For example, Stuart Wecker of Symmetrix Incorporated observed that "it is hard for me to tell what is a business user," noting that people now install second lines in residences at higher than expected rates. Moreover, the increasing exposure to computing and networking in work, study, and other institutional contexts will both broaden the customer base and lead to the use of tools mastered at work or in school for other than business-related tasks.[8] The explosive growth of experimentation, particularly in the context of the Internet, underscores how the simple pattern of an end user at home performing the same work-related tasks as otherwise would be done at a place of employment does not capture the full range of transference of information technology-enabled capabilities.

WHY THE NII MUST REACH THE HOME

Particularly in plans for technology deployment to and network access for the end user in the home, the steering committee found areas of uncertainty and confusion. In one view, advanced network services will penetrate into the home because some one application is so important and desirable that it alone can drive the economics of deployment. This "killer app" economic model has, for residential networking, most commonly anticipated entertainment services as the dominant driver. But the problem with the "killer app" metaphor is the expectation that one activity will saturate the market.[3] Communications and content providers contributing to the NII 2000 project did not quantify the analysis, but their comments suggested that an application need only capture a significant percentage (even 10 percent) of the national market for telecommunications to justify the necessary facilities investments.[4]

Entertainment has appeal as a "killer app" for residential use for several reasons, including the obvious one that broadcast and cable are in the entertainment business already and understand it.[5] As a result of their efforts, the principal application of communications technology for the nonworking home consumer has been television entertainment. Even for sectors such as telephony that are only contemplating entering the entertainment business, there is a proven market that can at least justify financial speculation. Home entertainment is an important segment of the U.S. communications industry (see Figure 2.1)[6] and will continue to grow with the transition to digital technology. As a set of businesses, however, home entertainment represents only a small percentage of the U.S. economy. One reason is that strictly personal use of information infrastructure for entertainment is a function of disposable personal income (including competing demands on household resources) and discretionary time.[7] By contrast, business-related use depends on the shift of activities to the home that traditionally or otherwise require a person to be at a different and specific location—literally, a place of business.

The perceived inability of providers to construct a business case for investing in residential information infrastructure in the absence of a "killer app" was a basis for frustration expressed by representatives of various business domains. As examined in Chapter 3, comments from infrastructure builders (excluding cable and terrestrial broadcast television providers) indicate that they are slowing their investments for fear

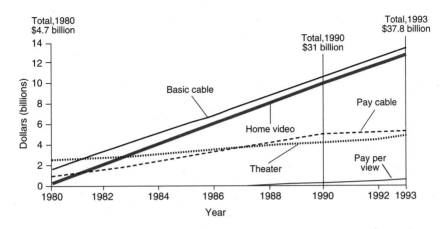

FIGURE 2.1 Consumer spending on entertainment, 1980 to 1993.
SOURCE: "The NII in the Home: A Consumer Service," a white paper contributed to the NII 2000 project by Vito Brugliera, James A. Chiddix, D. Joseph Donahue, Joseph A. Flaherty, Richard R. Green, James C. McKinney, Richard E. Ottinger, and Rupert Stow. Data from P. Kagan.

that home entertainment may not yield a sufficient return after all (Mills, 1995c). Pessimistic about consumer market prospects, Paul Green of IBM's T.J. Watson Research Center concluded that "the only way that I see that we are ever going to be able to get fiber to the home, barring some discovery of the 'killer app,' is via smaller and smaller businesses installing their own private fiber or renting it from the telephone company. Eventually it will just become slowly democratized." For user domain representatives, it was one matter to hear about infrastructure being built for what they felt was the wrong "killer app"; it was quite another for them to hear that it might not be built for many decades, given that the speculative "killer app" might be dead on arrival.

Evidence of growth in the amount of business that will be conducted to and from the home supports the conclusion that the vast majority of information infrastructure use will involve interaction with industries and government: finance and banking, health care, government services (benefits, information, taxation), manufacturing, and dozens of other domains, each of which has, to varying degrees, been assimilating networked infrastructure into a variety of business processes. Inputs from these sectors indicated that business uses in the home, and not leisure uses, should be driving the plans for deployment of bandwidth to the home. This insight is consistent with the slow rollout of fiber reflecting expectations for communications traffic based primarily on conventional use of telephony (see Chapters 3 and 5). It is not clear, however, whether slow deployment of non-television bandwidth reflects anticipation of gradual growth in the market for miscellaneous business uses, or instead reflects lack of recognition of the eventual market role of these uses. The small body of current knowledge about deployment of application services compounds the uncertainty. Over the long term, however, business-use financing (treating infrastructure as a cost of doing business) should be at least as important as consumer financing in driving deployment (see "Economic Models" in Chapter 3). Overall, business uses will drive the deployment of information infrastructure because they give rise to interactions that will take place in large institutional settings, small business settings that resemble homes in terms of resources, and homes.

Together, inputs from infrastructure suppliers and users suggest that no one application domain is expected to drive more than a small percentage of the activity on the NII. Further, the evolution of different product and service elements—such as voice telephony, electronic mail, and various forms of video distribution—is too uncertain to allow reliable predictions about which, if any, might dominate. It is the steering committee's view that NII technology deployment will be driven by the collective needs and aggregate economics of many domains. In other words, the search for a holy grail of information infrastructure does not lead anywhere, but everywhere.

EVOLVING DEMAND FOR NII CAPABILITIES

User familiarity with information technology and user demand for NII capabilities will co-evolve, a process that will take time and that may also yield unanticipated results.[9] The beginning of such a co-evolution is evident in people's increasing willingness and ability to talk about the Internet, as well as in other indicators that user involvement is greater today than a year ago and still growing:[10] more people using information technology at work, school, and at home; more advertisements, articles, and business cards including links to a network or World Wide Web (Web) address; and more movies, popular books, and other mainstream media with computer and networking themes.

Yet making the transition from interest in and acquaintance with information technology to fuller acceptance, implementation, and use is not necessarily a natural process. In many instances, end users do not quite know what they want,[11] and their perceptions often differ by age. Further, it is difficult to make full use of technologies whose potential end users cannot imagine when they are still unfamiliar with the technology.[12] Additional barriers to widespread implementation are both technical—how to incorporate legacy systems, how to ensure interoperabil-

---

BOX 2.2
Electronic Commerce and Legacy Systems

The electronic commerce domain has a large quantity of legacy systems which it needs to interface to, and ultimately phase-out of as it evolves to more modern systems, applications, and processes. These legacy systems and processes (e.g., paper checks, mainframe-based settlement and payment systems, and electronic data interchange value-added networks) will not go away overnight, and a successful electronic commerce infrastructure must allow the user to easily and transparently transfer between and switch back and forth between the new all-electronic and the older, hybrid legacy systems and processes.

—Daniel Schutzer, "Electronic Commerce"

---

ity—and cultural. Daniel Schutzer (in a white paper) and others underscored the difficulty of accommodating legacy systems in the near term to facilitate communication among different domains (Box 2.2) as the information infrastructure evolves. White papers by Thomas Rochow et al. and by Robert Mason et al., for example, commented on difficulties with introducing use of information technology in manufacturing that are also applicable across the board to the several user domains examined during the course of the NII 2000 project (see Box 2.3).

A majority of user domain representatives at the workshop and forum indicated that the primary issues inhibiting greater NII use were not infrastructure-specific. In fact, several of the speakers commented on their satisfaction with current communication services, and it is also the case that networking in at least some form is being used increasingly in essentially all industries and sectors (see Box 2.4 and Chapter 5 for observations on business networking trends). Enormous opportunities for savings have long been part of the appeal of business networking applications such as electronic data interchange (EDI) and also underlie, for example, power-utility investment in energy demand management systems as discussed in the white paper by John Cavallini et al. Widespread implementation and use of information technology, however, are complicated by ongoing fundamental changes in nearly every user domain that have as much to do with the information itself as with how it is communicated. In the 1980s, for example, EDI attracted attention as an advance beyond internal corporate networking to support interenterprise communication using standardized trade-related documents. In the 1990s, discussions of electronic commerce have reflected extensive changes in activity within and among enterprises and individuals that now have greater flexibility in exchanging information. Current accounts of indus-

---

BOX 2.3
Adaptation to the Use of Information Technology in Manufacturing

Nothing is harder to facilitate than the change of a work process. This is cultural change, often a change from what has been a successful process in the past. Human beings, perhaps as a result of a built-in predisposition to protect the species from the unknown, are strongly resistant to change.

—Thomas C. Rochow, George E. Scarborough, and Frank David Utterback,
"Electronic Integrated Product Development as Enabled by a
Global Information Environment:
A Requirement for Success in the Twenty-first Century"

. . . [T]here is concern that the learning cycle for small manufacturing enterprises (SMEs) . . . to implement information technology is too long and too costly for them to effectively make the transition to the NII environment. The solution to the problem is not simply one of assuring that every SME can purchase and install a new information system. Instead, the solution requires an understanding of how a complex combination of structural, technical, managerial, and economic factors affects the diffusion of information technology in SMEs and puts at risk a significant component of the nation's manufacturing base.

—Robert M. Mason, Chester Bowling, and Robert J. Niemi,
"Small Manufacturing Enterprises and
the National Information Infrastructure"

---

try- and sector-specific problems concern how different industries conduct business and/or evolve, both in terms of overall structure and business processes and in terms of the assimilation of all kinds of information technology into those processes.[13,14]

Within each domain the barriers differ, but contributors to this project delineated some broad themes. Data formatting standards and legacy systems are pervasive concerns. Difficulties have surfaced in the context of EDI, collaborative databases, and other applications that involve document handling and exchange, and the white paper by Stephen Zilles and Richard Cohn speaks, for example, of the need for standards to support all steps of document use—production, viewing, reading, reusing, annotating—and links standards to architectures. Another cross-cutting concern is labeling and identifying people, places, and organizations, as Ed Hammond points out in a white paper. Yet another related concern is lack of cohesiveness within industries and organizations themselves. Richard Sharpe of the Hartford Foundation explained at the January workshop that health care "information is totally fragmented. The business is

---

BOX 2.4
Demand for Networking in the Business Domain

Many business and public sector domains have made significant investments in networking, as reflected in their purchase and use of private networks—local area networks, wide area networks, virtual private networks, and so on. A May 22, 1995, International Data Corporation analysis (IDC, 1995a, Figure 13) arrayed several different industries according to their responses in three categories regarding networking:

1. The degree to which representatives indicated that they considered networking to be critical;
2. The number indicating that most electronic information is transferred by using computer-to-computer communications (as opposed to fax) among large business sites; and
3. The proportion deeming electronic commerce critical.

Each sector's responses to each of the three were as follows:

Sector	Response (percent)		
	(1)	(2)	(3)
Business services	74.0	25.3	26.4
Banking	71.0	22.1	13.7
Insurance	71.0	12.1	10.3
Retail	59.0	23.7	13.4
Transportation/communications/utilities	55.0	11.9	10.9
Process manufacturing	53.0	13.1	9.1
Discrete manufacturing	51.0	10.5	4.8
Education	49.0	20.8	9.4
Government	48.0	18.9	3.2
Health care	35.0	6.8	7.8

Notwithstanding perhaps predictable differences among infrastructure users by domain and by size of organization, there is evidence that the floor is rising. Growth in activity and sophistication among domains that came later to electronic networking and information services suggests that large interdomain gaps in networking are unlikely to persist, although some specialized needs are likely to continue or emerge (CSTB, 1993a,1995a).

---

not a system. It is a cottage industry, with each cottage having a different approach to the netware."

In addition, the cultural metamorphosis required in the transition to use of information technology within each of the several user domains is a reality that telecommunications providers must factor into their deployment decisions, according to project participants. Several speakers at the forum noted that infrastructure providers' involvement in helping end users to accept advanced communications capabilities and use them in new ways might accelerate the demand for services. As Thomas Rochow of the McDonnell Douglas Corporation pointed out with regard to manufacturing, "We are talking about a sector of our economy that really has to learn how to crawl before we can walk and then run. If you help us do that, you might be surprised that we can help you co-evolve with us for our mutual benefit." Fostering the adoption of information technology is arguably a task for both the user domains and the facilities providers, given that infrastructure providers have a business interest in being responsive to customers' needs. From the providers' perspective, each application domain has its own language, perspective on its problems, and need for a somewhat tailored approach—all factors that can slow progress.

Whether or how well assimilation proceeds, it may also pace the rate of market growth, inasmuch as it speaks to the problem of market penetration in a given domain. In their white paper, Mason et al. note that smaller manufacturing enterprises that may be only at the beginning of the so-called "learning curve" are responsible for up to nearly 40 percent of the nation's manufacturing employment. Richard Sharpe remarked, "Health care is a sleeping giant. This is a major sector, a trillion-dollar business opportunity for you folks who are selling your wares."

Variations in requirements imply, in particular, that there is no coherent voice through which users can express their needs up front. It also implies that no one domain may have sufficient clout to sway investment choices one way or another to meet its needs. Thus, when infrastructure builders aim for a constituency that represents a common denominator or compromise among different flavors of demand, it is easy for users in any domain to feel that "they're not talking to us."

The lack of specific requirements or variation in perceived requirements could be a problem for those who must decide what infrastructure to build through processes involving up-front commitments to long-lived facilities characterized by economies of scale that are paid back through volume use. As David Messerschmitt of the University of California at Berkeley observed at the forum:

> Do the needs of various user groups, such as doctors and hospitals and Joe Six Pack, differ radically? If so, we need to think of perhaps different network solutions that are somehow "gatewayed" for these different communities. Or are their needs actually very similar, and not different enough to justify that segmentation, so that we can benefit from the economies of scale of defining a more homogeneous NII network infrastructure?

The discussion here (see Chapters 3 and 4) does not conclude that separate networks are required.

THE END USER AS CONSUMER

In the effort to stimulate consumer demand for information technology, affordability, ease of use, and interoperability of available devices stand out as basic considerations. Affordability is a concept that applies to a product's entire life cycle; it includes both the initial purchase price and other costs incurred over a relatively long expected period of use (consumers generally cannot recover the costs of their durable goods in the same way that businesses can recover the capital of past investments and invest it for modernization[15]). Joseph Flaherty of CBS Incorporated summed up the situation as follows: "So while the network questions might be bandwidth, bandwidth, bandwidth and access, access, access, the consumer questions are cost, cost, cost and life, life, life of the facility."

Project contributors associated with television manufacturing and services emphasized the consumer experience with electronics: relatively low price points, long-lived products (especially in the case of the more expensive items), and compatibility. In contrast, contributors associated with the computer industry observed that consumers are investing in personal computer (PC) equipment even though it costs more than entertainment devices, although given the relatively high initial costs, customers are unlikely to upgrade regularly.

Costs for equipment are only part of the challenge in increasing consumer demand. Another is the price of service. While broadcast television involves no service charge, Brugliera et al. note in their white paper that basic cable service averages about $300 per year and premium channels an additional $100 per year each, levels that consumers are aware of and can factor into their expectations. Average monthly rates for basic telephone service, according to Federal Communications Commission (FCC) statistics, are about $11 for residential customers and about $43 for single-line business customers (FCC, 1994, pp. 304-305).[16] In contrast, on-line service pricing has been volatile, currently averaging around $10 per month for about 10 hours of "basic" service. Price levels affect willingness to move from one pattern of consumption to another (e.g., from videocassette rental to use of video on demand) and to use new kinds of products.

In addition to the issue of overall cost are the issues of predictable cost and easy payment for services, as emphasized by Leonard Kleinrock of the University of California at Los Angeles in the context of nomadic computing needs, which combine portable and alternative computing and communications arrangements (see Box 2.5). The features sought by

---

BOX 2.5
Predictable and Easy Payment

I do not want to make a query out over the network and have a 15-megabyte videoclip downloaded to me on my 14-kilobit modem. I want to be warned about the cost in time, delay, dollars, and storage and maybe get some approximate picture, maybe just the title of the picture, or fuzzy image, or a slower frame rate. In order to create this, we need a variety of capabilities. We need the ability to handle replication services, file synchronization, predictive caching, adaptive database management, location services, tracking of people, devices, resource discovery, and profile discovery.

In order for me to use [the telephone system] anywhere, all I need is coin of the realm and an empty telephone booth. I do not have to identify myself, register ahead of time, or pay for it ahead of time; I just go and use it.

—Leonard Kleinrock, University of California at Los Angeles

Kleinrock imply corresponding accounting mechanisms—well established for telephony and various subscription television services but currently in flux for computer-based services.

Growth in consumer acquisition and use of PCs provides evidence that at least more of those who can afford to purchase PCs are opting to do so. At the January workshop, Tora Bikson of the RAND Corporation cited research showing that the proportion of income spent on access to PCs or access to network services has increased (Anderson et al., 1995). Similarly, the growth of cellular telephony suggests a willingness to alter household budgets to cover the cost of a valued service. The cellular pricing structure, which makes handsets very cheap and calls quite expensive (though prices are beginning to fall), gives people the opportunity to experiment with using the service. Growth in volume suggests that many find it more useful than they expected, fueling the transfer of this technology from business-financed use to more personal use.

In addition to cost, ease of use was described by project contributors as a primary consideration in consumers' willingness to use information technology. The white paper by Oscar Garcia discusses the issue. The user interface is clearly a crucial component in information technology use and one for which research could bring needed improvements (see Chapter 6 for a discussion of research needs). Experience with telephones and televisions, which are generally recognized as easy to use, illustrates that user interfaces can be tailored to a single use. Similarly, the common wisdom on fax is that it was accepted because it had a single-use interface and worked over telephone lines. In contrast, tasks associated with more complex and emerging service objectives such as accessing and using the Internet are still perceived as complicated, with more variables and harder-to-use interfaces.[17]

Although technology advances have enabled dramatic improvements over the last several years, the general-purpose PC is not yet as easy to use as either the television or the telephone, largely because many of the tasks to be performed with the PC are intrinsically more complex. This is a significant barrier for many, and is likely to be one for many years to come.

Some of the difficulty in learning to use new technology is being offset by the emergence of new service businesses that offer, for example, the capability of hosting Web pages for customers who do not want to configure and operate their own Web server. Such businesses provide the storage for Web pages, as well as the service that translates the names for the Web pages (the universal resource locators) into the appropriate address on the network. Customers pay monthly fees for such services. Other service providers intend to sell a turn-key capability that a client can install to operate a Web server.

Despite the need for continued improvement in ease of use, it is important to emphasize that expectations for user friendliness should not be unrealistic. A local, consumer market assumes that people will know what to do with the capabilities available. The basic user will be able to accomplish a great deal with navigation tools built into current and future television services, for example, but skillful use of interactive environments, beyond entertainment applications, will require training—which is already taking place in the corporate setting, in social groups for adults, and in the schools, especially for the next generation of users.

Elaborating on Paul Green's characterization of the popular desire for ease of use as a point-click-results capability, Irene Greif of the Lotus Development Corporation suggested the need to prepare for a greater level of sophistication by building systems that accommodate the sophisticated as well as the limited:

> We do not want to build user interfaces so simple that the user who needs to undertake a more complex task, for example to issue a sequence of requests—some of which depend on the outcome of previous requests—cannot do so at all. A simple point-and-click interface cannot easily express these more complex objectives.

Another issue for providers is responding to the need for access to the same information from different user interfaces. People have different sets of skills for finding and visualizing information, and they need different user interfaces to allow them to make the best use of those skills. Group systems that take into account users' varying capabilities can be very valuable in making teams more productive and smoothing out the problems inherent in people seeing things differently.[18]   Different kinds of interfaces may also be needed to support access by people with certain physical limitations. Of particular concern are the vision-impaired, whose needs are not addressed by the many activities aimed at producing a more visually rich interface, whether via television or PC.

ACCESS DEVICES

In homes, the three main access devices deployed at this time are the telephone, the television (TV), and the PC. Ninety-four percent of U.S. households have a telephone (FCC, 1994, Table 8.1), about 97 percent have a TV (McConville, 1995; Veronis, Suhler, 1995, p. 313), and 32 percent have a PC (Veronis, Suhler, 1995, p. 313). At work, the access devices are telephones and PCs. On the road, it is again the telephone (perhaps wireless) and the portable PC, with TVs ubiquitous in temporary accommodations. Communication occurs over public and private networks. It is logical to start with this installed base to understand how people will access future information infrastructures, even though current devices will evolve over time.

The "inevitable" merging of the various access devices into one, either the TV or PC, has been forecast. Notable in the January workshop, however, was the expectation among participants from the computer, television, and telephone industries that these access devices would coexist, albeit with an increasingly powerful and flexible set of capabilities. Despite interest in speculating about futuristic consumer devices, the roles of the principal access devices are not likely to change for at least several years. The PC-TV combinations now coming onto the market appear to be basically a PC with augmented capabilities for television reception. The television is not becoming a PC, although the PC may be used as a television (and also as a telephone).

Given the enormous installed base and the substantial volumes of existing devices that will be delivered in the next several years, it is likely that televisions, PCs, and also telephones will remain the only access devices deployed in enough quantity to qualify as consumer items. Changes will take place, but, as has been seen before, a new service will not completely supplant an established one: as television service emerged, for instance, radio service did not die, because it had a well-defined set of user modalities that continued to provide value; as television emerged, movies did not disappear. The PC is a new medium whose capabilities can be exploited to provide new services, such as those associated with the Internet, as well as mature services whose operators understand and know how to capitalize on PC capabilities.

The Personal Computer

Given the various uses anticipated for the NII—including work, learning, business and commercial transactions, and entertainment—the PC's role as an access device will become increasingly important (see Box 2.6).[19] Close to 60 million PCs were deployed in the U.S. workplace at the end of 1994, with close to 80 percent of them connected to a network (IDC, 1995f). About 32 million were deployed in the home.[20] Millions of portable PCs are used by mobile workers. The most rapidly growing industry segment is the installation of PCs in the home (*Business Week*, 1995).

The PC's importance for access to current and future information infrastructure raises concerns particularly about cost and ease of use. Consumers now pay about $2,000 for a new computer, a price that has increased slightly over the last several years—as has the volume of PCs purchased. Current industry trends are to keep prices relatively constant while delivering increasing power and capability in the machine. Improvements in processor design and integrated circuit manufacturing techniques have consistently lowered the cost for a given amount of memory or processing power,[21] a trend likely to continue. These added capabilities are important both in improving ease of use (graphical user interfaces, for example, require substantial processing power and memory) and in delivering multimedia capabilities.

Although the PC thus provides the greatest and most general capability among the common access devices, as an access device it is relatively expensive. Consequently, the computer industry continuously asks the question, Can we create a useful, under-$500 access device? Such a "Model T" or "Yugo" could boost the household penetration rate of PCs closer to 80 percent. To date, no such device has proved popular, in part because the compromises required in features and capabilities would be severe, but companies are experimenting with limited-feature, low-price devices, and their experiences will help calibrate the market.[22] The improvement in features at an approximately constant real cost will likely pace the replacement (or augmentation) rate. Compounding the costs for equipment and software purchase are other costs relating to network access and support, which may raise the effective cost of a networked PC to several thousand dollars, or in large institutions, tens of thousands of dollars.

Given the expectation that PC costs will remain relatively constant at about $2,000 per system, what steps can be taken to ensure that the widest possible cross section of society benefits from this technology?[23] What is likely to happen has an analogy in how needs for transportation are satisfied: while not everyone owns an automobile, most have access to transportation. Similarly, electronic access to information is being made avail-

---

BOX 2.6
The Growing Role for the Personal Computer

• *The personal computer (PC) is interactive in both stand-alone mode and on a network.* Interactivity is fundamental to its design and use. When the PC is compared to other access devices, such as the television, there are and will continue to be significant differences in what is meant by interactivity, driven primarily by the differences in usage modalities: one sits about 2 feet from a PC and about 10 feet from a television.

• *The PC is mass-produced.* The installed base of workplace PCs in the United States is almost 60 million units, according to International Data Corporation (IDC, 1995f); IDC forecasts a base of 80 million in 1999. Home PCs represent the fastest growing market segment, with shipments increasing from 6 million in 1993 to 9 million in 1995 (McWilliams, 1995). Jupiter Communications estimates that there are 34 million households with PCs in 1995 (Maresca, 1995). Market research suggests that factors behind growing household PC use include increases in working at home, falling relative prices, increasing ease of setup (due to more fully equipped hardware and preinstalled software), and new choices of software and applications (Kirkpatrick, 1994).

• *The PC is a de facto worldwide standard.* In the computer industry, the volume of sales sets de facto standards, and hardware and software compatibility are relatively good. Furthermore, there are no geographic barriers to PC use; over 50 percent of purchases are outside the United States.

• *PC technology advances.* Over the years the PC has evolved in CPU performance, quality of the user interface, storage capacity, and connectivity, among other characteristics. Hardware improvements have been accompanied by advances in applications. The rate of technological change is accelerating, with rapid improvement in such areas as multimedia capabilities, connectivity, and mobility.

• *The PC is adaptable.* The PC is both a business and a consumer product that has business, education, entertainment, and other uses. With the emergence of real-time video communication capabilities, the PC will become a communication device augmenting existing voice services. Simultaneous transmission of data, video, and audio is a practical possibility.[1]

---

[1]Chapter 5 presents statistics concerning introduction of new products that augment the capabilities of PCs for communication, including modems and network equipment.

---

able increasingly in libraries, schools, business establishments, and other public centers where PCs can be utilized by many. Kiosks provide a means for access in public places, although usually for a specified set of services accessed through specialized interfaces (and with less privacy than is possible in the home or individual office).

The Television

About 97 percent of all U.S. households have a television, and about 62 percent out of those have cable service (McConville, 1995). Television is clearly a ubiquitous access device, one that provides communication services for substantial periods of time. It is part of our culture; much of our entertainment and information comes from watching television. With the widespread use of cable services, there is also an existing infrastructure to manage the interaction between users and service providers. Consumers can purchase premium services, either on a monthly basis or on impulse, via the set-top converter, which is the gateway between the television and the cable service providers.

Terrestrial broadcast television uses wide bandwidth that potentially could help to enable other services, via broader access to the bandwidth. The greatest source of bandwidth to the home is terrestrial TV, but its 6-MHz channels provide 20 Mbps only for one-way communication into the home, supporting only a fraction of the activities that can leverage the NII. Broadening of access is more evident in cable television. As digital video transmission is deployed, cable service providers will be able to increase the capacity of their networks and will also be able to offer additional, including interactive, services. In such an environment, a customer would be able to access (purchase) content—such as video programming—more or less on demand from a server. The set-top box will play an increasingly important role and will likely go through rapid technological evolution over the next several years.

The likely first step in migrating toward such an environment is the evolution of existing cable systems to hybrid fiber coaxial cable (hybrid fiber coax; HFC) systems, as discussed in Chapter 4. The use of HFC will allow the coexistence of digital and analog signals and will enable two-way, asymmetric transmission of digital data (NIST, 1994c; Hodge, 1994). This is a basic infrastructuren capability that, if properly deployed, will allow the network to connect a number of access devices: television (via set-top box), the PC, and the telephone. While some in the industry would like to see a quick migration to an all-digital delivery paradigm, the television community is concerned about the migration path from analog to digital transmission, combined with the rise of interactivity. In a white paper, Allen Ecker and Graham Mobley voice the expectation that digital set-top boxes will "also have analog tuning capability because you do not want to do away with the analog services that are currently providing most of the revenues that cable systems enjoy, and most of the consumer demand at the current time." Advanced analog set-top boxes have the capability of sending digital applications such as on-screen displays of program guides, virtual channel information, and other digital data along with the analog video and audio. This capability allows an analog set-top box to bridge the gap between analog and digital services that will evolve in the future.

As the television industry moves forward, costs will increase. Television equipment will continue to become "smarter," requiring processing power, memory, and software. Furthermore, modulation techniques to support digital video transmission require high-performance and complex integrated circuits. The cost of such equipment is several times the cost of current set-top boxes. It will take many years before cost goals acceptable in the consumer market will be realized. In the meantime, modest steps are possible such as expanding the channel capacity by the addition of digital delivery to the current analog service.

In summary, an upgrade of the cable plants to HFC, coupled with the development of advanced consumer systems, should allow for advanced television services and an expanded use of broadband networks reaching the home. While this will provide added business opportunities for the service providers, it is highly likely that the role of the television will continue to be what it is today: an entertainment device (CSTB, 1995c).

Advanced Television

Digital television channels provide more broadcast capacity as well as increased data bandwidth in the available spectrum. They make use of compression techniques to allow up to four times the usual number of program streams to be transmitted within a single broadcast channel bandwidth. In addition, efficient channel utilization is likely to link digital high-definition television (HDTV) transmission with unused data stream capacity that could be used for transmission of additional programming or a data service.

HDTV has been the subject of significant levels of corporate and research investment in recent years. It is also the subject of FCC activities in terms of both standards setting and spectrum allocation. Experts are divided about the future of HDTV per se, with some believing that it will provide a very attractive human interface and set of capabilities and others foreseeing a much less significant role. The steering committee generally discounted the impact of HDTV as a force shaping communications and information-related behavior and markets for the next 5 to 7 years, given HDTV's high initial prices and very limited sales, and believes that it will be even longer before a significant amount of HDTV-compatible programming will be available.[24] Even then, the steering committee considered the availability of new spectrum for other uses to be more important than the availability of a higher-fidelity television viewing experience. In the meantime, TV programming displays on PCs are growing, presenting prospects for enhancing and otherwise using those images.

The Telephone and Other Access Devices

With about 94 percent of all U.S. households having telephone service, telephones rival televisions as the most widely used device for gaining access to the NII and will continue in that capacity for the foreseeable future. Although the functionality of a telephone can be found increasingly in PCs and its eventual integration into television and set-top box installations has been variously proposed, it is unlikely that such developments will affect the widespread installation of telephones. The telephone is an inexpensive and highly versatile consumer device that has become an integral part of our lifestyle, and the ongoing introduction of a variety of telephone-based services further increases its functionality.[25]

Cellular and personal communication service (PCS) telephones now provide increasing communications mobility to a broadening slice of society.[26] Initially expensive business tools for senior executives, real estate agents, and other business managers who must operate untethered to landlines, cellular telephones are now becoming commodity items for the general consumer; PCS "telephones" are expected to follow suit. Over time, these telephones, too, are becoming "smarter," linking into computer networks for data access or for basic telephony over broad regions of the world that have central billing.

Combining a range of computing and communications features in a highly portable package, personal digital assistants (PDAs) promise to provide "anytime, anywhere" communication capabilities of a broader nature than can be found in pagers or telephones or a hybrid of the two.[27] If that promise can be realized, then PDAs may constitute a cheap ($200) PC with communications capability. Greater support for wireless, mobile systems may spur development and use of such small systems, although their impact may be limited in this decade.[28]

Toward a Fully Integrated Home System

An important question is how the three separate classes of access device—the telephone, the television, and the PC—will interconnect and interoperate with the various networks coming into the home. Currently, there is no clear or consistent model for how (or even whether) to achieve interconnections): the consumer must obtain a separate interface unit for each access device being connected to each type of network. A PC requires a stand-alone device (a voice modem, an integrated services digital network (ISDN) interface, or (now emerging) a modem for the cable network); a television requires a leased or purchased set-top box, satellite decoder box, or simple antenna to receive television signals. The consumer must hook all these pieces together correctly. This task is, at present, a significant source of user frustration that is often compounded by the failure of the various parts to work well together. For example, televisions cannot offer advanced features such as "picture inside the picture" through many set-top boxes.[29]

Any business sector that provides infrastructure components must work to ensure that there are suitable standards and interconnection interfaces in place so that the consumer can assemble a system from parts or pay an expert to provide the assembly service. Failure to provide and implement such standards is perceived as a barrier to market penetration (see Box 2.7), yet premature standardization also remains a concern. Some industry players see the set-top box as evolving to serve as a central point of interconnection for all networks and applications. This capability would require that the set-top box (which might at that point be too large to actually sit on top of a television set) have some internal modularity so that interfaces to different networks could be plugged into it, much as network interface cards today are plugged into a PC. See Box 2.8. Other project contributors cautioned against projecting the characteristics of today's set-top boxes into the future. General Instrument's Quincy Rodgers noted that set-top boxes divert attention from "the real issue, which is where different functionality is to be performed in a network." Additionally, Robert Aiken of Lawrence Livermore National Laboratory questioned whether "what gets deployed [in the home] becomes a separate choice from what gets deployed in the access network."

A well-elaborated concept for staged evolution toward home-based integration is offered in the white paper by Ecker and Mobley. They describe the potential for a two-part home communications terminal (HCT)—one part specific to the particular network (network interface module) that could be rented and one general part that could be purchased with features to meet the needs of the consumer (see Figure 2.2).[30] In the forum, Mobley explained that a network interface module would be necessary "in order to come up with a box that a consumer can buy and know would be compatible in the future." The final phase of integration would be a fully integrated home unit or home set of equipment that would connect broadband PC modems to the cable system, provide for power consumption monitoring, support telephony, and provide access to digital interactive entertainment. According to Ecker and Mobley, the rate at which full integration occurs will be governed by a number of factors, including migration to digital transmission, development of multimedia operating systems and user interfaces to support multiple applications, design for "full interoperability at critical interfaces and [to] oper-

BOX 2.7
The Need for Consumer Interface Standards

Consumers have a very interesting habit. If the industry is confused, think about how confused consumers are. They simply sit on their wallets. If we want to make the NII useful, we have got to deal with standards.

—Vito Brugliera, Zenith Electronics Corporation

There will be opportunities for communication of applications between appliances within the home. That means that whatever we design in terms of a network has to comprehend access into the home, out of the home, and within the home within the architecture.

[There is a need to develop] something I would call the moral equivalent of the RJ-11 for broadband. By that I mean a lot more than just the physical connector. What the RJ-11 has done symbolically for the telephony industry is turn on a very large set of creative applications of telephony, ranging from modem applications in the data space to all sorts of remote voice mail with touch-tone entry, and all sorts of answering machines. . . . [T]here is a national market in which a consumer can go down to . . . the local supplier, buy equipment, and know that it will plug in and work not just in his current home, but also in whatever home he moves to. We need to achieve something like that for the broadband world. We need an architecture that will generate a standard consumer way of interfacing with the broadband network, which is independent of all of the choices we know we are going to have to make in the access network.

We have heard arguments about the differences between various hybrid fiber coaxial cable-type deployments, between that and fiber to the curb, asymmetric digital subscriber line, and various wireless technologies for reaching the home. Ultimately, I think the consumer is not going to care a lot about the access technology. What he is going to want to be able to do is have his PC or his other information appliance capable of plugging into the NII in a standardized way. That is going to require the definition of a standard for connectivity both at a physical level and at an electrical level, and a protocol level that is common across at least a national market, perhaps a worldwide market.

—Kevin Kahn, Intel Corporation

If you believe the PC is the device, then the answer is a 10-base T Ethernet plug: it is an RJ-45. It is the logical successor to an RJ-11. The wireless modems have that plug on the back, the ISDN modems have that plug on the back, and the T-1 modems and the RF modems. Guess what? PCs already come with Ethernet plugs on the back and you plug them together and you are done. They are in fact routers. The set-top box should be a router; it is a media converter. That is what it is. We are done. It is Ethernet.

—David Clark, Massachusetts Institute of Technology

BOX 2.8
Computer-based Set-Top Boxes and Multisignal Conversion

Given the several digital data delivery media entering the home, including cellular, broadcast, cable, telephone, and direct broadcast satellite, practicality, economy, and convenience demand a single "set-top box" for the description, decoding, and processing of the signals for display. Further, the increasing need for interactive upstream communication suggests that, if it should ever achieve universal penetration, the computer, with its associated telephone modem, is the most efficient location for the multisignal converter functions. The convenience of the armchair remote control facing the television display will remain for the viewer of entertainment programs, but some of the switching functions it originates would be performed in the computer-based signal converter. In this concept, the leads from the terrestrial antenna, the satellite dish, and the cable feed would all terminate at the computer box where appropriate circuits would process the signals for display at, in many cases, multiple viewing locations in the home, each requiring different signals for display. This aspect of convergence will minimize the cost of equipment to be acquired by the consumer.

—Vito Brugliera, James A. Chiddix, D. Joseph Donahue,
Joseph A. Flaherty, Richard R. Green, James C. McKinney,
Richard E. Ottinger, and Rupert Stow,
"The NII in the Home: A Consumer Service"

---

ate efficiently within the regulatory environment," and in particular the cost of the fully interactive HCT. Currently such units do exist, but they are quite expensive, in part because of the high-density integrated circuits needed to handle the "complex digital and analog signal processing inherent in any interactive terminal."[31]

WHAT INCREASING USE OF GENERAL-ACCESS DEVICES IMPLIES FOR NETWORKING TECHNOLOGY DEPLOYMENT

The increasing use of general-access devices such as PCs has implications for architecture, facilities, and service offerings (see Box 2.9). Also important are basic expectations about how access devices will be used and by whom, including the degree of end-user control over bandwidth and content selection.

What technical capabilities should an advanced information infrastructure have to support expected end-user needs? Chapter 4 discusses options for residential network access that are now under consideration or are currently being deployed. In this section, the steering committee identifies several essential service features for an NII:

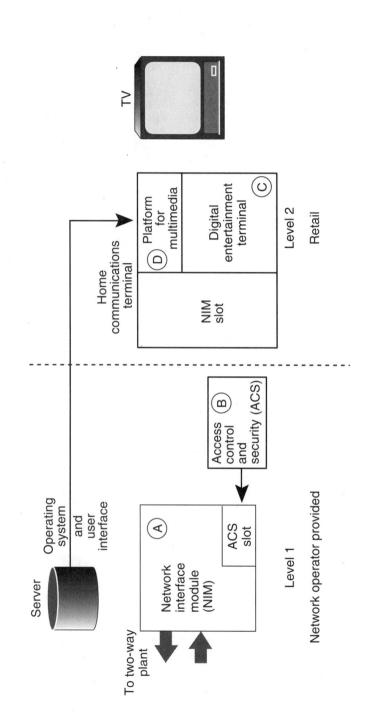

FIGURE 2.2 Proposed two-part broadband digital home communications terminal. Architecture to resolve interoperability and retail sales issues.

SOURCE: "The Evolution of the Analog Set-Top Terminal to a Digital Interactive Home Communications Terminal," a white paper contributed to the NII 2000 project by H. Allen Ecker and J. Graham Mobley.

BOX 2.9
User Behavior and Architectural Support

If I really wanted to be interactive, I would talk to my wife instead of watching television. Most people watch TV. We've had (since 1950) 45 years that have demonstrated pretty conclusively that a lot of people want to have a fair amount of passive entertainment. And I don't think it's necessarily because there is an unavailable interactive alternative. In fact it may be due to the availability of the interactive alternative that you want that passivity. We may be bumping up against a basic constraint on human demand.

—Steven Wildman, Northwestern University

But the Web is based on a different model where the people of the world are creating the content. It makes a great deal of difference in the architectures of the national information infrastructure as we move forward as to where you assume the content is coming from. If it really comes from people everywhere, then you need a two-way, broadband infrastructure. . . . However, if the content is primarily provided by Hollywood and the likes of the current content providers, if the primary market is pay per view, then you can have servers that broadcast essentially to the people.

—Robert Lucky, Bell Communications Research

[There is] value out of being able to present views, present them to one or many specific others, and to communicate as a participant in varied interactions . . . . [T]his implies an architecture quite different from the kind that would mainly support downloaded entertainment. It also implies a set of addressing mechanisms that we do not necessarily get with other kinds of connectivity.

—Tora Bikson, RAND Corporation

In the future you will see much more sophisticated things of that nature, where the content is created on the fly by the user in a collaborative sort of an application, collaborative design, or whatever, where you are mixing graphics and simulation with voice and video, and so on. So I would actually characterize it as three generic kinds of applications. I think that you are either going to have three separate networks for those purposes, or you are going to have a single network that accommodates them all in a relatively cost-efficient way.

—David Messerschmitt, University of California at Berkeley

It all depends upon who gets clicked. If I am at home and I get clicked [by a distant Web user], I need bandwidth back into the network to respond to that click.

—Leonard Kleinrock, University of California at Los Angeles

- High data rates to the end-point,
- Adequate bandwidth in both directions,
- Multiple-session capability,
- Continuous availability of service,
- Real-time, multimedia communication,
- Nomadicity, and
- Security.

Associated with these service features, to make them viable in the market, are ease of attachment and low cost. None of these capabilities are static; they will evolve with the technology and its uses. There are strong ties among the various components: the applications, the computing capability at the end point, and the network capability.

High Data Rates to the End Point

The network connection, or "last mile," must be able to support high data rates (high bandwidth) in order to allow the use of rich, multimedia data types. In the corporate setting, this level of access via local area networks is taken for granted. However, to the home, most users currently use conventional telephony-rate data communications, with current data rates at or below 28.8 kbps. Enhancements to cable TV systems offer the potential of receiving data at 20 Mbps, but that bandwidth is not available to subscribers to transmit with. The capabilities of the video delivery systems are being further expanded. For example, inherent extra capacity in the television vertical blanking interval is now being used by service providers to carry content other than conventional broadcasting, from program-guide information to Web pages linked to broadcasts through the Intercast technology. Yet even with Intercast, a telephone return path is needed for interactive applications.[32]

Many contributors identified ISDN, which offers a data rate of 128 kbps, as the next obvious step in upgrading link speed to the home. ISDN is the cheapest way to gain a factor of 5 to 10 in bandwidth without having to rewire the home; it allows reuse of the existing infrastructure at a relatively small incremental cost.

While these speeds are applicable for tasks such as exploring the Web or exchanging mail, they can constrain more advanced jobs involving access to higher-resolution images or video. These services are better served by data rates similar to those for today's local area networks, with peak transmission speeds between 1 and 10 Mbps. The steering committee concluded that residential bandwidths in this range would be very desirable to serve emerging applications needs.[33]

Adequate Bandwidth in Both Directions

In a typical corporate network environment the end user is able to receive and send data at the same rate. This symmetry is also present at lower speeds when a PC is connected to a network via a modem through conventional telephony or ISDN circuits. However, because of the features of some advanced technologies such as those used by the cable industry, the service that cable providers are anticipated to provide is typically highly asymmetric: users are able to receive data at a higher rate than they can send data. Chapter 4 gives more details on the performance to be expected. Although this upstream or reverse-channel speed is adequate for many applications, many believe that it may become an increasingly limiting factor in achieving the promise of an advanced NII.[34] It is important that network architectures take such potential limitations into consideration and allow for future upgrades to assure that demand for ever-increasing bandwidth can be satisfied economically.

Multiple-Session Capability

Network access must be able to support multiple sessions simultaneously. Corporate networks are able to provide this capability today. For such a capability to be available to the home, some sort of packet switching is required. Packet switching allows a user with a single telephone connection to communicate with multiple remote sites. Inexpensive packet switches are now being marketed for the home or small business that will allow multiple individuals (workers or family members) to have network access simultaneously without having to sign up for multiple service connections. Increasingly, ISDN and conventional telephony modems are being used from the home to carry data packets exactly for this purpose. Current data modems for cable now being evaluated also use the packet mode of transmission to support this objective.

Continuous Availability of Service

Continuously available service is important because it saves having to dial up to be able to receive information. For example, a user can be notified of received mail as it arrives, not just when the user thinks to check for it (the assumption is that the user is not billed for passive connect time). When availability is continuous the user can offer a service on demand—the user can become a provider. Continuous availability of service is often found in large business or institutional settings. In the home today it is most evident in televisions left on for long periods of time.

Real-time, Multimedia Communication

The network must be able to support advanced, real-time, multimedia communication capabilities. Audio and video will become increasingly useful modes of information delivery. Consider, for example, video clips as a part of a Web page advertising some product or a component in an electronic mail message. Another important application area is teleconferencing, especially video conferencing, which many think will be a key facilitator of "telework." The requirement for multimedia, real-time communication implies a need for adequate bandwidth (ISDN may not be enough), bidirectional bandwidth (the teleworker will both send and receive a teleconference), and specific tools for bandwidth management. Improvement of compression is allowing better and better video to be supported on comparatively narrow bandwidths. Video conferencing on 128 kbps looks much better and is much cheaper today than a few short years ago.

Nomadicity

Network access must be available from multiple points—at work, from the home, on the road—whether tethered to a wireline system or through wireless capabilities. Different mechanisms for access will most likely have different characteristics, both in the physical and logical connection, but the applications must be able to scale with available resources. Nomadicity (any time, anywhere access) is a critical capability for an advanced information infrastructure (see Katz, 1995). It bears on lower physical and services levels of the architecture as well as middleware and application levels. The challenges of providing for nomadicity were outlined in forum comments and in a white paper by Leonard Kleinrock; see Box 2.10. Nomadic users must adapt to differing bandwidth levels from different locations and increasingly will embrace wireless and wireline transmission at different times and locations.[35] Supporting them places a premium on interoperability and accommodation of differences in the nature of the error rate, fading behavior, interference levels, and so on between wireless and wireline networks as well as accommodation of multiple wireless architectures that may or may not involve base stations.

Security

Security considerations will be increasingly important. Although the need for security is currently appreciated more in businesses than in homes, even in businesses there is limited awareness. The topic of security is well beyond the scope of this project, but contributors clearly noted

---

BOX 2.10
Nomadicity

The kinds of parameters we have to worry about are the usual ones: bandwidth, latency, reliability, error rate, delay, storage, processing power, interference, interoperability—and, in addition, size, weight, and battery power, another set of key concerns in the things we carry around with us . . . . We have to deal with the unpredictability of the user, of the network, of the platform. We have to deal with graceful degradation. We have to scale with respect to everything: number, size, quality of service, and so on.

—Leonard Kleinrock, University of California at Los Angeles

---

the need for capabilities that allow for the protection of individual privacy, the security of funds transfer and protections for intellectual property, and the integrity of material transmitted. Several contributors commented on how this issue is being tackled within industry domains (e.g., banking and finance, manufacturing), including attempts to use the Internet more securely; deployment issues relate to securing of infrastructure links and end-to-end applications and therefore affect all levels of the architecture and all players, including users themselves.

Dependence on networking activities in more and more social and economic activity will broaden concerns about security. Irene Greif described this process at the forum:

> Once your community is all hooked up so that everybody can talk to everyone else, if you volunteer to organize a PTA committee to do a surprise party for the teachers, you are going to have to figure out whether the discussion bulletin board that you have put in place for that process can be read by all of the teachers, the principal, some of the students, all of the parents. You will be doing access control and database design, and building a whole application. That is not easy. We have had quite a bit of success in the business world with groupware products, getting some of those kind of capabilities out of the hands of the skilled programmers, MIS [management information systems] departments, and into the hands of office workers. But that is still very far from what home users will want.

CONCLUDING OBSERVATIONS

As outlined above and based on many inputs, the steering committee concluded that the following capabilities are essential service features of an information infrastructure evolving to meet end users' varied and increasingly general-purpose needs: high data rates to the end point, adequate bandwidth in both directions, multiple-session capability, continuous availability of service, real-time and multimedia access, nomadicity, and security. Together, they compose a very different set than is currently available.

Comments by representatives of various user domains suggested concern about two alternative and undesirable prospects. On the one hand, decisions regarding financing, timing, bandwidth, symmetry, standards, services, and virtually every other aspect of residential and small-business access appear to many to be driven today by the presumption that home entertainment is the residential "killer app." Industry and government service representatives, concerned about their business or functional needs, are unsure what will result under this scenario. Would the infrastructure deployed as a result be of sufficiently low generality to lock out either some currently viable applications or deployments, or some future ones? Or would deployment of any sort be slowed because of uncertainty about the viability of this business model?

On the other hand, responses by different infrastructure providers to varying business pressures might result in an NII characterized by heterogeneous technologies and architectures, interoperating poorly, if at all. Investment in the reengineering of access facilities to the home will be slowed by the difficulty of making an integrated business case for infrastructure deployment, because the potential uses for infrastructure appear in a number of business sectors and are difficult to evaluate. At the same time, development of multiple delivery systems can foster innovation in technology and businesses and can provide more choices to meet diverse user needs and wants. Will citizens and sectors of the economy, as they become sufficiently sophisticated in their use of a range of applications, recognize the implicit cross-application demand for general-purpose capabilities too late to motivate timely provision of such capabilities?

The disconnect between users and infrastucture providers must be resolved largely by the user and application domains better articulating their needs and making clear the importance of enabling broad infrastructure use. This is something the user domains have not done well. A second approach to bridging the gap is to bring the infrastructure builders into the industry or sector planning and implementation processes so that the two can deal jointly with the technical and financial models required to serve both. A good example of this approach is represented by the North Carolina Health. Information and Communications Alliance established by the state legislature but funded almost entirely by private industry. This project, truly a joint effort of state government, health industry professionals, health industry information vendors, and infrastructure providers, illustrates that installing infrastructure can be handled more quickly and easily than can working through the political, social, and high-level barriers to use—problems that are expected to take several years to resolve.

Despite real concerns and choices, the near-term barriers to end-user access are not the technical features of the access infrastructure. A modern modem and Internet access from a Macintosh or "Windows" PC constitute a sufficient baseline for the next stage in widening access to general-purpose information infrastructure. Users today have concluded that they can experience the World Wide Web quite successfully from a home or a school over telephone lines. One possible path forward involves encouraging further use so that people can learn how to benefit more fully from the information technology. Rather than emphasizing the need for more bandwidth as a minimum, users should perhaps focus on minimizing barriers related to cost, ease of use, a natural process of familiarization and acceptance, and maturation of standards and interfaces, so that the consumer is better able to purchase and integrate the needed components.

The enduring issue of standards and interfaces for consumer equipment has ramifications that range to the competitive position of U.S. companies, given the international nature of information infrastructure goods and services. For data access, the steering committee sees a trend toward an Ethernet interface, the so called 10Base-T standard, as the connector for consumer data devices.[36] In the television industry, the organization of the next generation of product (e.g., the eventual role of the set-top box and the television) is not currently clear. A number of developments point to progress in the area: the Advanced Television Systems proceeding at the FCC is likely to settle on a wide range of characteristics of digital systems for broadcast television,[37] the preponderance of which will apply to all methods of network distribution; MPEG-2, while not a complete system, has standardized a wide range of digital video characteristics, and the Advanced Television standard is expected to be consistent with MPEG-2; telephone companies have begun the process of procuring video equipment, several settling on an architectural structure consistent with that described in the white paper by Ecker and Mobley and based on a separation of security and network functionality into two parts—network equipment (a network interface module) and other features in consumer equipment (a digital entertainment terminal); and standards bodies (such as the Digital Audio Visual Council) are currently working toward standardizing digital video over cable television systems. It should be noted, however, that there are advocates both for the marketplace setting the standards or for technologists seeking to do the same by setting standards prior to the introduction of a given technology. Both approaches have advantages and disadvantages.

NOTES

1. See CSTB (1994c) for a discussion of technology needed to support telework. According to a recent survey of Internet users, over two-thirds connect to the Internet from the office as opposed to from home (see Swisher, 1995).

2. These comments apply primarily to white collar work, but the increasing role of service activities in all manner of industry and sector implies that the kind of work that can be done from the home composes a growing share of the occupational mix.

3. "Killer app" is a term of art that refers to an application that enables the information infrastructure environment in a way not economically possible before. This is in marked contrast to "killer technology," a term in the electronics industry that refers to a new technology that drives prior technologies out of the marketplace (e.g., what solid-state electronics did to vacuum tubes).

4. The need to generate adequate return on investment fuels the search for the elusive "killer application." While derided by some, it is a simple expression of the business appeal of something that sells in large (enough) volume to support the kind of traffic aggregation that makes increasing bandwidth supply cost-effective. The value of simply covering a significant percentage of the market seems particularly apparent in the cable industry, which, while considerably smaller and more cash-poor than the telephone industry, appears committed to extensive and expensive facilities upgrading to hybrid fiber coaxial cable systems based largely on the revenue expectations associated with entertainment.

Wendell Bailey and James Chiddix observe in a white paper that the networks being deployed are sufficiently general-purpose that they could support other applications besides video entertainment if the market demands them. For example, Time Warner is now providing wireline telephone service to customers in Rochester, New York, in competition with the incumbent telephone carrier. Bailey and Chiddix calculate that with 15 percent penetration of homes passed, the incremental cost of supporting telephony will be under $1,000 per customer in the short term. Increased penetration and improvements in hardware price-performance could lower this cost further. (Cable and telephone company entry into one another's lines of business depends, of course, on regulatory issues in addition to economic and technical factors.) Cable systems originally designed for delivery of video to the home do not typically have large numbers of connections to business premises or to facilities of interexchange carriers; interconnection with the local telephone company is necessary to provide these connections, as has occurred in the Rochester case.

5. Because of the video component, entertainment is linked to higher bandwidth than is conventional telephony, leading some to argue that if the infrastructure is built to support entertainment it will support other applications. The amount of support it can provide will depend on architectural parameters (e.g., symmetry).

6. Terrestrial television broadcasting revenues are derived overwhelmingly from advertising and size the industry at about $30 billion annually (Veronis, Suhler, 1995, p. 104).

7. New information and entertainment services coexist with currently available services in competing for the consumer's attention and resources. In 1993, the average U.S. adult spent 3,304 hours using communications media, such as television, radio, recorded music, newspapers, books, magazines, theatrical and videotaped movies, and video games. (These data, from Veronis, Suhler & Associates, do not include time spent using telecommunications services such as telephony.) This total has varied within a 3 percent band since 1989, and Veronis, Suhler predict only a modest 1 percent increase in the next 5 years. The most popular media in terms of time spent were television (1,560 hours, almost half of the total), radio (1,102 hours), music (294 hours), and newspapers (169 hours). Educational software and consumer on-line and Internet services are the segments projected to increase most rapidly in terms of consumer use over the next 5 years, at over 20 percent and over 36 percent per year, respectively. Because both start from comparatively minuscule shares of consumer time, they have the capacity to grow substantially without having to drive out mature services such as television and radio. (See Veronis, Suhler, 1995, p. 15)

Another recent survey (Hamlin, 1995) by NPD Group found that respondents recorded about 4.5 hours daily spent on "entertainment," which included television-video-music, reading, hobbies, visiting friends, or out-of-home entertainment, and just under 3 hours daily on "other" activities that included such disparate categories as gardening and on-line networking. The contrast between the results of these studies underscores how little is really understood (or consistently described) in terms of consumer behavior.

8. Kraut's Home Net project shows that the methodologies developed in workplaces are being taken into homes as well (Kraut et al., 1996).

9. Key issues concern speed of change, kinds of change, perhaps obstacles to deployment due to naive analysis—or absence of analysis about cost-benefit distribution (as documented in Olsen et al., 1993). See Greif (1988) for historical background and technical and social papers. An instructive example concerns the Version Manager added to Lotus 1-2-3: early focus group evaluators disliked the idea of a group spreadsheet but could grasp immediately the need for alternative versions of ranges in their individual "what-if" analyses. Sometimes during the course of a single 2-hour session, some subjects' attitudes about group spreadsheets turned around completely as they talked through for themselves how having personal "versioning" would then make it more likely that they could share their spreadsheets. Incremental change and perceived personal payoff paved the way to acceptance of a technology that initially seemed unfamiliar and of benefit primarily to others.

10. The rise of the magazine *Wired* may be emblematic: it "has become the totem of a major cultural movement" (Keegan, 1995).

11. According to Irene Greif, Lotus Development Corp. has learned about the advantage of supplying more features than a developer can sell at the outset. People who thought that they were buying into LotusNotes to share information later learned the value of the access control and authentication features. The

design tools also come into play in fairly short order, as end users realize that their group needs something slightly different than other groups.

12. The majority of individuals who use PC software may utilize only the basic capabilities of that software, without taking advantage of its more advanced features. Similarly, there are those who hardly use video cassette recorder features beyond hitting "on" and "play" for a rented video. Even years of exposure to personal computers have left most end users uncomfortable with the information-sharing potential of NII technologies. Groupware systems have been installed at many forward-thinking corporations only to be rejected by users who were not ready to embrace such technology.

13. In many instances, these issues reflected major changes taking place within a particular domain and hold significant implications for the NII (e.g., the trends toward managed care and home-based patient care will have profound effects on the health care domain as well as its NII-related requirements). With regard to health care, for example, the Council on Competitiveness observed that "telemedicine will not be used until it is considered a proper standard of medical care, and it will not be considered acceptable care until it is more widely used" (COC, 1994, p. 7). Even industries with considerable experience using networked systems, such as banking, continue to innovate. For example, a new effort to interconnect banks, the EDI Bank Alliance Network Exchange, has been described as an alternative to more traditional forms of electronic data interchange that will provide more flexibility to banks but also affect internal bookkeeping and reporting (see Messmer, 1995a).

In institutional settings, in particular, the accumulation of technical infrastructure relates to service demand and use. For example, one of the biggest obstacles to deployment of LotusNotes has been lack of infrastructure. Sales initially were made to large customers who could show installed and working PC LANs and serious support for networking, on the grounds that otherwise the customer would have to make too large a change at once and would not be able to separate issues of infrastructure deployment from those of application-level deployment.

14. Federal program attention to health care and other major domains that have been called "national challenge" areas has fostered progress in scientific and technical applications of information infrastructure in those domains. As noted in the project white paper by Randy Katz et al., those applications involve small numbers of dedicated (and motivated) users, but they help to validate the promise of information technology and illuminate domain-specific challenges. Addressed as one of the goals of the federal High Performance Computing and Communications Initiative, National Challenges include work in digital libraries, public access to government information, electronic commerce, civil infrastructure, education and lifelong learning, energy management, environmental monitoring, health care, and manufacturing processes and products (CIC, 1995). See also CAT (1994a,b).

15. Businesses, too, are unhappy with current tax law on depreciation. The mandated 5-year depreciation cycle on computer hardware means that new technology purchases are often delayed while thousands of PCs complete their depreciation term. Says one chief information officer, "You have a tax accountant

driving IS [information systems] policy, and that's bizarre." As a result, some companies are quietly expensing their computer hardware, while others are exploring leasing options. See Halper (1995).

16.   Affordability is a concern for small businesses as well as residences.

17.   The U.S. Chamber of Commerce and others recently launched a business-service suite (a set of bundled specific services) aimed at small businesses (see Anthes, 1995b) that includes such resource-location functions.

18.   For example, users of collaborative software might be confused in a real-time conference if they are unable to make "here" and "there" references, unless a system translates these for separated users.

19.   The white paper by Avram Miller and Ogden Perry discusses this point further. Early reports of the end-of-year sales patterns suggest that consumer purchases of high-speed modems for home PCs grew, reflecting an estimated increase from 70 to 90 percent of (all) PCs sold with modems, most also featuring installed software for on-line service access (Templin, 1995).

20.   See Veronis, Suhler & Associates (1995), p. 313. Some sources offer a higher estimate, up to 35 percent; see, for example, Maresca (1995).

21.   Other PC components, not central processing unit (CPU)- or memory-related, that carry significant costs include the color display, power supply, communication interface, and disk storage, which have improved more rapidly than the CPU. A breakthrough in the cost of the display unit would rapidly contribute significantly to the prospect of developing a cost-reduced data access device. The white paper by Brugliera et al. notes that the display and cabinet constitute 75 percent of the total cost of television equipment.

22.   See Clark and Rigdon (1995), Ziegler (1995a), and Burgess (1995). Oracle has proposed a $500 "network computer" intended to allow Internet access over telephone lines (see *Wall Street Journal,* 1995c). Apple Computer has developed Pippin, a multimedia player and Internet access device that attaches to the television. Pippin is expected to be available in 1996 for less than $1,000 (Hamm, 1995).

23.   Attaining universal access was the focus of a RAND Corporation study that called for universal electronic mail (Anderson et al., 1995). There is an obvious economic barrier facing a portion of households that would like to own a PC. One study reported that while 59 percent of households with income of at least $50,000 own a PC, the number is 29 percent for those in the $30,000 to $49,999 range and 19 percent for those below $30,000 (KRT Graphics, 1995).

24.   Each week, 50 hours of HDTV-compatible programming is available now in the form of 35-mm film used in most prime-time productions.

25.   Voice messaging, call forwarding, caller identification, and other services are obvious examples.

26.   The white papers by Robert Roche and Mary Madigan give details.

27.   By extension, various wearable computing and communications devices are also expected to reinforce use of information infrastructure. Features and costs are even more speculative for these products than for larger portable communications and computing devices.

28.   Philips Electronics recently announced plans for a video telephone that could be worn on the wrist and offer Internet access (Bloomberg Business News, 1995).

29. This kind of incompatibility between cable service offerings and advanced consumer electronics features motivated the cable compatibility element of the 1991 Cable Act (P.L. 98-549), amending 47 USC Sec. 544. It required that "[w]ithin one year after October 5, 1992, the Commission shall prescribe regulations which establish minimum technical standards relating to cable systems' technical operation and signal quality. The Commission shall update such standards periodically to reflect improvements in technology. A franchising authority may require as part of a franchise (including a modification, renewal, or transfer thereof) provisions for the enforcement of the standards prescribed under this subsection. A franchising authority may apply to the Commission for a waiver to impose standards that are more stringent than the standards prescribed by the Commission under this subsection." The provision led to standards-setting activities (and associated debates) within the cable industry.

30. The inclusion of both rented and purchased components assumes some continuation of current business practice whereby some service providers, such as cable multiple system operators, supply equipment to facilitate upgrades, protect against theft of service, and influence how consumers use their offerings.

31. A fully interactive HCT requires about nine custom-integrated circuits, 975,000 gates, and more than 1,500 interconnections between the integrated circuits. With advances in integration, the number of required integrated circuits may be improved to perhaps two by 1998, which would improve the marketability of the HCT to consumers.

32. Eventually, technology (e.g., plug-in boards) may support consumer access to the vertical blanking interval, thus facilitating more direct interactivity (Intercast, 1995).

33. As discussed in Chapter 4, there are a number of options for more advanced transmission services to the home. In addition to copper wire, 60 percent of U.S. homes have cable television service. Since 93 percent of homes are passed by cable service, further deployment of coax access, as for HFC, is relatively easy in these neighborhoods. The evolution of traditional cable systems to hybrid fiber coaxial cable increases the potential for provision of advanced network services with higher bandwidths.

Broadcast is another path to the home. There is today limited ability to carry data in the unused portions of the video signal (e.g., the vertical blanking interval), and the anticipated move to digital video broadcast will provide much greater capacity. The rapid emergence of direct broadcast satellite is another path to the home, with similar opportunities for general information delivery. Interactivity for these two paths is hampered by the fact that the telephone is the most likely back channel for the foreseeable future.

Cellular, and eventually PCS, telephones are also points of access from the home. However, they are low-bandwidth connections and are likely to be used for data access only when alternative wire services are not available.

34. ISDN is used to support video and data conferencing, for example, but it is difficult to upload a great amount of data.

35. Meanwhile, software to support nomadic users is providing options for conserving on bandwidth (e.g., through compressed file transfer and transmis-

sion of only changed portions rather than the entirety of files) as well as remote control of network nodes (e.g., printers) and security (Watt, 1995).

36.   Ethernet is a mature and inexpensive technology. As other technologies, such as asynchronous transfer mode (ATM), mature and become widespread, it is conceivable that they would be used for such purposes.

37.   The FCC will be building on voluntary standards setting that is ongoing in industry.

3

Where Is the Business Case?

FACTORS SHAPING INVESTMENT IN
INFORMATION INFRASTRUCTURE

Perceptions of business opportunities pace deployment of information infrastructure—how much money can be made, with what investment and risk, over what period of time? In and around 1993, when the administration released its *National Information Infrastructure: Agenda for Action* (IITF, 1993), private and public discourse seemed to reflect greater confidence concerning directions and opportunities. In 1996, however, the inputs to the NII 2000 project suggest that the only aspect of the business case for deployment on which there appears to be broad consensus is uncertainty compounded by a focus on associated risk.[1]

The current uncertainty is accentuated by a combination of ongoing or anticipated transitions in technology (see Chapters 4 and 5), regulation and public policy, and industrial organization. Key technology transitions include the shift in computing power and functionality from the center to the edge of networks; the separation of services from the physical infrastructure; and the shift from analog to digital storage, transmission, and processing. The key public policy shifts relate to relaxation of regulation and other changes in competition policy, plus associated business incentives (e.g., permissible depreciation schedules). Supply and demand are complicated by regulation, which variously (1) affects who can enter which markets, the cost of interconnection, capital formation, and product and service pricing in some but not all segments of the national information infrastructure (NII); (2) has different implications for incumbent and new-entrant enterprises; and (3) motivates some investment decisions based on anticipation that the framework will change. Shifts in industrial organization draw on both technology and policy trends and are fed by the declining costs of bandwidth, increasing consumer investment for infrastructure (cable, end nodes, information services), and surging commercial interest and activity in the Internet.

Among market participants and analysts, there is agreement that markets for information and communications goods and services will grow continuously and that there is a variety of markets, with many kinds of investments, costs, revenue generation models, and buying patterns. There is also recognition that market growth is a function of cumulating purchases and uses that, in turn, build on technical foundations (e.g., expanding price-performance of microprocessor-based devices) and behavioral ones (e.g., growing comfort and sophistication in the use of personal computers (PCs)).[2] Nevertheless, the lack of agreement on how much of what kind of services will likely be purchased (at a given price and time) leads alternately to hedging, experimentation, or stalling.

The clearest trend is toward considerable experimentation by network, service, and content providers now and extending perhaps for another 5 years. The foundation for various experiments is a solid business case in telephony, television delivery, and (more variable) on-line services. At this time, though, corporate commitment to a complete strategy relating to network-based services appears unrealistic, and even companies that had made public strategic commitments have been backing off. For example, among the regional Bell holding companies (RBHCs), enthusiasm has diminished for video dial-tone systems, extending to cancellation, deferral, or alteration of plans for deploying video delivery systems.[3] The market reaction to the Netscape initial public offering may be emblematic of the current ambivalence: despite considerable uncertainty, there is also considerable investor interest, some of it reflected in almost incredibly high initial stock prices.[4]

Technical, business, and regulatory uncertainty is yielding a degree of business paralysis as well as experimentation. The difficulty of expanding the market is seen in the fact that many proposed and attempted information services are alternative methods of delivering known products (e.g., (near) video on demand vs. video cassette rental). Robert Crandall of the Brookings Institution cautioned that where capital investment requirements are high, competing wireless investments may retard progress inasmuch as they drain potential revenues from new wireline facilities by targeting similar applications. By analogy, he noted that "cable evolved not in the novel ways that some of the pie-in-the-sky optimists envisioned in the 1960s and 1970s, but rather by providing us

---

BOX 3.1
A 20-year Horizon?

[W]hat is wrong with 20 years? If you look at the evolution of infrastructure, 20 years is close to a microsecond. If you look at how long it took for digital technology to roll out just into the telephone switching plant, that was a 20-year process. If you look at the development of the PC, which we tend to think of as happening overnight, that was literally a 20-year process as well. If you look at the time needed to introduce any of the fundamental technologies over the last three or four decades, it has been a 15-, 20-, or 25-year process. Indeed, if fiber optics in the home was 20 years from now, I would say that would be a revolutionarily short time, given the fact that the marketplace is going to have to pay for all of this. And if you tried to make it faster, you would probably be distorting the marketplace. You would have to do it with some sort of premature subsidies. Consequently, I am listening to the conversation and saying I do not really understand why we are bemoaning the 20-year period. We should really be rejoicing.

—Howard Frank, Advanced Research Projects Agency

---

more sports, more movies, more replays of sitcoms, and perhaps more news programs." On the other hand, comments generated by the project suggest that such variations on a theme are more likely to come from the obvious players, the existing businesses, and that newer ideas hatched by entrepreneurs may be less visible, at least at first.[5]

Confident of the potential for innovation, James Chiddix of Time Warner Cable observed that "there are thousands of people who will begin to put creative energy into trying to find ways to harness these technologies to find some new wonders and surprises. It is very hard to predict what those things are and what their social implications are. But I think that time is the only issue, whether it is 5 years or 20." Howard Frank of the Advanced Research Projects Agency (ARPA), reflecting on the forum discussions, maintained that 20 years seems reasonable. See Box 3.1.

Information infrastructure businesses can be split roughly into two categories—facilities and services—and the investment required accordingly can be incremental or "greenfield," can support processes that are capital- or labor-intensive, or can be long- or short-lived or sunk.[6] Particular investment choices will drive the amount of bandwidth available, the features that can thus be provided with the bandwidth—especially openness and symmetry giving the capacity for upstream communication—and the application services enabled for the public as a result. Caution and anxiety about the size and profitability of the market increase with the degree to which a business is dominated by facilities, and therefore by capital investment. Investments in facilities are crucial for expanding the deployment of bandwidth, while investments in services that make use of the facilities and in devices that make use of the services are lower in magnitude and shift at least some of the cost away from the facilities providers. The greatest cost—and the highest level of risk—appears to be associated with deploying access circuits, facilities serving homes. Three alternatives seem to be seen for the near-term deployment of network-based infrastructure:

1. Some people will spend large amounts of money to take the infrastructure (especially access lines) one big step forward, installing technology we will live with for a long time; or
2. We will live with access technology that evolves continuously, not in big jumps or after long pauses; or
3. We cannot afford to do what companies or commentators are contemplating.[7]

The remainder of this chapter outlines several issues: the investment challenges associated with evolving the NII, the role of the Internet, and alternative models for generating revenue to recover and drive future investment. A number of themes emerged from the different inputs to the project; this chapter reports, as well as comments on, some of the tone or flavor imparted by different types of facilities and service providers (and by industry analysts) to the debate on information infrastructure investments. Who said what is sometimes as meaningful as what is said at all.

INVESTMENT IN FACILITIES

The Problem of How Much Bandwidth to Invest In

Fiber is being deployed by many parties, setting the stage for competition, since as noted in Chapter 4, sunk investments in fiber facilities can support multiple application services. The investments are being made despite uncertainty that was captured somewhat cynically by Jack Thompson of Gnostech Incorporated when he observed:

> . . . [T]he telephone people are saying, I can't make money in telephony anymore—I have to get into cable. And the cable guys seem to be saying, I can't make any more money in cable; I have to get into telephony. So why is everybody trying to get into a business where there is no money left?

J.C. Redmond et al. of GTE Laboratories address this query specifically in a white paper, noting two possibilities: either current participants can modify their networks "to handle the total communications needs of customers (voice, data, video) by relatively modest incremental investments"—fostering competition to dominate and survive—or unprecedented growth and demand for new services may occur, fostering entry into adjacent or complementary businesses. Given these possibilities, and moderated by the difference in the costs to upgrade a cable TV system to support telephony or to upgrade a telephone system to offer broadband services (*Telecommunications Reports*, 1995i), companies are both posturing and making actual investments in the hopes of reaping the advantages that may accrue to successful first movers.

In the context of investment in facilities for access to information, the problem of whether, when, and where to gamble on fiber is emphasized by telephone companies, because deployment of fiber represents a high fixed-cost investment—creating the desire for high-volume use to recover costs.[8] See Box 3.2. In telephony, despite compelling arguments for fiber in backbone facilities, the lack of local traffic volume may make deployment of fiber to the household unlikely in the near future outside of high-density urban areas.[9] For cable companies, the upgrade path to fiber is clearer. Because they already have coaxial cable networks reaching into homes, cable firms are building fiber out from the center toward homes in a hybrid architecture (see Chapter 4).

Noting that net capital stock has been declining with changes in accounting measures, if not in economic terms in the telephony business, Robert Crandall underscored the need to "keep the flow of new funds coming into this sector of the economy if we hope to build these extremely risky—particularly if they are to be wireline—systems with a substantial amount of fixed costs." With a nod to the major presence of telephone companies, he estimated that "if the NII is to be built by established telephone companies with technology now under development, it would probably require a near doubling of these companies' assets."[10]

The scale of the investment, combined with both competition and constraints on the nature and remuneration provided by business activities to generate revenue, poses the threat of asset stranding to telephone companies. Stewart Personick of Bell Communications Research expressed the problem in the context of sustaining demand, in a competitive environment, for two-way communications capacity:

> If I had to spend $30 a month personally to operate a server, and I found out that for $20 a month I could put my material on someone else's server, with a 155-megabit-per-second incoming line, redundancy, and everything else, why would I month after month pay the $30?

Hal Varian of the University of California at Berkeley explained that the problem is one of survival over the long term, given the underlying economics of the business. He spun scenarios (see Chapter 6, Box 6.4) that

---

BOX 3.2
In Search of Volume

Joel Engel of Ameritech explained that "fiber is an extremely cost-effective transmission medium. It is not cost-effective because it is cheap, but because it has very high capacity. The unit cost is very low, so anywhere you can aggregate traffic, where you can share among many users, the unit cost is quite cost-effective. But, if you run fiber out to the individual subscribers, individual homes or small businesses, they do not generate enough traffic to support that cost, and they have to pay the cost of the whole thing because it is dedicated." In his white paper BellSouth's Robert Blau describes the regional Bell holding company (RBHC) environment as one in which competitive entry into the relatively lucrative exchange access and intra-LATA (local access and transport area) toll markets has both constrained RBHC traffic growth and led to lower prices, depressing growth in earnings. In addition, increases in RBHCs' fixed costs as a proportion of total costs (as may occur with upgrades) may make earnings more volatile.

Jim Chiddix of Time Warner Cable spoke of his company's Full Service Network experiment in Orlando, Florida, as "an expensive project. But if there is a volume market there, the nature of the technologies that we are discussing will force prices down very quickly." John Redmond, reflecting on GTE's experiment in Cerritos, California, emphasized the need for low prices to induce use: "It was not clear that people were going to pay that much more for anything that they could get free off of the television now." Intel Corporation's Kevin Kahn related the problem to mass production in the businesses of information appliances and services: "At the end of the day, the fewer the choices, the higher the volumes; the higher the volumes, the lower the prices, and the more ubiquitous—therefore, the more attractive as a consumer product—it is."

---

might arise if "chronic excess capacity" were to result from "two or more broadband wires to the house providing essentially the same service." Other things being equal, there would be price wars, producers could not cover fixed investments in facilities, and there would be financial distress.

Risk aversion pervades the comments and concerns expressed by the biggest players in the NII arena, the telephone companies (especially the local exchange carriers; LECs), which appear to face both high costs for the associated access circuit investments and high uncertainty in expected circuit use.[11] See Box 3.3. In his white paper Robert Blau of BellSouth points out that telephone companies can and do choose to invest in apparently less risky "opportunities outside local networks," and he suggests that "decisions by Bell company managers to accelerate the introduction of advanced network gear did not have a positive effect on shareholder returns."[12] His analysis points out that investment is deterred by the prospect of delays between deployment (and associated investment) and the generation of returns on that investment. (Invest-

---

BOX 3.3
Risk Aversion and Investment in Circuits

Business says you spend money where you think you can make money. You do not spend money today to make money 25 years from now.

—Edmond Thomas, NYNEX Science and Technology Inc.

Even in a noncompetitive environment, if you invest the capital significantly before the revenues come in, you are in deep trouble, because typically the interest that you have to pay when you borrow the money is about equal to the rate of return when the revenue starts coming in. When there is a 2- or a 3-year gap in between those two events, you never catch up.

—Joel Engel, Ameritech

If shareholders believe that risk-adjusted returns on investment in advanced network technologies will remain competitive with returns on alternative investment opportunities, then those technologies will be deployed and the new service features they make possible will be brought to the market in a timely manner. If, on the other hand, shareholders do not regard prospective returns on network investment to be high enough to compensate for risk incurred, then lesser amounts of discretionary capital spending will be committed to new network technologies.

—Robert Blau, BellSouth Corporation

---

ment advisors Alex. Brown & Sons Inc. (1995), however, have recommended against considering earnings as the key valuation metric for online service providers because they are "investing heavily ahead of expected revenues"; revenue (subscriber) growth and projected cash flow are better indicators. Other financial analysts reportedly expect delayed returns and advise postponing profits in the interest of investing for growth and position (Higgins, 1995b).)

Investment posture also reflects the nature of the business; the degree of optimism and the aggressiveness of investment prospects voiced by contributors to the NII 2000 project varied with the speaker's affiliation. Leslie Vadasz of Intel Corporation related the differences in attitudes about financing to the differences in culture between the computing and communications sectors: "I go to computer meetings, and we don't talk about how much we are going to invest in this, or how much return we are going to get on that. We don't ask, Is there a market? Is there no market? We run as fast as we can." Vadasz expressed concern that absent comparable attitudes among telecommunications providers, "the capability of the access device is going to go up, and up, and up, and up, and the bandwidth available for a [public switched] network environment is not going to keep up with it." The conservatism voiced by telephone company executives corresponds to their observed pace of investment; the impatience voiced by computer companies, among others, begs the question of whether a different outlook, combined with prudent investment strategy, might accelerate deployment. Yet cultural differences do reflect some fundamental differences in the computing and communications markets, such as the greater uncertainty in communications markets; differences in market power and industry structure (e.g., monopolies may be slower to innovate); and regulatory constraints, all of which contribute to a tendency of communications providers not to run as fast as many computer firms.[13]

Federal Licenses as an Influence on Deployment of New Wireless Systems

In contrast to the uncertainties regarding deployment of wireline facilities, the minimum investment in facilities for wireless cellular and personal communication service (PCS; also paging and other mobile radio) systems is more or less determined by spectrum licensing build-out requirements and by competitive pressures.[14,15] While licenses and competitive pressures drive the minimum rate of investment, license holders may also invest in upgrades relative to licensure requirements, which may affect the number of cell sites, interoperability (capability for roaming), and other features; the terms set forth in licenses do not precisely determine deployment.

Licenses do not obviate the risks associated with investment (and arguably could increase them to the extent that deployment proceeds faster than apparent demand would justify). Industry representatives privately acknowledge great uncertainty regarding the evolution of wireless systems, as noted by one project reviewer: "The industry is growing so fast and in so many directions that few people really have a grasp of the whole." One indicator is the reported scaling back by licensees (0.5 MHz) of interactive video and data services of their expectations for the original target markets. Moreover, while attempting to reconceptualize the services they can offer and reduce financial risks, they may transmit only test signals to meet Federal Communications Commission requirements—an illustration of the fact that investment and deployment do not necessarily add up to commercial service availability (see Arlen, 1995a; and Mills, 1995b).

Although cellular license holders were not allowed to bid for PCS licenses in their own territory, the two markets are expected to co-evolve, with the PCS share of the combined market increasing and interoperability growing to help sustain the cellular market base.[16] A key positioning element was the success of the top broadband PCS license winners in aggregating bids to achieve nationwide geographic coverage and contiguous spectrum coverage. Private mobile services (including those for police and fire protection and the growing industry for unit-to-unit communications for personal and business use) already support tens of millions of units in service worldwide, with leading-edge technologies in use and planned.

While regional small wireless systems involve industrywide and major-city investments on the order of $20 billion,[17] space-based satellite systems aimed at provision of global telephony (voice and data) include Teledesic's $9 billion, 840-satellite, low-earth-orbit system; Hughes Communications' $3 billion, 8-satellite system; Motorola's 66-satellite Iridium system; and many more (Samuels, 1995; Cole, 1995). These global systems will be able to provide "cellular-like" service throughout the United States. The white paper by Robert Blau cites a WEFA Group forecast that suggests that excess capacity will result from commercial wireless investments.[18] However, since some unused capacity is normal for lumpy infrastructure investments, the key unknown is the size and duration of the gap between capacity and demand.

Investing to Achieve Infrastructure Generality

Compounding the problem of how much bandwidth to invest in is the problem of deciding to what extent that bandwidth should be provided in a general and flexible form. Decisions about providing for generality affect deployment of services, over and above deployment of facilities. See Box 3.4. The computer industry designs and builds computers that are used for a wide range of applications, not just for a single predetermined application such as word processing. Uncertainty about the eventual application forces the development of devices with general and flexible characteristics. As discussed in Chapter 4, the Internet similarly attempts to be a general infrastructure that can support a range of applications. This generality provides insurance against the unpredictability of demand. A specific example that came up in several discussions at the workshop and forum was whether it was justifiable to install significant bandwidth for traffic from the user into the network, usually discussed as upstream, back-channel, or symmetric bandwidth. Symmetry is a quality inherent in telephony (albeit with limited bandwidth). A related issue is the extent to which the capabilities of the network should be provided in an open manner.

Open interfaces may stimulate the creation of new applications but may also open the door to unwelcome competition. At the forum and in

BOX 3.4
Investment for Generality

The real question is, are we going to have enough capacity in this basic hardware infrastructure and some of the supporting application software that makes possible differentiation so that we can have appropriate differentiation where it is needed?

—Steven Wildman, Northwestern University

The most important characteristic of the NII from the perspective of users is probably the flexibility to accommodate new applications in the future, most of which we cannot anticipate today . . . [allowing] application developers to target a broad set of NII infrastructure and terminals with new applications without having to deal with an exponentially growing set of new cases as new technologies are developed, but rather . . . develop generic applications that can target the entire infrastructure and all of the terminals out there, no matter whether they are wireless PDA[personal digital assistant]-type devices or desktop supercomputers or standard telephony devices. That is not very easy to achieve. It requires a very careful definition of architecture, and scalability of applications to the capabilities of terminals and to the capabilities of the transmission infrastructure. One of the key characteristics is the capability to deploy new applications without any modifications to the network itself. Because once you require modifications to the network, then that puts a huge obstacle, economic and otherwise, in the way of new applications.

—David Messerschmitt, University of California at Berkeley

I would like to see systems that allow upstream bandwidth from individual homes to be considerably higher . . . , and then deal with the aggregate upstream bandwidth on the HFC [hybrid fiber coaxial cable] system, for example, as a traffic engineering problem. If we do a fixed static allocation of upstream bandwidth, we have precluded any reasonable way of saying, "I am going to put a media server in my home because I have a really clever idea for serving media on the Internet." On the other hand, if it is strictly a question of doing traffic analysis on a deployed system, and then deploying additional spectrum or changing the bandwidth reservations around in order to increase the upstream bandwidth when it becomes available, then that is a much more hopeful situation. . . . I have some difficulty believing that in a system with 125 homes you are going to find 125 Web suppliers that are running full media out of their homes. What I have no difficulty believing is that you will find, within the relatively near-term future, some people out there who are doing that. If the allocations are static, such people are precluded from running full media out of their homes. If the allocations are dynamic allocations, then it is reasonable to experiment and to let people have that kind of outbound bandwidth while others are simply sitting there, pointing and clicking with their infrared control, and we will not have precluded part of the space for purposes of experimentation.

—Kevin Kahn, Intel Corporation

his white paper, David Clark of the Massachusetts Institute of Technology related observations from the Internet environment to the evolution of the telephone system (see Chapter 4), describing its process of opening up certain interfaces:

> The reason we want to look at architecture is that the decision to provide an interface, both in a technical sense—whether to implement it at all—or in a business perspective—whether to open it—is in fact a critical business decision. . . . If you open an interface, then that is where your competitors show up.

Providing for such openness may have broader business ramifications as well. For example, the steering committee noted some concern in the business community lest open access for new services be invoked as political grounds to force provision of mature services in an open way. (Some cable providers, for instance, have expressed the concern that providing open access services such as the Internet might establish a precedent suggesting that video services should be similarly open. The extreme form of this concern is fear that the eventual consequence of open access to specific service platforms will be the imposition of a common carriage status on all services.)

Openness and bandwidth symmetry were focal points of discussion in the January workshop; the inability of people to quantify markets for these qualities seems to lead to market trials and deployment plans with limited openness and limited upstream bandwidth. Overall, comments by representatives of various industries suggested that more closed and proprietary service packages seemed to offer more promise for profits, a view anecdotally supported by reports that Wall Street attaches higher value to ventures with some element of proprietary, differentiating technology. Other participants, notably those associated with the computer hardware and software industries, suggested that the open nature of the Internet model may provide more stimulation for innovation.

Uncertainty about the market looms large when it comes to forecasting demand for general infrastructure qualities and associated services. Considerable skepticism is expressed by telecommunications industries and industry analysts about the demand for symmetric communication.[19] Observed Graham Mobley of Scientific-Atlanta:

> What will the consumer really want to do with the interactive services, and how much is he willing to pay? There have been projections that show that, with interactive services, you could probably increase revenues by a factor of two between broadcast and incremental interactive services. On the other hand, nobody really knows what those interactive services are yet. Therefore, cable systems are not sure how much cost and investment to put into providing full interactivity.

According to Joel Engel of Ameritech, part of the confusion on this topic comes from a failure to distinguish symmetric applications from symmetric networks. Networks will support multiple applications, which will have differing requirements for symmetry. Engel argued that the overall demand is for asymmetry:

> [D]uring any prime time period pick up the fiber or the coax and cut it and look at the bits going in both directions. You are going to see that in the aggregate, the total traffic is going to be highly asymmetric because of all of the services that do not require any upstream at all.

The cable industry's plans to incrementally provide greater upstream capacity (see the section "Incremental Increases" below) reflect its uncertainties about consumer demand for symmetry and about the costs and revenues associated with providing more generality.

Inputs to the project attested to telecommunications providers' beliefs in the profitability of infrastructure that is not fully open or symmetric. For example, Tim Clifford, previously with Sprint, questioned the extent of the need for openness and interoperability, and AT&T Corporation's Mahal Mohan argued at the forum that interoperability mattered most at lower architectural levels. See Box 3.5.

The problem telephone companies see with openness is the seeming inexorability of being reduced to a commodity transport business: those who make investments face free-rider competition and the prospect of being unable to recover costs.[20] By contrast, closed systems provide more of an incentive to innovate and be a first mover, and the various experiments with more or less closed systems offering different combinations of services suggest a competition to be first with the winning formula. Hal Varian suggested that this was the problem with "plain old" Internet transport service: "There are no barriers to entry. There is no proprietary technology, no special inputs. Since Internet transport is an undifferentiated commodity, consumers are going to buy on the basis of price." However, several Internet service providers do use proprietary technology (e.g., some in routing—Advanced Networks and Services Inc.; some in security—UUNET, ANS; and some in network management—MCI, ANS), which raises questions about the relative costs and success of technology-based attempts to differentiate service offerings. More generally, these examples illustrate a variety of options for Internet service providers to differentiate their services without getting into the content business, such as control of bandwidth, security, private virtual networks, alternative access (e.g., wireless), roaming, multicast, and (good) network management.

Viacom's Edward Horowitz cautioned that "the incentive is to build these networks to the point where there are maximum barriers to compe-

---

BOX 3.5
Interoperability

Service providers want to differentiate themselves through advanced technology (such as better service) and through information services (or content). That tends to drive one away from interoperability. So, as we move into this environment of competitive services, I think we have to start thinking about what the real need for interoperability is. Does it truly have to be globally seamless or can we allow essentially closed groups to provide interoperability through a limited set of interconnect points?

—Tim Clifford, DynCorp (formerly with Sprint)

The interoperability is at a transport level, being able to get messages across, back, and forth. But the feature functionality is at a different dimension.[1]

—Mahal Mohan, AT&T Corporation

---

[1]As illustration, discussions are ongoing in industry to minimize incompatibility among early PCS systems, possibly by developing hardware to support multiple protocols. See Csenger (1995) and Wexler (1995b).

---

tition for a network vis-à-vis another one and not go further." Horowitz noted that there are many points (such as operating system, storage, transport) in his content-creating and content-distributing business at Viacom where he could face higher costs because of the constrained choices of services that arise as a consequence of "only one solution for a network." He emphasized the need for open access to the set-top device, explaining that "it is not a box per se; it is the process by which you extract information from transportation and you get it displayed or [converted] into usable form."

Horowitz's concerns are examined in the context of alternative industry and government perspectives in a white paper by attorney Jonathan Band. Commenting on how Microsoft's competitive success has inspired arguments and action by different industry groups, Band observes:

Microsoft hopes to dominate the market for the operating system for the "set-top box"—the entry point to the information infrastructure into individual homes or business. By controlling the standard for the set-top box operating system, Microsoft will be able to exercise control over access to the entire infrastructure. Microsoft wants to encourage third-party vendors to develop applications that will run on its operating system; the more applications, the more desirable the operating system becomes and the more likely that the market will adopt it as a de facto standard. At the same time, Microsoft wants to prevent the development of a competing set-top box operating system that is compatible with all the Microsoft-compatible applications.[21]

Band discusses how the word "open" has been used by various industry sectors to describe interfaces that are controlled or protected in some way in support of particular business interests. An important issue is that innovators of new features, functions, and interfaces may view these as valuable intellectual property and may wish to derive revenues from their use. Standards bodies that specify open network standards must balance the rights of creators with the need for users to have assured right to use the standards on predictable and reasonable terms.

Building on the implied potential for unbundling, James Chiddix argued that "when our capacity is not limited, it is not in our business interest to impede our customers' access to any service that they want to pay for." Also reflecting on the changing cable environment, General Instrument's Quincy Rodgers observed that "the customers are demanding open systems. They are demanding licensing. . . . People are insisting that their networks will, for instance, support multiple operating systems." Wendell Bailey of the National Cable Television Association pointed out that the facilities by themselves do not guarantee openness, which also derives from business strategies:

> Cable modems are about supplying wideband access to data service, [also including] multimedia clips or video in motion. But . . . they will not give you access to cable channels that are not carried by your cable operator. The fact is that had there been such a model 15 years ago, you would not know what to ask for now, because there would be no programs or services. People like those in the cable television industry paid to create them, to put them up there to run on their platforms. Now you would like a switched network to get at all of them. Someday you will have that: you will have that when the incremental cost of providing that is reasonable—when there is a business to be had for providing that.

As Chiddix acknowledged, "Clearly fiber to the curb with one fiber taking traffic in each direction lends itself well to totally symmetrical traffic, whereas hybrid fiber coaxial cable, as it is being implemented, is significantly asymmetrical in its capacity." Similar observations can be made about broadcasting, which delivers considerable bandwidth that is controlled by the broadcaster.

The issue of who controls access to and use of circuits and who benefits from associated revenues is key. Mused John Redmond, "We are going to have to bundle our services, because we are going to have to go to customers and put together things they want. It may not be all our services. It may be some of yours, and you may have to work with someone else to put a package together that someone wants." These comments appeared to focus on bundling with content providers, but they could apply equally to services associated with other kinds of applications, as anticipated in Chapter 2.

Stewart Personick, noting that internetworking does not have to imply full integration of services, suggested that part of the problem was one of getting started:

> There are two different meanings of interoperability. I can have large vertically integrated suppliers that represent closed systems internally, and they can always gateway to each other so that they can exchange messages. Customers on one system can access information on another. The question is, Will large, integrated, competitive suppliers voluntarily allow niche players to leverage off of their investments? That is, will they open up inside their system so that someone who has a better server, application, or user interface can just use that limited advantage and start a business? I think that it is certainly not likely that we will have that type of openness, where there are open interfaces everywhere, in the near term. However, it may be a very good long-term objective because, as we know, that type of openness does promote innovation and does promote driving prices down.

Consistent with Personick's speculation, the Web and even the telephone system appear to provide counterexamples to arguments favoring closed systems.[22] Thus, telecommunications executives also acknowledge the change in incentives provided by expanding bandwidth. As suggested above, greater bandwidth raises questions about how to maximize the use of the deployed capacity. Noted Engel, "Perhaps sharing the cost to the individual customer across many, many services may be the way to break the code on the last mile."

FROM FACILITIES TO SERVICES AND APPLICATIONS

Although the facilities owners dominate the public debate over telecommunications policies, they are only a part of the process of deploying the NII. Separate innovation and roll-out are also needed in services, especially services other than commodity transport—those relating to content delivery and a variety of communications and information applications.

Compared with deployment of facilities, deployment of services and applications involves a larger number of players, in part because such players need not own their own facilities. Market entry is cheaper, since it is driven more by software and human resources; capital to supply some services (the canonical high school student in the home basement) may be relatively small, involving leased circuits, switches or routers, and various servers.

Balancing Investment—Software "Capital"

Stanford University's Gio Wiederhold suggested in a white paper that "[t]here is an optimal trajectory in balancing investments in the systems infrastructure versus software application support." In at least the health care arena, the focus of his paper, he recommended moving "support to the information processing infrastructure, so that relevant applications can be built easily and the customers can be satisfied." Duane Adams of ARPA noted that the conceptual framework for that balance remains uncertain, in part because of uncertainties surrounding software system interoperability. He remarked on opportunities for providing services that are basically tools to help the developers create products that will become available over the NII. That prospect was echoed by Edward Horowitz of Viacom Incorporated, who characterized five environments provided (or constrained) by information infrastructure for generating and distributing content, relating their value to users to their degree of openness (Box 3.6). Similarly, Charles Ferguson of Vermeer Technologies maintained in a white paper that software and network interoperability both depend on unbundling "viewers, servers, tools, operating systems, specific information services, and/or Internet access provision with each other."

Adams' observations also seemed to anticipate the explosion of interest, in late 1995, in Sun Microsystem's Java programming language for developing distributed applications. Java programs can be transferred from a server to a remote site over the network as needed, which expedites the deployment and use of new applications. Ferguson echoed the general point about software-based tools in his paper; see Box 3.6.

The Separation of Services from Facilities—
Broadening the Potential Content

The applications business is the umbrella under which fall concerns about "content." Inputs to the NII 2000 project underscored that the information infrastructure is an arena for both content as a product and content as a byproduct of other activity. Content includes not only "packaged" content provided as a business activity, but also informal or amateur content in the form of material shared by individual creators in varying formats (voice, numerical data, image, video), and content communicated as an adjunct to other, higher-value activities (e.g., for electronic commerce or distributed and telework; see CSTB, 1995c).

BOX 3.6
Software and Other Tools

State-of-the-art commercial technologies applicable to the Internet include visual tools and WYSIWYG [what-you-see-is-what-you-get] techniques that enable end users to develop applications that previously required programming, client-server architectures, on-line help systems, platform-independent software engineering techniques, and systematic quality assurance and testing methodologies. Adobe, Quark, Powersoft, the Macintosh GUI [graphical user interface], and even Microsoft have used these techniques to make software easier to use. If these techniques were applied to Internet software, the result could be a huge improvement in everyone's ability to use, communicate, publish, and find information.

—Charles H. Ferguson,
"The Internet, the Word Wide Web, and Open Information Services:
How to Build the Global Information Infrastructure"

There is [1] an authoring environment, how you get your ideas and visions developed; [2] storage; [3] the transport; [4] deciphering for use or display; and [5] . . . invoicing, collecting the money. I look to the NII as being able to support multiple operating systems, competitive operating systems, in all five of these environments without permitting one operating system or one set of users to block those of another.

—Edward Horowitz, Viacom Inc.

Content as a product is the emphasis of publishing, entertainment, and other businesses. As Edward Horowitz argued, "You have no bytes and bits without intellectual property; you have no business without something to convey." Some market analysts have gone so far as to suggest that the value of information about a service can exceed that of the actual service.[23] Horowitz's comments on the importance of packaging and marketing to content providers showed that information infrastructure can be important for distributing both information-based products and information about those products.

Ongoing developments suggest that the information infrastructure plays a key role in such trends as marketing goods as streams of services. The NII facilitates direct contact between advertisers and consumers, and in the process it is producing changes such as those observed for product "branding."[24] A key development—or sign of NII maturity—will be the shift in emphasis away from the tools of access (appliances, networks) to the services and functionality delivered. Market success on the NII may require figuring out how to sell computing and information profitably, much as manufacturers seek to sell a lifetime of clean clothes instead of packages of soap, ongoing oral care instead of toothpaste, pet care rather than dog food, and so on.

Depending on who is speaking, "free" or no-fee information can be a product (as for scholars), a loss (where intellectual property is appropriated in a way that bypasses a compensation system sought by the owner), or a complement to a product that is intended to motivate the buyer. As Terisa Systems/CommerceNet's Allan Schiffman noted, "In cyberspace there is the possibility of having a good deal more shelf space, but still the necessity of competing for the attention span of prospective purchasers."

Perhaps because of the Internet's legacy as a source of no-fee information generated in the research, education, and library contexts, and perhaps because of uncertainty about how to charge for intellectual property, several people spoke of the Internet's value as a source of complementary information about commercial products. Andrew Lippman of MIT spoke generally about the Internet's potential for navigating various reservoirs of information; Daniel Lynch of Interop Company and Cybercash Inc. spoke about the potential for the Internet to foster global brand identification. Edward Horowitz described actual uses of the Internet as a marketing and promotion vehicle (see Box 3.7). Similar experiences and ambitions have been chron-icled in business press reports on a wide variety of efforts to use the Internet and Web for advertising and promotion, with some degree of contention among directly generated and advertising agency efforts.[25]

Peter Huber of the Manhattan Institute cautioned against assuming that the content tail would wag the infrastructure dog, inasmuch as communications transport businesses are the largest information infrastructure businesses in terms of revenues. Even factoring out known levels of data traffic over telephony networks, their size attests to a huge market composed of humans talking to each other. Other contributors commented on the enduring strength of communications relative to sharing of packaged information. For example, past president of Prodigy Ross Glatzer reminded forum participants that "all people communicate, but only a small percentage of the population really cares about any one topic of information."

Consistent with Glatzer, Michael North of North Communications asserted that rather than assume that the market will favor "network-centric versus user-centric" services, we should expect people to be both "consumers of information sometimes and . . . producers of information sometimes. Sometimes we are in read-only mode, and we like to see what others have to say, and sometimes we would like to be publishers ourselves." The separation of services from facilities enables both kinds of

---

BOX 3.7
Promotional Information Uses of the Internet

There are certain things that go over the Internet which we love. We are promoting a new movie. We throw it up on the Internet, on our home page. When a Star Trek movie came up, we had half a million visits in six weeks through two million or three million pages of scripts and various other things downloaded during that period of time. The people who design the home page were ecstatic. . . . . You do not get any money for it. The cost of creating that content comes out of the marketing budget, the marketing and promotion budget to manage the expectation. Simon and Schuster, for example, has huge amounts of educational programs. When you sell a program that consists of textbooks and ancillary material, the textbooks are what they want to get paid for and the ancillary material comes along with it. We are probably going to put the ancillary material up on the Internet.

—Edward Horowitz, Viacom Inc.

---

behavior (assuming some degree of symmetry), and both will fuel market growth.

THE INTERNET AND ITS USE FOR BUSINESS

Effects on Provision of Goods and Services

How will the Internet or other information services affect the basic economics of content-providing businesses, which have historically been quite risky, with a much higher rate (and expectation) of failure than, say, telecommunications? Steven Wildman of Northwestern University explained that Hollywood economics recognize that "for motion pictures, 10 percent of them make a profit; 90 percent fail. Television programs aren't much better. CD-ROMs are looking similar." He suggested a need "to develop a financial infrastructure to average or aggregate those risks," as is currently done for motion pictures and television programs. Wendell Bailey described how this riskiness is apparent in cable program turnover: "At the 1995 National Cable Television Association convention in Dallas, Texas, there were 27 new [program producers] seeking access to cable networks. I have been in the cable industry for 14 years, and I counted up 181 programmers that I had seen at that show over the last 14 years that no longer exist today because no one wanted them." Yet the (current) cost of deploying a Web site is much, much smaller than the cost of making a movie or a CD. The result is much more experimentation and enthusiasm, since the definition of "success" (e.g., cost recovery) is much different. This differential risk may lead to changes in the overall mix of content available through the information infrastructure. In the short term, cost recovery is an issue here as well as in other information infrastructure businesses; on-line service providers, for example, have reportedly frustrated some content providers with revenue sharing terms that favor themselves, but these arrangements, like pricing of Internet service provider offerings generally, are volatile (Zelnick, 1994).

A broad view of the information infrastructure and of trends in information supply and demand provides evidence that one-to-many communications is beginning to lose some of its effectiveness and efficiency.[26] Trends in product diversification and customization suggest that if the slogan of the Industrial Revolution was the manufacturer's or retailer's statement, "This is what I have, don't you want it?"—the wave of the future is signified instead by the consumer's demand, "This is what I need, can you provide it?" The direction and nature of the flow of information may well change considerably, with a decline in the tendency of businesses to treat consumers as either target or database—rather, the manufacturer and the retailer will become both. Thus, for example, almost all print (and much television) advertising now contains an 800 number, even if the objective of the advertising is to enhance a brand image; this practice is now extending to Web and Internet addresses. The growth of the Internet and the Web themselves has been fueled by consumer-generated needs.

Drawing on his analyses of the television business, Wildman suggested that greater individual control over the selection of information products could have profound impacts on various kinds of content-publishing businesses:

> If the editorial function can be put in the viewers' hands, [to do] the picking and choosing, the viewers can find what they want. Then the power and the economic justification for being a network or a channel bundler is dramatically reduced. If we lose the networks, we have lost the major force in television over the last 50 years.

Wildman also suggested that changes could come as a result of ongoing audience fragmentation (arising from greater ease in targeting segments and the increasing difficulty of building a national audience).

At the January workshop, J.M. Tenenbaum of Enterprise Integration Technologies Corp./CommerceNet speculated about the evolution of Internet-based interaction to support more individualized services, including personal webs and group webs:

> [E]veryone is . . . going to be able to grab things over the net that are of interest, annotate them, link them into their own things, post them on their own Web server, and then selectively share some of those things

with their friends—initially by providing access to a server or posting them on a group server which has broader access out into the world.

Charles Ferguson argues that the Web offers "the opportunity to liberate computer users, publishers, and information providers from the grip of the conventional on-line services industry," which he likens to the mainframe computer industry because "it maintains its profitability only by charging extremely high royalties and by holding proprietary control over closed systems." Rhetoric aside, the Web clearly facilitates direct communications between information creators and consumers, which will affect the shape of a variety of intermediate industries, including publishing and advertising.

The trend toward greater individual control across different kinds of networks and media raises questions about prospects for provider-controlled service packages, including those associated with contemporary market trials. Similarly, notwithstanding existing provider comfort with asymmetry, one interpretation of recent shifts in broadcast company ownership is that despite their imperfections, interactive services and other uses of computers are shifting consumers' attention away from broadcast media, constraining expectations for growth in the business value of broadcasting.[27]

The Internet—Layering, Incrementalism, and Diversification

The development of the Internet epitomizes the separation of services from facilities. The rise of a variety of Internet access providers derives from layered infrastructure architecture, which is described in Chapter 4. One layer's materials are the next layer's framework. Activity is happening at all layers at once, beginning with a teasing apart of low-level services from physical infrastructure in the form of simple Internet access business. This situation complicates assessing who owns what, who resells what, capitalization and risk levels, entry requirements, and so on. On a rough basis, however, business opportunities can be seen in the area of transport service and access supply, "middleware" services, and applications.

First there are the Internet service and access providers. Although there is no clean categorization, some of these are commodity providers and some add higher value (e.g., information service providers that provide both communications and information services); some target individual users (aiming for large numbers of small accounts) and some organizational units (aiming for modest numbers of large accounts). Telephone, cable, and other facilities-based providers have moved over the past couple of years from strong reservations about the viability of the Internet to increasing willingness to provide and package Internet access, with some kind of added value (as illustrated by earlier comments on the proliferation of suitable cable modems).[28] Concentration among on-line service providers has been increasing; the largest three (America Online, CompuServe, and Prodigy Services) served 89.3 percent of the market as of December 1995, and the largest six together served an estimated 96.9 percent of the 11.3 million subscribers (Arlen, 1996). Increasing concentration may underlie a movement for some smaller service providers to become content providers serving customers through larger players (see Arlen, 1995b). In their white paper, Jiong Gong and Padmanabhan Srinagesh comment on the economics behind different categories of Internet service providers, themselves displaying different degrees of layering depending on whether they own their own facilities:

> The variety of organizational forms in use raises the following question: Can ISPs [Internet service providers] with varying degrees of integration coexist in an industry equilibrium, or are there definite cost advantages that will lead to only one kind of firm surviving in equilibrium? The answer to this question hinges on the relative cost structures of integrated and unintegrated firms. The costs of integrated firms depend on the costs of producing the underlying transport fabric on which IP transport rides. The cost structures of unintegrated firms are determined in large part by the prices they pay for transport services (such as ATM and DS3 services) obtained from telecommunications carriers. These prices, in turn, are determined by market forces. More generally, the layered structure of data communications services leads to a recursive relationship in which the cost structure of services provided in any layer is determined by prices charged by providers one layer below.

Next come the middleware providers, notably those firms springing up to offer products based on the World Wide Web—Web-based publishing facilitators, browser providers, and so on[29]—and Internet (or Web) directory services (Higgins, 1995b). CommerceNet, for example, is a consortium that owns a Web server for which it develops and supports applications; it does not own network facilities, per se.[30] Although middleware includes mass-merchandised, consumer-oriented, and corporation-oriented products, the segments and the providers are already appearing to consolidate (Goff, 1995).

Also in this category are the security protection service providers, some acting as part of browser offerings (e.g., Terisa Systems); some separate (e.g., RSA Data Security Inc.), albeit possibly functioning through business alliances. Another example of middleware services, again tied to the Web, are the on-line equivalents of credit card verifiers, which mediate financial transactions between purchaser and merchant. Middleware business seems to fit into a new kind of "intermediate product" category (just as sheet steel is an intermediate good between the materials and automobile industries).

Then come applications, such as business services (e.g., Lexis/Nexis) and on-line games (e.g., Sierra On-line). These range from final products (e.g., games) to intermediate products (e.g., business services).[31] The proliferation of application services that are themselves inputs to other activities illustrates the difficulty of categorizing the products and businesses associated with information infrastructure. It also underscores the fact that infrastructure-related businesses are increasingly enmeshed in other, possibly higher-value, activities (e.g., education, commerce, research, work of different kinds), much as are other kinds of infrastructure.

Although activities can be examined from the perspective of different layers, Stephen Wolff of Cisco Systems Inc. cautioned that a holistic perspective is also important. Wolff noted that Internet growth will not remain very high unless facilities providers "increase their investment at commensurate pace, because the Internet is a value-added service on top of the underlying bitway structure. So it's all got to go together or it's not going to go at all." Similarly, @Home's Milo Medin noted that despite its growth, the Web's "potential is not going to be realized unless we can really scale up the level of bandwidth in the network." In his white paper, Robert Blau describes the Web as a driver of network market growth that could challenge local network capacity:

> As new resources come on-line, demand for access to the WWW will increase along with its value to users as well as information service providers. Similarly, as the value of the WWW increases (e.g., by the square of the number of new users added to it during any given period), on-line sessions also should increase in duration (e.g., from current levels of 25 minutes per session versus an average of five minutes for local telephone call) for the simple reason that there will be more users and services to interact with. The combination of more businesses and residents spending more time on-line, accessing increasingly sophisticated multimedia services that require substantially larger amounts of bandwidth to transport, could press the limits of many local telephone networks within a relatively short period of time.

Blau's speculation about the Web as a driver for demand and revenue is notable, given his otherwise conservative assessment of the investment and revenue horizons for telephone companies. On the other hand, he also notes that Internet traffic can increase the efficiency of network facility use, suggesting that such traffic "could help recoup the cost of deploying wider-band technologies that Internet users will need" if "priced properly."

As fast as the Web's growth has been, the entire flow of Internet traffic is vastly less than the capacity of the telephone network—probably less by two orders of magnitude.[32] As a result, even with modest growth in local access capabilities, supply and demand for bandwidth may be in reasonable balance.

Hal Varian provided a broader holism, relating the economics of network markets, which depend on the presence of multiple users (who find value in direct proportion to the number of other users), to adequate distribution of complementary goods and services:

> My favorite candidate for the "killer app" is multimedia video conferencing and wide area collaboration. But it is very hard to create critical mass in this kind of industry, as ATT found out years ago with their Picturephone initiative. People are not going to invest in the hardware, software, or learning costs until the technology is widely enough deployed to warrant their investment. But this leads to the standard chicken-and-egg problem: overcoming that conundrum will be the big problem for the industry.

Robert Crandall also emphasized at the forum that services will evolve with the information appliance (and other equipment) base, including access equipment and other elements of applications.[33,34] Part of the growth of fax, for example, reflected the transition in equipment from telex as well as the acquisition of fax equipment by more and more people as a function of declining cost.[35] Recognizing this problem and taking advantage of the relatively low cost of reproduction for software, on-line service providers (e.g., America Online and Prodigy) have given away access software. Similarly, market-leader Netscape has made Web browsers available for free or at low prices in the interest of selling more expensive software for servers; the Web server market is forecast to grow dramatically yet still remain small for several years.[36] Notwithstanding the rate of growth of the Internet and the World Wide Web, user equipment cost and difficulty of use constrain the level of use of emerging features and services, as noted in Chapter 2.[37]

Both applications and middleware involve some kind of framework for organizing material (content) that may be produced or distributed as part of the application. A white paper by Randy Katz et al. captures the perspective voiced by several in arguing that "a critical element of NII development is the fostering of appropriate commonalities, with the goal of achieving broad adoptability while promoting efficient competition and technological evolution."[38] Middleware standards (for example, standards for data format and service invocation[39]) enable a common application development framework; application standards enable implementation by a variety of providers and, ideally, access by users operating in a variety of environments. For example, a white paper by David Schell et al. describes needs associated with geographic information sys-

---

BOX 3.8
Middleware Standards Needs

Commercial need for better spatial data integration is already clear in areas such as electric and gas utilities, rail transport, retail, property insurance, real estate, precision farming, and airlines. Given the critical nature of applications positioned to combine "real-time" and geospatial attributes—emergency response, health and public safety, military command and control, fleet management, environmental monitoring—the need to accomplish the full integration of [spatial data] resources into the NII context has become increasingly urgent.

—David Schell, Lance McKee, and Kurt Buehler,
"Geodata Interoperability—A Key NII Requirement"

[Digital libraries] are leading to significant advances in the generation, storage, and use of digital information of diverse kinds. The range of underlying services and technologies includes advanced mass storage, on-line capture of multimedia data, intelligent location and filtering of information, knowledge navigation, effective human interfaces, system integration, and prototype and technology demonstration.

—Randy H. Katz, William L. Scherlis, and Stephen L. Squires,
"The National Information Infrastructure: A High Performance
Computing and Communications Perspective"

---

tems, while the one by Katz et al. explains needs associated with digital libraries. Katz et al. underscore the importance of developing appropriate software, as noted above: they relate cross-cutting applications to the emergence of "a common service environment" for building domain-specific applications, complemented by application development and support tools and "a marketplace of reusable subsystems." See Box 3.8.

Alleviating concerns about standards will depend in large part on attainment of consensus within an application domain (see Chapter 2), but that process should build, to the extent possible, on common or cross-domain standards at the middleware level. This use of common middleware standards will maximize the prospects for compatibility between implementations at the domain level and will facilitate the eventual integration of inter- and intra-domain communication.

The Web provides an illustration: it embodies a framework and a set of standards that have made the Internet more useful to more businesses, organizations, and individuals; it works through standards, and it has given rise to businesses that implement and advance those standards. Whereas conventional or paper publishers own their own presses, trucks, and so on (or subcontract to businesses that own such equipment), the

Web and the Internet make use of more broadly shared distribution infrastructure. Another lesson from the success of the Web is that an open standard like the Internet's TCP/IP protocols can be a very fertile field for innovation, allowing experimentation with multiple applications.

The inclusion in Microsoft's new operating system, Windows '95, of software for accessing an information service package, including Internet access, reflects a business strategy based on tying two layers together: the software provides the interface to physical network facilities (typically owned or resold by others); it also provides TCP/IP support for customers already having Internet access. This development seems to go beyond the bundling of TCP/IP software with computer and network operating systems (Higgins, 1995a)[40] and the distribution by information service providers of access software with PCs and directly to consumers recently. The broader Microsoft strategy appeared initially to tie three layers together by integrating various applications with networking (Zelnick, 1994). Microsoft Network is an illustration of the growing emphasis on software to implement information infrastructure access.

More broadly, Hal Varian suggested that the joint evolution of content and transport businesses may well lead to some form of integration, raising questions about the market structures that are economically sustainable given the product or business and possibilities for competition that technologies are creating. He commented on recent instances of cooperation and alliances among broadcast, cable, telephony, and entertainment companies, which embody integration that may or may not endure, at least in terms of which business dominates:

> [V]ertical integration with the content providers seems to be the most popular solution. We have got considerable evidence of this happening already. There is U S West, Time Warner, Disney, Ameritech, BellSouth, MCI, Rupert Murdoch. America Online just announced some joint agreements and mergers yesterday. It is not obvious that it will really work in the long run. These days, the cash is going from the transport providers to the content providers, because it is the transport providers that have all of the money. But, if the market for transport becomes very competitive in the future and it becomes a commodity business, then the money is going to have to flow the other way. You are going to have to have the content cross-subsidizing the transport. What you buy is the content; the transport is thrown in for free. The big question is whether content providers will stick to their joint agreements once they have competing transport providers clamoring for their business. That remains to be seen.

Consistent with Varian's analysis, Milo Medin described how his new venture, @Home, will combine Web servers with cable facilities and cable and other media programming.[41] Taking a broader view of integration, there are already signs of the integration potential of telecommunications companies and banks, and yet other instances of integration may emerge.[42]

INCREMENTAL INCREASES

Reacting to the risks, uncertainties, capabilities, and costs of various technologies, contributors to the NII 2000 project seemed to favor investments that allow for increases in bandwidth, openness, and symmetry on an incremental or expandable basis. David Messerschmitt of the University of California at Berkeley related incrementalism to architecture: "I would try to define an architecture that had the characteristic that I could initially save money by deploying an asymmetric situation, but hedge my bets by having a rather simple upgrade path to a more symmetric situation." Decisions on architecture as well as facilities affect how easily decisions and investments made today allow for or support the next increment—how easily evolution will occur. For example, putting extra fibers in a bundle conveys significant extra capacity wherever they go. As Robert Powers et al. explain in their white paper, the capacity of a fiber pair has grown substantially over the past 15 years "based only on changes in electronic and photonic equipment attached to the fiber, not changes in the buried fiber itself." That situation relates investment in fiber to incremental investments in associated equipment. Decisions on architecture also relate to the split between incremental investment by providers and by customers (see "Economic Models" below). Thus, at the January workshop David Messerschmitt related integrated services digital network (ISDN) and the telephony activities associated with the Advanced Intelligent Network initiative (see white paper by Stewart Personick) to architectures that allow more intelligence in terminal devices and thereby provide more flexibility in provisioning new services than do architectures that contain all service functions in centralized switches.

In view of the uncertainties associated with the economics of investment in fiber, telephone companies have been paying significant attention to technologies that allow them to better leverage existing copper plant and digital switches (through software and appropriate line cards), providing significant bandwidth advantage relative to conventional telephone service, albeit less than that available through fiber.[43] Two technologies dominate this approach: asymmetric digital subscriber line (ADSL) and ISDN.

ISDN is a phoenix technology, having been touted and then dismissed by experts but now appearing to be relatively easily supplied.[44] In the absence of alternatives, both providers and business customers cite ISDN as a vehicle for telework and other data-intensive home communications.

Commented Edmond Thomas of NYNEX Science and Technology, "There were no terminals or applications for a very long time. . . . With the Internet, terminals now becoming available, and, more importantly, application software to call on it, [ISDN] is starting to find almost ubiquitous application." Les Vadasz emphasized ISDN's bird-in-the-hand value: "The technologists are enamored with the next generation and the generation beyond; they are not realizing what benefit we could get from [ISDN's] bandwidth, which is available now."

To make the point that incrementalism is relative, Robert Blau argued that at about $3.4 billion (42 percent of the company's total capital expenditures between 1988 and 1993), making all of Southwestern Bell's access lines ISDN-ready would be a major commitment. Edmond Thomas argued for diversification even in the short term: "You have got to try them all: the technology right now is at best a first generation. And you could make a very big blunder by choosing incorrectly." Nevertheless, router, modem, PC, and on-line service vendors all seem to be moving to support ISDN access, trends that should sustain some level of growth in ISDN availability.

ADSL represents a way to reuse the existing copper plant for delivery of video and some interactive applications to the home. Mahal Mohan explained in a white paper that ADSL makes use of existing copper plant by installing matching equipment at both ends of the loop. An incremental deployment, "ADSL devices can be disconnected from one user and moved to another user as, for example, when the first ADSL user decides to upgrade to a higher bandwidth medium such as fiber or fiber coax access."

Similarly, other forms of digital subscriber loop technology allow the copper loop to be reused for other forms of new service. The symmetric high-bit-rate digital subscriber line (HDSL) may represent a way for the telephone companies to use their copper loops to sell interactive data services to the home at speeds of up to 2 Mbps. While products for this application are not yet fully mature, it is possible that this service might actually be less expensive to deploy incrementally than the lower-speed ISDN service, because it could be specialized for data only, rather then needing to support both data and voice service through the switch.

Edmond Thomas related incremental investment in ADSL to the different costs associated with providing service to different areas. See Box 3.9. In his white paper, Francis Fisher of the University of Texas at Austin underscores the importance of relating deployment to area. He notes that there are relatively low costs of entry in dense downtown markets, fostering openness, whereas in the residential market it is more difficult to assure universal service, let alone open service, by a single provider. The

---

BOX 3.9
Potential Uses of Asymmetric Digital Subscriber Line Technology

Asymmetric digital subscriber line (ADSL) technology probably will have, in the early days, two major applications. One of them is in congested urban areas, such as in apartment buildings, where you have conduit congestion and there is no way to get to a customer's apartment without knocking down the walls. If you want to provide interactivity, ADSL may in fact be a way to do that. The other application is at the opposite end of the spectrum, in rural areas where you have a low population density. You would like to provide those customers some interactivity and you cannot afford to put in fiber initially, but the copper is already in the ground. Right now, our view is that fiber to the curb looks like it has potential in the very dense urban areas, and hybrid fiber coaxial cable probably in the suburban to the moderately dense urban areas. But my bet is also that our assessment right now is probably wrong. As volumes increase and technologies improve, the areas of applications of these technologies may, in fact, change dramatically. If we make a big investment today in one area, I think we could be very, very wrong.

—Edmond Thomas, NYNEX Science and Technology Inc.

---

incentive and profitability problems, of course, are exacerbated in the even sparser rural areas due to limited traffic aggregation.

The television industry has perhaps the strongest tradition of incrementalism, in part because of expectations—reinforced by a history of regulatory requirements for back-compatibility with the installed television set base—regarding consumers' limited ability and willingness to upgrade television sets. Thus, Scientific-Atlanta's Allen Ecker pointed out, "Analog is going to pay the bills for a long period of time for the investment to get the infrastructure, certainly in the entertainment part . . . ." Some kinds of information infrastructure require relatively modest incremental investments for consumers, some require more, and, as discussed in Chapter 2, the increase in intelligence and functionality in end-user devices suggests that more and more of the total investment is migrating to the periphery of the network and into users' environments. Graham Mobley noted that an associated issue is ownership and distribution of access devices: "[I]n the cable environment there may well be situations where interactive terminals would be leased from the cable company on a trial basis. If someone did not like the terminal, he or she could give it back and go lease a lower-cost or lower-featured box. These things will come along with time."

The theme of evolution in cable (see Box 3.10) was extended into the future by Don Dulchinos of Cable Television Laboratories, who described

---

BOX 3.10
Incremental Expansion of Cable Service

[T]he roll-out of home digital terminals or high-speed data modems . . . is a very evolutionary process. Only those customers who demand service, as they demand service, can be supplied with the terminals. The roll-out of the technology would be closely matched with the revenue made possible by that technology. Then, by the year 2000, you start looking at broadband types of full-service networks, add video servers and media servers in general, either at a head-end location or distributed throughout the network, and provide service that way.

—Don Dulchinos, Cable Television Laboratories Inc.

Since we have got this broadband pipe in place, we can reinforce it with a little fiber, make it work a lot better for our core business, and then get into digital businesses, whether they be telephony, PC modems, or interactive video, on an incremental basis, where most of the subsequent investment is variable. And it goes into the modem, into the routers, into the set-top boxes, or into the telephony interfaces. It is largely a *traffic engineering* problem; we can keep pushing fiber deeper, and making it more and more granular, and getting fewer and fewer homes per fiber trunk. And then we can reconfigure which part of the spectrum in the coaxial cable we use. Those are not great problems, because they are forced by demand, which means revenue.

—James Chiddix, Time Warner Cable

[In 1975,] basic cable was about $7 per month. They introduced HBO for another $7, a service that took effectively no bandwidth. They were able to double their revenue and put in a simple box on a variable cost basis. We have a very similar situation right now. You can add lots of digital information on a cable system today using an asymmetrical modem. I define "asymmetrical" as meaning broadband for downstream communication and twisted copper pair coming back. You can charge probably $15 or $20 because you are going to a particular kind of user to deliver very-high-speed data uniquely to that computer. It takes very little bandwidth, and your capital expenditures are one box at a time.

—Edward Horowitz, Viacom Inc.

---

hybrid fiber coaxial cable upgrade plans that will support delivery of about 80 analog video channels and at least 100 digital video channels, and growth in interactive applications (implying upstream capacity). He related capacity supplied by cable providers to home equipment and demand. James Chiddix also commented on the fit between supply and demand, further suggesting that the evolving cable architectures do provide the flexibility sought by David Messerschmitt.

In response to a question, Chiddix indicated that it would be possible to provide a choice of data-oriented radio-frequency modems supporting different degrees of asymmetry: "The beauty of having this radio spectrum in our coaxial cable is that we can have coexisting transport structures that behave very differently. We will build different businesses around them. In fact, we need to find ways to get more revenue out of high-value services than out of lower-value services in exactly that way." Edward Horowitz cautioned against expecting too much too fast, observing that "the only thing that was displayed at the [1995] cable show of any value was the fact that there is a move by the cable community to install broadband modems." Significantly, a number of computer hardware manufacturers (e.g., Hewlett-Packard, Motorola) are seeking to supply these modems.

Wireless nonbroadcast networks have been incremental for consumers. At the outset of availability of cellular and PCS services consumers have had a larger wireline base of equipment to receive calls, while providers must develop sufficient infrastructure to support wireless service. PCS can be considered a kind of incremental improvement over cellular, with digital cellular as a closer improvement over analog cellular. There was some speculation among project contributors about the value of PCS and other wireless systems as a vehicle for relatively near term experimentation with different product and service concepts.[45] Mused Harvard University's Lewis Branscomb, "Let the wireless services try to capture these new markets, and then see how fast the cable firms and the local exchange carriers get into the competition for the business."

The comments of both cable and telephony providers referred to business calculations and "traffic engineering" intended to manage and minimize investments in anticipation of delayed revenue growth. For example, in discussing with other forum participants how to interpret deployment statistics, Joel Engel explained that providers do not assume that every home passed will be a customer, which has implications for the translation from aggregate bandwidth to a neighborhood to bandwidth delivered or accessible to an individual household, especially during the first stages of service introduction, but also when the offering is fully mature.

Engel said that Ameritech has "engineered our system to take into account what we think is a reasonable distribution across these services to allow symmetry for those applications that require it." Andrew Lippman cautioned against excess conservatism: "Start small if that is the economic answer. But do not view the ultimate design as one that still will be potentially too small for what is really going to be there."

ARRANGEMENTS FOR INTERCONNECTION

Although technology may facilitate unbundling, the business arrangements surrounding interconnection, which reflect underlying network economics and superimposed regulatory regimes, are key to associated investments and offerings. These arrangements, which relate to both interconnecting networks and gateways or other forms of connectivity to nonnetwork content and service providers, affect the incidence of cost and the levels of revenue and profit. Many questions arise, such as the following:

- Who wholesales and who retails what in local and interexchange connectivity and information access?[46]
- How balanced will traffic flows be among interconnected systems?
- What capacity exists to charge different fees in different directions where flows are balanced or unbalanced?
- How will financial compensation (settlements) be governed in areas where traffic flows are unbalanced?
- How will end-to-end impairments be allocated amongst the various service providers? and
- How can quality of service be maintained in a distributed network with multiple providers?

The arrangements for interconnection constitute a topic on which economics research and analysis are under way, building from the experience in telephony.[47] Not surprisingly, telephony-experienced participants in the project were the most vocal contributors on this topic. For example, Teleport Communications' Gail Schwartz and Paul Cain describe in their white paper the elements of central office interconnection facilities: interconnection electronics, cable, and services, plus local access and transport area (LATA)-based local exchange routing guides and the line information databases (associated with Signaling System 7) and other databases (for directory assistance, 800 numbers, and so on). They relate those facilities to business arrangements, noting that in the Internet "commercial service providers hand off traffic to each other with no settlements, no exchange of money, on a sender-keep-all or bill-and-keep basis."[48] At the forum, Schwartz asked,

> Are competing local exchange carriers terminating traffic on each other's networks going to pay each other or are they going to do a sender-keep-all arrangement? If they are going to pay each other, given that the traffic will be unbalanced for a long period of time (that is, the incumbents will be terminating a lot more traffic than the new entries will be terminating), what terms will they adopt for doing that? If it is not bill-

and-keep, which might not be feasible because of unbalanced traffic, then the economic basis for the exchange of traffic would normally be, absent a heritage of regulation, a capacity-based charge rather than a minutes-of-use charge. . . . If a new entrant has to price its own services in a manner that is tied to the discount plans and the other rate schedules of the incumbent, then the new entrant is economically impeded from using its portion of the interconnected network of networks to its full capability, and therefore recovering its own investment. . . .[49]

Although both established and new providers argue regularly in regulatory proceedings about the balance of traffic flows and cost incidence,[50] there is a tendency over time for flows to and from most areas within the country (and the providers that serve them) to be balanced, at least in voice communications.

The terms and conditions for interconnection are becoming a pressing issue as more and more networks connect with the Internet and with each other. Tim Clifford noted that arrangements between local exchange and interexchange carriers involve business mechanisms to track traffic flows and translate that information into financial settlements that are designed for switched voice and private line services; because the experience in telephony tends to exclude interconnection between competitive service providers, the past models may not apply. In their white paper, Powers et al. note that among the factors leading to greater interexchange carrier (IXC) provision of end-to-end services is "the interest of both IXCs and their customers in cutting the costs of the last-mile links, which are now such a large portion of the costs of providing long-distance telecommunications." Greater competition in local exchange or regulatory requirements for cost-based access charges will also affect those costs.

Local access charges also reflect another issue that has become urgent in the telecommunications reform debates: costs associated with unequal provider obligations. Baumol and Sidak (1994a, p. 196) argue that the costs of serving as the carrier of last resort and other regulatory "obligations are appropriately treated as sources of common fixed costs for the firm; the costs must be covered legitimately by the firm's prices."

Resolving the issue of settlements is far beyond the scope of this project, but contributors familiar with the Internet identified Internet-related interconnection arrangements as a sleeper that could have an enormous impact in the future. The commercialization of the Internet explicitly involves so-called network access points (NAPs). The NAPs interconnect Internet backbones (interexchange components) and are federally supported now but will not be indefinitely; there is also a Commercial Internet Exchange, which has connected member providers without settlement charges. Although NAPs provide a convenient location for interconnection, they offer no new mechanisms to facilitate settlements.

Internet protocol functionality makes settlements much more difficult to implement than in historical telecommunications systems, most obviously because the Internet has no concept of a "call" against which individual data packets can be counted and billed. This has been a major reason that many Internet service providers have not been able to craft agreements: even providers that have agreed to the principle of settlements still have not figured out how to act on it. In their "Economic FAQs About the Internet," MacKie-Mason and Varian (1995) assert that a system of settlements is inevitable for the Internet, because "resource usage is not always symmetric, and it appears that the opportunities to free-ride on capacity investments by other network providers are increasing." They caution that as of mid-1995, "the necessary technical, accounting, and economic infrastructure is not in place for NAP-related settlements."

ECONOMIC MODELS

Deployment of high-capacity and more general facilities raises questions about how much revenue can be generated, and how fast, to pay back the investment. An unfortunate consequence of the term "national information infrastructure" is the tendency for most people to assume that it implies something monolithic and uniform as a bundle of services or businesses. But just as it is increasingly clear that the NII embraces combinations of technologies that are optimized for the delivery of multiple services or service groupings, it is also clear that the NII does and will continue to contain multiple business and social models. Complicating the debate, the new constituents entering the national information infrastructure discussion bring with them different models and motives. These models drive experimentation with pricing schemes, which in turn drive the flow of cost recovery from end users and from information and on-line service providers that make use of facilities and even other services owned by others.[51] End-user pricing arrangements can and probably will differ from the way carriers are or will be compensated for providing underlying network capacity to information service vendors. The pricing of intermediate components (e.g., access to fundamental communications facilities, interconnection among networks) will be an important determinant of market conduct and performance, and itself calls for more analysis.

Padmanabhan Srinagesh, an economist for Bell Communications Research, related the telephony investment posture to a business model that recoups large up-front investments through streams of small payments (see Box 3.11). Telephone (or cable) companies deploying fiber face a problem of asset specificity: the wireline access circuits, in particular, link the provider to an individual consumer who may or may not want to

---

BOX 3.11
Cost Recovery in the Telephony Model of Communications

If customers were willing to pay $1,600 for optical fiber and symmetric band-width to the home, the way they pay for a computer, a competitive market with many kinds of suppliers might emerge. The fact is that the communications industry works in a different paradigm, where the one-time costs of facilities are recovered through a steady flow of monthly charges. The risk that the asset may be stranded remains with the provider and not with the consumer. This is a major reason for slow change in the communications infrastructure.

—Padmanabhan Srinagesh, Bell Communications Research

---

generate enough use to pay back the investment in a "timely" manner. Some kind of forward contracting (long-term commitment to pay) could offset the uncertainty, although that is not a conventional market mechanism outside of satellite service or certain kinds of private networking, possibly because of regulatory constraints. However, in their white paper, Gong and Srinagesh note that "there appears to be an empirical trend toward term/volume commitments that encourage consumers of private line services to establish an exclusive, long-term relationship with a single carrier." A consequence appears to be evidence that non-facilities-owning Internet service providers with such multiyear leases are themselves beginning to offer long-term pricing options to their customers.

Both NII 2000 project components (workshop, forum) and popular debates tend to characterize the telephony model as one that involves increasing consumer cost with increasing usage. Robert Crandall pointed out that the incremental charges themselves reflect quirks of the regulatory history:

> In the case of the way states regulate telephone, we subsidize people's access to the system, but then charge them prices which are far in excess of costs to use the system. As a result, there is far too little usage of the communications networks we now have. . . . The assumption [appears to be] that we all subscribe to a telephone service in order to sit and either look at our telephone set and not use it, or to wait for some telemarketer to call us, so it doesn't cost us anything to pick up the telephone. Presumably if you want to use it, you should be allowed to use it at a price certainly no greater than the incremental cost to society of using it, and that isn't what we do today.

In short, the telephony price structure is not directly related to the cost structure, which confounds the business challenge facing telephone companies that are contemplating how to proceed with information infrastructure.

The business models associated with the NII involve different combinations of, and investments in, several key components: network facilities (e.g., circuits, switches, routers, base stations, antennas and receivers, head ends); content (e.g., text documents, still and moving imagery, data files—presented as articles, photographs and videos, databases, and so on) and associated facilities (e.g., storage servers, browsing and search systems); information appliances (e.g., telephones, televisions and set-top boxes, personal computers, personal digital assistants); and skills (implying time and training) of people developing, producing, delivering, and using the information infrastructure. They differ in terms of who bears what costs and risks to deliver and use information infrastructure, including what costs are internal to customers or providers and what costs a provider can pass on to customers.

Cost incidence is particularly relevant to understanding what it takes to achieve some degree of equitable access, since users vary by income, education, and other indicators of willingness and ability to use a given service. Provider costs are themselves uncertain. For example, early entrants in the on-line shopping business have found that "just being there" is no prerequisite for success. There are significant investments that must be made in back-end systems as well as linking the manufacturer to the consumer via on-line access. The process of figuring out what technology is needed, where, can take time, producing a lag in matching business opportunity to consumer demand.[52]

Overall, variation in cost level and incidence as captured in different business models allows different parties to experiment with different offerings (goods, services, and price structures) at the same time, and it allows different kinds of providers to serve different kinds of customers with a range of prices, levels of performance and quality, and commitments of resources. Variation is a logical business response to the absence of a "killer app" and the enormous uncertainty about market demand. How much and what kinds of variation are sustainable over the long term, however, will depend on how the underlying economics of the information infrastructure evolve with the deployment of new technologies as described in Chapters 4 and 5. Another important but uncertain issue is the cost of accounting mechanisms necessary to support different approaches to intermediate and end-user charges. Such costs affect the relative appeal of charging on the basis of time of use, quantity of use, and/or access. Subject to applicable regulatory constraints, a range of business models should be observable over the next several years.

At least five models (and probably more), representing different combinations of cost recovery for content and for infrastructure, are evident today:

- *Metered telephone:* the consumer pays by the minute (for time using the network and level of traffic);
- *Embedded or domain-specific:* cost is hidden in some other service;
- *Broadcast TV and radio (advertising):* the advertiser pays (by the minute), and the consumer does not pay for service;
- *PCs:* the consumer pays for unlimited use of a device (including stand-alone use, independent of network-based services); and
- *Cable or flat-rate telephone subscription:* the consumer pays by the month.

The discussion below addresses how these various models are being applied to the evolving information infrastructure service menu. It highlights the emerging uses of the Internet, which is changing conventional charging and other business practices. Although the models overlap somewhat, they are intended to reflect different emphases and approaches to recovering the costs of services deployment.

Usage-based Fees for Communications and Information Services

The model of usage-based fees for services is most like the metered telephony model, which involves monthly payments on a volume-of-usage (e.g., message service units) basis. In this model, which embraces network-based services that are both special-purpose (Lexis and Nexis are good examples) and general-purpose (CompuServe and America Online are good examples, in the context of use beyond a monthly base level), the information user is the key economic factor. Market growth and competition pit perceived value against cost. Information consumers weigh the factors, and they vary sufficiently that the market has supported both special- and general-purpose, and both no-frills and high-value-added, services.[53]

Competition has kept the prices declining, and services continue to improve in both usability and value. Perhaps 7 million U.S. homes now subscribe to some kind of on-line service, and frequency of use in those homes continues to increase.[54] Communication, chat and electronic messaging, and common-interest bulletin boards and consumer information continue to attract large volumes of traffic and growth. Electronic transactions such as investment activity, including stock transactions and electronic bill paying, while modest activities, continue to grow and proliferate.

Embedded or Domain-specific Services

Under the NII umbrella a number of domain-specific applications or services are being developed. It may increasingly be the case that the communications between businesses and between businesses and homes will be "included" in the pricing for core products and services. Embedded deployment of computing and network capability in the private sector is driven by the strategies of the businesses to which the infrastructure application contributes. Financially, such outreach by businesses may accelerate diffusion (assuming available facilities provide the necessary capabilities) inasmuch as their investments are amortized in a relatively short period of time. Associated costs for distributing information or communicating may become viewed as an element of overhead (somewhat analogous to climate control or electric power). This prospect suggests that much of the information infrastructure will become deeply embedded, like motors or solenoids, so that its costs are submerged.

For example, remote access to medical instruments and specialists targets physicians in their offices, providing rural and other hard-to-serve areas with greater resources via information infrastructure. Such services may provide PC-type hardware devices, software, and wide-area communications for physicians without charge.

Most of the currently envisioned health care uses of the NII in the home will be paid for by providers and payers of health care or suppliers such as drug companies. They will be "free" to consumers. In the context of home banking, an example of a domain-specific service model is the recent introduction by Citibank of home banking services "free" to its customers with some supply of software and necessary equipment (modem, or terminal).[55] Obviously Citibank feels that this service will increase its competitive position, and it can absorb these costs through its core business revenues. Another example is provided by Pacific Gas and Electric Corporation, which is experimenting with an "energy channel" on cable television that allows users to more easily control their home appliances, lighting, and heating and other climate control functions. Although more efficient monitoring and control of energy consumption will ultimately save on utility costs, meter readers, and other costs, Pacific Gas and Electric currently plans to charge consumers about $10 per month for this optional service. On the other hand, Kansas City Power and Light plans to offer a similar service "free" to its customers because it believes that doing so will be profitable.

Although time will tell, domain contributors to the NII 2000 project expressed the belief that the Kansas City model would dominate. One reason is that support will also be provided by intermediate service suppliers. For example, Mastercard and Visa plan to use a software standard supporting electronic credit card transactions that will not involve charges to consumers (Hansell, 1995b). Communications arrangements for that credit card system are left to consumers.[56] That condition illustrates that a key to progress for embedded or domain-specific services remains the underlying or complementary relationships between consumers and communications providers.

The Broadcast Model

In the broadcast model, based on the traditional radio and television broadcast environment, the advertiser pays. In several instances both before and during the forum, contributors commented on broadcast model applications of the Internet component of the NII, for example, to bring information about products and services to niche and casual users without a fee, at least for access to and use of the information. The World Wide Web was the locus of much of this activity in 1995 and appears to be the place where this model is developing most rapidly. However, there are a number of other instances associated with specific businesses. For example, pharmaceutical companies are exploring on-line delivery of applications and networked information, which they intend to deliver free of charge, with advertising, to the doctor or clinic. One service—Physicians Online—has more than 50,000 users (*Electronic Marketplace Report*, 1995). The motivation is simple—facilitating the marketing of more quickly developed and more complex pharmacological compounds—and economically sound; it can be equated with the airlines' motivation in making computerized reservation systems available.[57] The ubiquity of the Internet infrastructure adds the reach and efficiency of shared network infrastructure as the enabling ingredient. In the broadcast model, the user—for example, the medical professional—sees only the service; costs come in the time and training needed to gain the familiarity necessary to get to the information, in a real-time way, but there is no direct out-of-pocket cost to the end user.

Robert Crandall, speaking on behalf of an advertising group, commented on the historic role of advertising revenues in the growth of various media, despite regulation, and relative to subscriber-funded telephony. He argued that advertising should continue to be exploited as a source of financing for new information infrastructure, speculating on possibilities for a mix of advertising and direct subscriber payments—between services and for the same service: "[I]nvestors should be permitted to explore all possible sources of revenue from the marketplace if we expect them to commit such large amounts of capital to so risky an enterprise." Crandall's assessment is corroborated by a financial analysis for video services by Veronis, Suhler & Associates. Veronis, Suhler (1995) estimate that most households (which already pay more than $20 per month for basic cable and $35 if they subscribe to premium channels) will be unwilling to pay a monthly incremental subscription fee of $10 to $15, a fee that would be necessary for recovery of investment in interactive video capacity at a rate of 10 percent per year. Hence they suggest an alternative strategy of offering interactivity at no extra subscription cost and paying for the upgrade with revenues generated by video on demand, a lower access fee (perhaps $5 per month), and advertising.[58]

Reflecting on his experience managing Prodigy Services, Ross Glatzer suggested (while tacitly accepting the broadcast model) that

> even the best of the on-line service advertisers—and some are very good—must get a lot better when they go on the Net, because most of their customers will be paying for the time to view their applications. . . . On the Net I believe the advertiser will end up paying for the number of footsteps that cross his threshold, and the amount of time that those feet stay in the store. . . . This then puts a premium on closing a very high percentage of sales.

As Glatzer's comments suggest, the nature of advertising will have to evolve to meet new service contexts. With the exception of telephony and possibly mail, all current media were developed in the service of a mass culture. Newspapers, magazines, and radio and television with mass audiences were encouraged and supported by mass advertising. Little commercial information was targeted to specific audiences or individuals. While the public paid part of the cost of media such as newspapers and magazines, this revenue represented only part of their economic value. Advertising did and still does provide the bulk of media revenue. Mass advertising in mass media represented the ultimate in downstream information in a society and economy driven by mass production, mass distribution, and mass consumption.

The case for advertising on the NII must be made in the context of what advertisers and consumers seem increasingly to want: direct contact with each other. These contacts will, through interactive information infrastructure, become dialogues. These dialogues have the potential to become enduring relationships among manufacturers, service providers or retailers, and the ultimate consumer. Unable to identify or separate loyal users from trial purchasers or identify heavy users of other brands who would be well worth converting, manufacturers have lacked the capability to create different advertising programs for each. It is the ability to acquire and build a base of loyal, long-term customers—suggesting a new definition of branding plus the ability to better measure what action or behavior either advertising or new product introductions have stimulated—that provides the profit leverage for manufacturers of products, providers of services, or retailers.

How information is used and the direction of its flow are key. Because real accountability requires real information, abstract criteria such as "share of voice" and "share of mind" will give way to a brand's "share of customers." Information infrastructure will provide manufacturers with the information they need to convert products into long-term services. In the future a brand may identify the quality of the relationship as well as that of the product. It will also help target both advertising and the charges for same: an increasing number of advertisers want to know what action or behavior their advertising has stimulated. Companies will not, in the future, manage sales, but rather customers: the blind spending of billions on advertising and promotion for product trials will be replaced by a more focused and longer-term discipline that will manage and increase the lifetime value of customers. Thus, the subscription and membership approaches to selling are already used to encourage the purchase of books, magazines, newsletters, audio recordings, video cassettes, participation in museum activities, telephone and cable service, on-line services, and even coffee and heating oil.

End-User Devices Paid for by Consumers

In the model based on consumers paying for use of a device, the information user invests the capital required to access the network (via acquired personal computers and modems). In the Internet or on-line services case, the user also pays for services; in radio and broadcast television the service is received without such fees. In both cases, advertising can be an important source of cash flow, reducing the charges to consumers. Consumer investments absorb some of the risk of obsolescence and of slower-than-forecast growth in demand; they also disaggregate the investment.

This economic model is subordinated to the broadcast and the consumer-pay (usage-based fees or access subscription) models. It assumes that consumers will possess more intelligent information appliances in addition to the nearly ubiquitous basic televisions and telephones.[59] It also recognizes that fundamental to the growth of the Internet and private networking has been the growing capital investment by individuals and organizations in computer equipment and associated local networks, modems, and related goods and services. As discussed in Chapter 2, the growth in number, diversity, sophistication, and cost of household information appliances is a major indicator; as discussed in *Realizing the Information Future* (CSTB, 1994b), the early growth of the Internet in the research, education, and library environments and the growth of private networking among corporations and other large organizations illustrate the varying willingness and ability of organizations of different kinds and sizes to make investments in intra-organizational network-related infra-structure (devices, local area networks, support, and so on), internalizing relevant costs.

Dependence on consumer-owned PCs raises two concerns, as noted in Chapter 2. The first is affordability. At $2,000 and perhaps three to six times the cost of a television set, the average PC system is beyond the reach of many consumers, who may need to depend on access via large institutions (places of work, employers, schools, government agencies, libraries) or public kiosks. A second concern is upgrading home equipment to match changing service capabilities.[60] Contributors involved with television made many observations about the long lives of television sets in homes, not least because consumers lack the investment incentive provided to businesses under the tax code to depreciate expenses for tax purposes.

One middle ground might come from more versatile software, but there is debate on this point. Queried Stewart Personick, "Is there a model that people will get used to the idea that these things are really disposable and throw them out every 3 to 5 years? Is the model that service providers will subsidize them like wireless cellular telephones, and it will be possible to get a new one for $29? . . . The theoretical solution of a programmable [and therefore upgradable] box is not very likely." Service-provider ownership of access devices is one response, illustrated by leased set-top boxes provided by cable companies or by the bundling (without separate fee) of equipment with services (see the discussion above of the embedded or domain-specific service model). Yet that path raises other concerns, such as the incentives for multiple service operators to minimize functionality to contain costs or the incentives to minimize generality to preserve profits via control over services.

The Access Subscription Model

The access subscription model is best described by the cable TV and on-line information and communications (including Internet access) providers; it can also be seen in flat-rate telephony (so much per month for unlimited calls). In both cases the cost to the information consumer is an attachment charge. That charge may include lease of reception equipment (e.g., set-top box) by the service provider.[61] Unlike the usage-based fee services, in this model one pays a flat-rate fee, usually on a monthly basis, for access to the facilities and information. Of course, illustrating the fact that these models are not pure, cable charges do reflect some offset from advertising revenues to providers, and they may relate to pay-per-view and/or premium services as well as the basic package. In the access subscription model there is a basic assumption that use time is not a cost factor. For example, in basic cable service, the basic investment and the cable signal delivered over it are there: if 100 or 1,000 subscribers tune in, there is no infrastructure cost element to factor into the price. Pay-per-view cable, on the other hand, equates to the usage-based fees model, in which the owner of the information or intellectual asset wants to recover the cost or value of that asset by charging for its use.

A key question with this model is the nature of the service itself. If it is essentially a commodity, it is hard for a firm to remain competitive if each provider offers essentially the same service. Thus, cable provider prospects are affected by the introduction of direct broadcast satellite (delivering cable-like programming) and on-line service provider prospects by the burgeoning entry into Internet access, including entry by providers offering little added value but low prices.

Payment Models and the Internet Phenomenon

As discussed at the forum, many economic projections relating to the NII seem to be building on the experience of the Internet. The Internet today embodies an infrastructure of sizable dimension, with perceived values in many areas of science, education, government, and commerce. It was built to one set of economic principles and is in transition to another set of economic principles, with all the attendant angst. In the recent past, the wide-area backbone of the Internet was provided through a contract from the National Science Foundation (NSF), reflecting the origins of the Internet as a research project within the U.S. government (primarily the Advanced Research Projects Agency of the Department of Defense and the NSF-funded use of the Internet in support of the academic and research community). But with the expansion of the Internet beyond these uses, and the entrance onto the scene of commercial providers, the NSF orchestrated a transition away from its backbone onto a fully commercial, competitive set of backbone providers. This transition has now occurred, and there are a number of Internet service providers that offer wide-area Internet service, as well as regional and local providers. Consequently, payment for services by users is increasing, through subscription services offering Internet access, while federal support (historically targeted to members of the research, education, and library communities but often overestimated by both beneficiaries and observers) via NSF is being restructured to further precipitate the maturation and commercialization process. This second-stage transition, like the larger development of the commercial market for Internet access, is still unfolding; financing for Internet access in research, education, and libraries continues to be a source of uncertainty and concern, as do other, technical and business, aspects of commercialization.

The Internet brings a unique perspective to this discussion from the unusual economic environment in which it exists. Fundamentally we have a very valuable and effective artifact and network of providers and systems that have been assembled according to a social benefit model. The costs of the infrastructure have been borne by the institutions, both governmental and private, that have desired the connectivity and services that the Internet provides. The information providers on the Internet likewise have contributed their intellectual assets and ideas freely, and the user or customer base in fact disdains, as evidenced by the tradition of "flaming," attempts by commercial enterprises to breach the free-flowing and noncommercial etiquette observed on the network. Based on this model, commercial interests have begun to take root, the growth and exploitation of the Web being perhaps the prime example.

The steering committee heard discussions reflecting a wide range of visions about how the Internet could be used in support of business. Some project participants spoke of the Internet as a vehicle among businesses: for electronic purchasing or joint design projects among several companies. Some project participants spoke of business needs that involved broad access to small business sites: offices of retail stockbrokers, insurance agents, or doctors. Some spoke of needing access to the home in support of their business: "telework," retailing, or home health care. And some believed that access to the consumer in the home *was* the business. As discussed in this report, these different visions have different implications for the business model and modes of payment, and for the needed infrastructure deployment. But the basic Internet services and functions can be provided in all these cases.

NOTES

1.   As Robert Crandall of Brookings noted: "[T]he number of competing technologies is growing and . . . the ultimate winner or winners is not known or even likely knowable at this time. . . . However one interprets the recent technological and economic developments in this sector, it is quite clear that building versions of the NII is not becoming less risky."

2.   Growth conforms to a diffusion model characteristic of network markets, often modeled with an S-shaped curve.

3.   See *Telecommunications Reports* (1995n). According to one assessment that focuses on technical difficulties, "Interactive fare from the Bells that combines video and telecommunications seems unlikely to reach even one quarter of U.S. households until well after the year 2000." See also *Computerworld* (1995). Even for some companies willing to make the investment, business case analysis suggests that break-even points will be reached only after 9 to 10 years, if at all.

Concerns raised by cable companies netted this response from U S West: "The key is not whether U S West or any other local exchange carrier can predict video dial-tone revenues and costs with any certainty—they cannot—but whether other telecommunications users will be harmed as a result of allowing LECs to provide video dial-tone service." See *Telecommunications Reports* (1994).

4. "Here was a company with negative earnings, $17 million in half-year sales—and a market capitalization of $2.2 billion at the close of August 9." See Hardy (1995), p. 206.

5. The problems of measuring and tracking new products and industries are well known; typically, relevant activities have to achieve some degree of scale or volume to be captured in reliable statistics.

6. Note that for existing entities there are investments to maintain or replace existing plant and equipment as well as investments for upgrades and growth, implying some need to net out what is investment for growth or upgrading.

7. The telephone companies, of course, would say that they do continuous upgrades, but the last 100 yards has not changed, in part because of regulatory constraints. They still offer the same service, and (again reflecting regulation) they still have very long depreciation cycles.

8. Stewart Personick of Bell Communications Research explained that alternatives for local exchange facilities investment are sensitive to relatively small (5 to 10 percent) differences in assumptions ("take" rates, actual applications, geographic density, supplier pricing).

9. John Redmond of GTE and Edmond Thomas of NYNEX drew from their companies' experiences and concerns to make similar observations. Also, there is some evidence that LEC supply of T-3 lines is growing, nurtured by falling prices that include discounts for fiber channel terminations rather than copper. See Rohde (1995b).

10. However, it is not clear whether recent or prospective changes may reflect enhanced productivity of capital in telephony, which would imply an ability to produce more with less capital than historically; similarly, it would be interesting to compare investment and productivity in wireless and/or competitive access businesses to those qualities in conventional wireline telephony.

11. In the report *New Age Media II* (Friedman, 1994), analysts with the investment firm of Bear Stearns predict that LEC investments in fiber deployment within the local loop will ultimately surpass cable company investments. Choices between hybrid fiber coaxial cable (HFC) and fiber to the curb (FTTC) architectures depend on firms' estimates of likely rates of subscription among the homes passed by the system. (Current penetration for cable television is about 60 percent of homes passed and for the telephone is nearly 100 percent.) Deployment of a new HFC network with full telephone-switching and video-delivery capabilities is estimated to cost about $1,000 per home passed (see the white paper by Stewart Personick). The cost to deploy only the basic transport infrastructure of an HFC transport network, excluding telephone and video, is estimated by Ameritech at approximately $300 per home passed (see the white paper by Joel Engel regarding Ameritech's plans filed with the Federal Communications Commission to deploy an HFC network in its service area). However, upgrading an existing coax network to HFC is estimated by Wendell Bailey and James Chiddix

in their white paper as much less costly, at about $120 to $130 per home passed. This would give cable television operators, who already have coaxial cable networks, a substantial lead in deploying HFC. The review by the steering committee of network deployment plans by cable and telephone firms tends to bear this out.

A July 1994 analysis by financial analysts at Veronis, Suhler & Associates estimated capital costs for deploying a new fiber-optic cable television network as being between $1,200 and $1,800 per household. They identify the cost of file servers and set-top boxes for two-way communications as variables that may drive the network cost higher than these estimates. As discussed in the white paper by Bailey and Chiddix, however, these are incremental costs; while the cost of building the basic transport infrastructure must be incurred completely before any services can be carried, incremental investments supporting interactivity and video on demand can be incurred gradually, while market demand for services builds.

12.   Blau presents an "inverse relationship between the ratio of network investment to operating cash flow from local telephone operations, and total shareholder return." It is not clear how much this analysis takes into account varying conditions among the regional Bell holding companies examined, including different initial capital stock, different geography, and other factors that might lead to variation in investment requirements and behavior.

13.   Robert Blau of BellSouth and Howard Frank of the Advanced Research Projects Agency noted the constraints on accounting rates for depreciation and amortization and for other sources of return on investment in wireline telephony.

14.   Note that wireless systems suggest a very different concept of facilities investment than do wireline systems. The public is a provider of spectrum, the use of which is licensed to the service provider, who in turn invests in transmission and other systems. Due to growing demand for spectrum resources, the Federal Communications Commission recently adopted rules to reallocate spectrum below 512 MHz. See Private Radio docket 92-235, cited in *Wireless Messaging Report* (1995b). The personal communication service (PCS) auctions represent a departure from past spectrum allocation practices, in which the public has arguably given away spectrum rights (in the form of operating permits for broadcasters) and in implicit exchange for performance obligations, to one where license fees imply greater private payment for use of scarce spectrum. Broadband PCS licenses grant broadcast rights to a pair of 25-MHz channels. Two licenses were auctioned off for each of 51 major cities, and carriers paid an average of about $15 per person (the maximum was almost $32 per person) for the licenses— a price that covered the right to launch a network, with construction and other operating costs over and above an additional expense. According to one calculation, with 50 million PCS customers, the cost per customer would be $154 to the provider, versus $1,500 if there were only 5 million customers in 5 years. See *Wireless Messaging Report* (1995d). See the white paper by Peter Huber et al. for a description of the nature and economics of licensing.

15.   Similar licensing rules will likely affect the digitization of television broadcasting by setting a date for the termination of analog transmission. In the broadcasting area, the problem is not one of local access, given essential saturation of

the market, but rather quality and other features of the service. The essential investment issues relate to movement to digital systems and eventually to advanced television (ATV) service(s). See *Information & Interactive Services Report* (1995a) and *Telecommunications Reports* (1995a,b,c,d,f,h,k,l, and m). Note that positive government reactions to PCS auctions has fed proposals to auction digital television spectrum.

16. See *Wireless Messaging Report* (1995d,e). Wireless data and local area network offerings are expected to help fuel the wireless market. See *Wireless Messaging Report* (1994).

17. This estimate is for a 5-year period, for nationwide major-player PCS networks, and includes license acquisition ($7.7 billion), radio and switching equipment, construction and installation, site acquisition and leasing, system design and engineering, and relocating current users. See Naik (1995a).

18. "[O]ver the next ten years, increases in network capacity available on commercial wireless communications systems (e.g., cellular telephone, PCS, etc.) will be large enough to accommodate not only natural growth in demand for mobile telephone services, but also nearly all narrowband voice and data traffic carried over wireline networks . . ." (see Blau's paper).

19. For example, a recent alliance among NYNEX Corp., Pacific Telesis Group, and Bell Atlantic Corp., doing business as Tele-TV Systems, announced plans in September 1995 to provide wireless cable television delivery via Thomson Consumer Electronics Inc. set-top boxes that will offer at least 120 channels but support only limited interactivity (Trachtenberg and Robichaux, 1995).

20. See, for example, the white paper by Jiong Gong and Padmanabhan Srinagesh.

21. See Clark (1995b). Band further notes that if Microsoft's set-top operating system were to become a de facto standard, there would be no entity or authority that could enforce the availability or fair terms of its licensure. However, since an operating system is just code, a new or compatible one could be written. The recent antitrust investigations of Microsoft suggest that the threat of enforcement action might itself motivate broader access.

Microsoft's reported plans and actions relating to Microsoft Network, its interconnection with the Internet, and its development of nonstandard extensions to its Web browser supported by its new content creation tool ("Internet Studio") appear consistent with Band's characterization. Although the introduction of Microsoft Network inspired various strategic responses by other on-line service providers, it did not command an initial market share as high as some had expected, and Microsoft's strategy is subject to change. Those expectations are a measure of the uncertainty and volatility that characterize the on-line service arena. See Clark (1995c).

22. This was a theme at the January workshop, and it is addressed regularly in the business press, conferences, and various policy forums. One bold perspective offered by Charles R. Morris and Charles H. Ferguson (now marketing Web-based products) is as follows: "In general, however, we feel that companies tend to underestimate the opportunities for increasing the space for proprietary architectures, in part, no doubt, because of two decades of often thoughtless propaganda for 'open' nonproprietary systems." See Morris and Ferguson (1993).

23.   Patrick McGovern, chairman of International Data Group, a market research enterprise, was quoted in an interview as saying that "the Airline Guide is more valuable than the airlines . . . . TV Guide was sold for $2.5 billion, [making it] more valuable than any TV network."

24.   According to one reviewer who provided many insights into advertising, "Branding was originally a way of identifying the manufacturer of a product so that consumers who liked it could repurchase it with the assurance of ongoing similarity.   This became necessary because in a mass production economy, the manufacturer and the ultimate consumer of his product were separated by several layers of distribution.   They never saw each other.   But branding too has entered the virtual world.   A product in action, whether it be soap, soup, automobiles, airline tickets, or financial services, is not the object seen at retail.   There it is inert and frequently meaningless.   Coffee is just a can with words on it.   Soap is only a package with words on it.   An airplane or car is a mechanical object.   But as commercial information, these products become services.   Soap is seen making clothes clean.   Brewed coffee in a cup makes family breakfasts joyous.   Automobiles are seen in motion.   Airplanes become the site of friendly service.   Commercial information has provided these objects with valuable 'brand personalities,' which are wrapped around products to prevent their commoditization."

25.   See Clark (1995a), Elliott (1995b,c), and Goldman (1995).   See Barboza (1995) for a discussion of the Internet as a medium for advertising.

26.   Many newspapers have closed or consolidated.   Magazines have had to fight harder to maintain circulation and advertising revenue despite their attempts at greater relevance.   Radio formats have changed.   "Talk shows" are the beginning of audio interactivity.   Network broadcast television is finding it more and more difficult to find programs with a mass common denominator.   "Mass mail" has become inefficient and its irrelevance has earned it the unhappy descriptor of "junk mail."   The growing public ability to consume information and related services at home, rather than going out for them, is reflected in pay-per-view television, with more than 1 million homes willing to pay $50 to view Mike Tyson's return to prizefighting.   In the future, "opening nights" or "you are there" political, sporting, and cultural events may well create enormous new revenues.

27.   Kessler (1995) noted that "the fundamental values of broadcasting licenses have topped. . . .   As PC screens become more televisual, they will attract still more eyeballs. . . . TV is not dead, but its economic model is subject to revision."

28.   CSTB has tracked this shift in perspective through a series of briefings and discussions revolving around its 1994 report *Realizing the Information Future* through major industry meetings (e.g., NCTA '95) and the activities associated with the NII 2000 project, which further engaged key industry leaders.

29.   See Anthes (1995a), Blodgett (1995), Gillin (1995), and Messmer (1995b).

30.   Personal communication, Cathy Medich, executive director, Commerce-Net. SmartValley and the associated Bay Area Multimedia Technology Alliance also provide infrastructure and technology support for applications development, feeding the proliferation of software-based services.

31.   For example, Intuit has contracted with several banks to use its Quicken software for individuals to transfer money between accounts, pay bills, and ex-

tract account data for use on PCs. Actual transactions will be processed through a service unit. See Flynn (1995).

32. Evaluating the actual volume of Internet, Web, and on-line service use is notoriously difficult. "[I]n cyberspace, . . . on-line firms massage membership figures, cloak their calculation methods in secrecy, snipe at rivals' claims and make their numbers impossibly hard to compare" (Sandberg, 1995c).

33. According to Crandall, "There is a huge incentive already to figure out how to make interactivity work, and then to provide interactive services. . . . Until there is a breakthrough, so that we all have interactive devices in our homes, I suspect that the major media types are simply not going to get terribly interested in it. The appeal is still to have things going through distribution channels such as HBO, motion picture theaters, whatever, because that's where the hardware is today."

34. See Liebowitz and Margolis (1994) for a discussion of the literature on and definitions of network effects and related phenomena, as well as work by Economides (1994) and Economides and White (1994).

35. For a discussion of fax, see Economides and Himmelberg (1995); see also Economides (1994).

Discussion of "killer apps" also appeared to be a proxy for some of the concerns about the need for greater ease of use for more advanced forms of information infrastructure. Cautioned Northwestern's Steven Wildman, "What's really going to slow things down or what has to come along is the development of a human infrastructure making it possible to take advantage of the new capabilities." According to Wildman, existing market trials illustrate the difficulties of integrating hardware, software, and human infrastructure at the provider and consumer ends. Quincy Rodgers of GI held out more hope, observing that increasing bandwidth provides "incentives to make the user interface as friendly as possible, because, in order to get back the investment that he has made in his network, [the provider] has got to have as many users as possible."

36. See Rigdon (1995b), Sandberg (1995b), and *Wireless Messaging Report* (1995a). Some observers note that the Web phenomenon may be less than reported: "Getting onto the Internet with your home computer is a lot like sex in junior high school: far more people talk about it than actually do it" (Mossberg, 1995).

37. The Windows '95 experience may be instructive: beyond the early adopters, who are usually willing to pay for the incremental investment needed to try new software, are the average consumers who may be interested in trying the product on a current machine and may require a sizeable investment to upgrade memory, and so on; others may combine software and new PC investments. See Farrell and Shapiro (1992) for a discussion of the diffusion of several consumer electronics technologies. They note, for example, that consumer acceptance of color television lagged broadcaster implementation until sufficient programming became available, pointing to the multifaceted nature of the diffusion process in that case.

38. "Commonalities," they continue, "include standard or conventional interfaces, protocols, reference architectures, and common building blocks from which applications can be constructed to deliver information services to end users."

39.   For example, secure electronic commerce has motivated a variety of standardization activities. See, for example, the discussion of "S/MIME, a specification that combines the Multi-purpose Internet Mail Extensions standard and RSA Data Security Inc.'s security algorithm, the Public Key Cryptography Standards (sic)" in Timmins (1995).

40.   Netscape is also facilitating Internet service provider access (see Booker, 1995b; Corcoran, 1995b; and *Information & Interactive Services Report,* 1995b), as are some PC vendors (see Zelnick, 1994).

41.   Cauley (1995b) and *Information & Interactive Services Report* (1995c). For other examples, see Robichaux (1995a) and Ziegler (1995c).

42.   In an analogous setting, banks are finding value in forming alliances with telephone companies in a kind of vertical integration: "Banks transmit huge amounts of data. Phone lines carry lots of data. So, why shouldn't a bank own this means of production, just as it owns branch offices. . . ." Although decreasing transaction costs may be the initial motivator, both partners often develop new lines of business. One bank, for example, has plans to use "mobile phones and a network of temporary computer kiosks to provide financial advice" to millions of tourists. NYNEX and Chase Manhattan recently unveiled a system to "handle payments over new interactive television systems"(Bray and Carroll, 1995).

Alternatively, direct links between retailers and manufacturers may diminish the role of banks; the directionality of the outcome, although constrained by regulations (themselves subject to change), is not entirely clear. See Bray and Carroll (1995).

43.   AT&T's Mahal Mohan describes in a white paper how the expansion of bandwidth in telephony is being accompanied by a steady expansion of service offerings in circuit-switched voice (and data) networks, including 800-number and other related services involving intranetwork databases, plus directory services and specialized security services. According to Mohan, "Currently these features are offered in rudimentary form as part of data and multimedia services, often to a limited base of users," but their deployment is expected to expand "rapidly over the next several years . . . supporting a broader user base."

44.   Recent FCC action reversing plans to require separate per-channel charges has helped to lower the effective ISDN charges, although state regulatory decisions remain critical. See Betts and Anthes (1995), Fitzgerald (1995), and Andrews (1995a).

ISDN remains imperfectly available, as noted in a recent commentary: "So why isn't ISDN as popular as, say, cable TV? There's still the half of the country that can't get it. Even if you are entitled to order the service, you will probably have to suffer through several phone company order-takers before you find one who knows what you are talking about. Also, your Internet service provider may not have ISDN at its end. Another hangup is the fact that you can't enjoy ISDN's benefits without replacing some of your hardware and software. And then there are the technical glitches. Although ISDN is supposed to be a standardized service, there are subtle local variations. . ." (see Shaffer, 1995).

45.   Bell Atlantic is taking this tack to experiment with "wireless cable"; see Mills and Farhi (1995).

46. See the white paper by Robert Powers et al.

47. For example, Baumol and Sidak (1994a, p. 202) observed that in network markets ". . . regulators must ensure that access prices enable the incumbent firm to remain financially solvent. The price of access, in other words, must cover not only the incumbent's incremental cost of providing access, but also the opportunity cost that such provision of access implies for the incumbent's ability to cover its common fixed costs, including its regulatory obligations to provide universal service." Tye (1994) adds that how this is achieved may depend not only on regulation but also on contractual arrangements between interconnecting parties, which themselves may be guided by regulation.

More generally, there is considerable discussion in economic and anti-trust legal literature about the applicability of the concept of an essential facility—to which access (as through interconnection) may be required. Problems relate to defining and measuring the quality of being essential and to the side effects (including discouragement of investment by free-riders) of compulsory access. See, for example, Areeda (1990).

48. For an in-depth discussion of interconnection pricing, see Brock (1995).

49. Schwartz explained that in New York, NYNEX and TCG have a relationship for exchange of local traffic using a capacity-based port charge, where loops and ports are unbundled and the inbound traffic is about a quarter of the outbound traffic.

50. Issues raised in regulatory proceedings include whether incumbents or competitors have higher costs for terminating calls. See *Telco Competition Reports* (1994a,b).

51. The interplay between network architecture and pricing strategy was the theme of an interdisciplinary panel on the topic "Architecture and Economic Policy: Lessons from the Internet" at the 1995 Telecommunications Policy Research Conference. As discussed there, economic theory presents principles for pricing goals and tactics; network architecture affects the feasibility and desirability (in terms of impacts on use and implications for provisioning) of alternative pricing approaches; and discussion among network architects and economists can contribute to better design of network enhancements to support flexible pricing policies.

52. A related challenge is adjusting traditional marketing strategies to the emerging on-line culture. Retailers who have enjoyed success on the Web appear to be those who pass savings on to the customer (as much as 10 to 20 percent below store prices) and who open themselves to "intelligent agents" used by consumers to search out Web sites with the best bargains. Other, less successful, on-line merchants often resist the use of such agents, believing global comparison shopping presents a major threat. See Rigdon (1995a).

53. There is some evidence that consumers prefer the flat-rate model. "When you're fooling around on-line and you're worried about minutes ticking by, you simply don't use it as much. . . . You see pennies going by your eyeballs." The implications of various pricing schemes for the future of multimedia communications are drawing service providers, users, and regulators into an ongoing debate; see Mills (1995a).

54. Since many subscribers use more than one service, the number of on-line

service accounts (approximately 11.3 million as of late-1995) overstates the number of households (Arlen, 1995b,c; 1996). By contrast, note that the increase between 1993 and 1994 in pager subscriptions was about 7 million (*Wireless Messaging Report*, 1995c).

55. See Corcoran (1995a), *New York Times* (1995), Singletary (1995), Rohde (1995a), *Report on Electronic Commerce* (1995a), Hansell (1995a), and O'Brien (1995). According to Citibank's advertising flyer for this service, there is a "free" 800-number modem line; customers can move money between accounts, check balances, check whether checks have cleared, pay bills, and obtain stock quotes without charge. Citibank has reported some 100,000 subscribers through the third quarter of 1995 (see Arlen, 1995b).

56. The concern here is with the business relationship; from a technical point of view, it is reasonable and even desirable for the credit card protocols not to be bound to a particular communications solution (i.e., a particular type of communications technology and therefore a particular class of provider).

57. See Booker (1995a) and Sullivan-Trainor (1995).

58. Perhaps because of difficulties guaranteeing cost recovery, they conclude that cable-delivered interactive services will be a choice available to only about 2.5 million households by 1998, but will accelerate and reach 40 million households by 2005.

59. While there is much discussion about interactive television (broadcast and cable), that alternative is not likely to rival services delivered via PCs between now and the year 2000. However, whereas with cable the providers make investments and spread costs among subscribers, with direct broadcast satellite (DBS) consumers bear substantial capital costs up front. Market research data suggest that consumers spent between $0.5 and $1 billion on digital DBS receivers in their first year of availability (*Communications Daily*, 1995d). This compares to a total U.S. business local-area network investment of approximately $5 billion (see Chapter 5 section, "Data Communications"). See Markoff (1994), Landler (1995), and Shenon (1995).

60. Some argue, however, that relatively modest levels of capability may be sufficient to support basic access; this is part of the argument behind the case for universal access to electronic mail as a first step in broader universal information infrastructure access (see, for example, Anderson et al., 1995).

61. As discussed at the January workshop, whether set-top boxes should continue to be leased or be made available for purchase is a matter of debate within the cable industry.

4

Technology Options and Capabilities: What Does What, How

The market cannot explore a space that technology has precluded.
—David D. Clark, Massachusetts Institute of Technology

The technology landscape of today is marked by rapid evolution, and advances in technology intertwine with evolution in the communications industry itself. This chapter offers an overall perspective on the drivers of change and on the capabilities of and trends in communications-related technology, with the goal of putting into perspective many of the specific developments of today. It also presents some of the steering committee's assessments of specific technology trends. Chapter 5 contains complementary statistics and an analysis of the deployment of these technologies.

THE CHANGING NATURE OF TECHNOLOGY AND COMMUNICATIONS

Communications services have been transformed by a long series of innovations, including copper wire, coaxial cable, microwave transmission, and optical fiber. Each has expanded the available bandwidth, and therefore carrying capacity, at reduced unit cost. Over many years the cost per voice channel has fallen annually by about 10 percent. With the huge increase in carrying capacity enabled by fiber and optoelectronics, the potential for cost reduction has become even greater—but only if the newly available bandwidth can be utilized profitably. During the same period, silicon integrated-circuit technology has allowed the price of computer performance to fall at a rate of 15 to 25 percent per year. This rapid progress in reducing the cost of computing is what makes computer technology the means to exploit the great growth in communications carrying capacity made possible by satellites and fiber technology.

Advances in the power of the general-purpose processor are easy to see and well understood; workstation speed has more than doubled every 2 years, and memory sizes have grown at equivalent rates. In the more specialized areas of communications, this increased processing power can be exploited in a number of ways—to achieve a simple increase in speed, for example, and to make computers easier to use (simplicity and natural logic in the user interface require very complex processes in software and hardware). Continued rapid progress assures continued advances in both function and usability. But increased processing power can also often be used to greater advantage to increase flexibility and generality, attributes that are key to much of the ongoing transformation of communications technology and thus the communications industry itself. Three specific trends relating to increased flexibility and generality are relevant to the steering committee's assessment: the increasing use of software rather than hardware for implementation of functions, the increasing modularity of design, and the increasing ability to process and transform the data being transported within the communications system.

Implementation of functions in software can reduce cost and permit modification of a function by upgrading the program. Costs can also be reduced by replacing a number of special-purpose or low-level hardware elements with a single integrated processor, which then performs all the same tasks as the multiple hardware elements by executing a program. Continuous cost reduction is central to the current pace of technology advance; it permits rapid technology rollover and restructuring of the hardware base. Implementation in software, however, has the added advantage of permitting the functions of a device to be changed after manufacture, to correct "bugs" or meet evolving user needs, whereas hardware, once manufactured, is frozen. The flexibility to change a product during its lifetime is critical, because of rapidly changing user requirements driven by new applications.

One way to build more generality into a system is to make the design more modular, dividing the system into separable elements that implement different parts of a function. These modules can then be used in different ways to create new services. Adding modularity requires the implementation of interfaces between the elements of the system, and this step adds cost, especially if the modules are physical hardware elements in the design, but to some extent even if the modules are software modules and the interfaces are subroutine calls. However, even though modularity and interfaces do add cost, current trends in design and implementation suggest (compellingly) that modularity, if properly done, has a powerful justification in the generality, flexibility, and potential for growth of the resulting system.

A third key trend resulting from increasing processing power is the ability to process and transform data carried in the communications system. One consequence is increased interoperation among previously incompatible systems. For example, the broadcast video formats in different parts of the world, NTSC, PAL, and SECAM, were a real barrier to interchange of video content until, as is now the case, it was possible to build economical format converters. Today, digital and analog telephone systems interwork, as do digital telephone systems with different voice codings, such as the several emerging digital cellular systems. In the future, as digital television broadcasting is deployed, digital and analog systems for television broadcasting will interwork.

These trends act in combination. For example, data transformations such as the real-time encoding and decoding of video streams or data encryption or compression are now migrating to software. Inexpensive digital signal processors permit the manufacture of $150 modems (today) that encode data at 28,800 bits per second (bps) for transmission down a phone line—an excellent example of the power of a processor chip and software to replace dedicated hardware.

These three trends together lead to a communications world with increasing generality and flexibility and increasing options for interoperability, with additional interfaces permitting the reorganization of the communications infrastructure to offer new services and support new applications. In turn, the increasing modularity of communications technology has transformed the whole landscape of the business environment. Interfaces represent a technological form of unbundling, which permits new forms of competition and new business strategies.

HOW TRENDS IN TECHNOLOGY ARE CHANGING COMMUNICATIONS INFRASTRUCTURE AND SERVICES

The various effects of technology on the nature of communications discussed above have three specific consequences, which represent major factors that shape the future of the information infrastructure:

1. The separation of infrastructure facilities and service offerings,
2. The construction of services layered over other services, and
3. The tension between supporting mature and emerging applications.

Separation of Infrastructure Facilities and Service Offerings

In the past, there were two important communications services, telephony and television. Each of these services drove the development of a technology infrastructure to serve its needs, and both of these infrastructures are today prevalent and of great economic importance.

Telephony and television have evolved considerably since their inception. The telephone system started with copper wires and mechanical switches; moved to modulating many calls on a wire, and then to digital representation of the speech channel and electronic switches, which together led to the current digital hierarchy; and next evolved to the use of fiber optics to carry the aggregated data and cellular wireless technology as an alternate access path. Television delivery (like radio before it) started as over-the-air broadcast but developed the cable infrastructure, and more recently consumer satellite dishes.

For both of these services during their initial evolution, the service objective remained the same: specifically, the delivery of a telephone call or a television channel. However, in both the telephone industry and the broadcast and cable industries, the trend now is to add modularity to the technology and to define explicit interfaces to the infrastructure that permit offering a wider range of services and applications over a common infrastructure.

Perhaps the earliest significant example of this trend toward separation of infrastructure and service offerings is the selling of trunk circuits by the telephone industry. These circuits, such as T1 at 1.5 Mbps and most recently DS3 at 45 Mbps, were first conceived to carry aggregated voice. But they are also sold as a separate component, to carry either voice or data for private customers. This splitting out of the lower-level infrastructure facility by revealing and marketing the interfaces to the point-to-point circuits is the single critical change in the facilities infrastructure that has created the long-haul data network revolution. It is these trunks that permitted the construction of the Internet and the switched packet networks such as frame relay and switched multimegabit data service, and in the past, X.25 networks. These trunks permitted the construction of on-line information service networks and the private networks that today serve almost all of the major corporations.

Recent developments more clearly articulate the separation of service from infrastructure. The telephone industry's new technology approach, called asynchronous transfer mode (ATM), will offer much greater flexibility in service offerings: ATM can carry voice, provide private circuits at essentially any specified capacity (rather than at just 1.5 or 45 Mbps), and also support more advanced services in the data area. Cable technology is following a similar path. While the early cable systems were practical only for the transport of video, their recent evolution to hybrid fiber coaxial cable allows the infrastructure to be used for a range of services, including telephony and data transfer.

The separation of facilities from service offerings makes good sense in the context of current business trends (see Chapters 2 and 3). The regulatory opening of more communications markets to competition, for example, puts a premium on infrastructure that facilitates rapid entry into such markets. Video and telephony providers alike wish to be poised to enter each other's business, as well as to participate in new businesses that may emerge. Also, as pointed out in previous chapters, the steering committee has concluded that the NII will not serve one "killer app" primarily, but rather will enable a wide range of objectives and applications arising from a broad set of business domains and societal functions. Many of these applications do not yet exist, and thus a critical objective for the NII is to be open to the development and deployment of new applications.

Building Services on Each Other

Just as the separation of infrastructure facilities from services permits the construction of a range of services on top of a common infrastructure, so, too, can one service be constructed by building it on top of another. This layered approach to constructing services is a consequence of the trends discussed above—increased processing power, and more modular design with defined interfaces to basic infrastructure facilities. In fact, a wide and sometimes surprising range of service offerings is being created by building one service on top of another. The teaching of networking often involves a simple, layered model of technology, in which infrastructure components are installed and then used as a foundation for next-level services, and so on in an orderly manner. Current reality is much messier and much less well structured. Neither the technology nor the business relationships show a simple order, but instead reflect a very dynamic and creative building of services on top of each other, with the players both competing and cooperating to build the eventual service sold to the consumer.

This layered building of services, of course, has been going on for some time, as noted above in the discussion of telephone trunk circuit sales. There are many other examples of service overlays, some of which are quite unexpected and at times confusing. With the expenditure of enough ever-cheaper computing cycles, one kind of service can be made into an infrastructure for another in quite creative ways. For example, software is available that permits the creation of telephone connections (with some limitations) over the Internet. The data stream that drives the

StarSight on-screen television guide is carried, for lack of any better transport service, in an otherwise unused portion (the vertical blanking interval) of the Public Broadcasting Service broadcast signal—an example of transforming, presumably with considerable processing power, an application-specific service (NTSC video; named after the standards-developing National Television System Committee) into a more general transport service. Perhaps the most confusing situation occurs when two services each can be built out of the other: the Internet can carry digital video, and video delivery facilities can be used to carry Internet service; frame relay service can be used to carry Internet packets, but at least one major provider of frame relay today uses Internet packets to carry frame relay packets.

Beneath these services and overlays of other services lie the physical facilities, such as the fiber trunks, the hybrid fiber coaxial cable and cable systems, the local telephone loops, and the satellites, as well as the switches that hook all of these components together. These are the building blocks on which all else must stand, and it is thus the technology and the economics of this sector that require detailed study and understanding.

The Tension Between Supporting Mature and Emerging Services

From an engineering point of view, the existing network infrastructure is still largely designed and constructed to achieve the objective of very cost-effective and high-penetration delivery of mature services, in particular telephony and video. While the separation of facilities from services has important business advantages, adding generality to the infrastructure, so that it can support a range of future applications, raises the critical concern of increased costs for infrastructure. The tension between cost-effective delivery of mature services and a general platform to support emerging applications is illustrated by the issue, often raised by participants in the NII 2000 project, of how much bandwidth should be provided to the residence, especially back-channel capacity from the residence into the network. A number of participants called for substantial back-channel bandwidth, often to avoid precluding new applications.[1] But the infrastructure facilities providers voice the real concern that adding back-channel capability in too large a quantity would add unacceptable cost to the infrastructure and could threaten the economics of their basic business, which requires considerable bandwidth to the home for video but only enough bandwidth from the home to support voice or low-bandwidth interactive control. They emphasize that new applications must prove themselves and that investment in new infrastructure capabilities can be undertaken only incrementally. From their perspective, it is important to have enough capability to allow the market to explore new sectors, but they cannot be expected to invest fully until an application is shown to be viable. This stance may limit the rate of growth of new applications, but there seems no economical alternative. Research, as noted in Chapter 6, may illuminate ways to reduce investment requirements or enhance applications to accelerate return on investment.

The steering committee concluded that the resolution of the tension between supporting mature and emerging applications was a key factor in determining the shape of the future NII. Two conclusions emerged from the discussions and materials presented. First, current technology plans show a studied balance between a cost-reduced focus on provision of mature applications and provision of a general environment for innovation of new applications, and second, there is broad recognition that the Internet is the primary environment for such innovation.

RESOLVING THE TENSION: THE INTERNET AS AN EXAMPLE

The simple approach to separation of infrastructure from service involves defining an interface to the basic infrastructure facilities and then constructing on top of that interface both cost-reduced support for the mature services and general support for new applications. Thus, the telephone system provides interfaces directly to the high-speed trunks, and the television cable systems define an interface to the analog spectrum of the cable. However, to support emerging applications, the interface to the underlying infrastructure is not by itself sufficient. New applications should not be constructed directly on top of the technology-specific interfaces, because doing so would tie the applications too directly to one specific technology. For example, a very successful technology standard for local area data networking is Ethernet. But building an application directly on top of Ethernet interfaces locks in the application to that one technology and excludes alternatives such as telephone lines, wireless links, and so on.

What is needed is a service interface that is independent of underlying technology options, and also independent of specific applications. An earlier report from the Computer Science and Telecommunications Board, *Realizing the Information Future* (RTIF; CSTB, 1994b), advocated an open interface with these characteristics to support innovation of new network applications. The report called this interface the technology-independent bearer service and called the network that would result from providing this interface the Open Data Network, or ODN. This interface would normally be effected in software; it is an example of a general-purpose capability that would be implemented in a computer as the basic building block for higher-level services and applications.

The architecture of the ODN was modeled somewhat on the architecture of the Internet, which has a form of the bearer service in its Internet protocol. However, RTIF was careful to discuss this critical interface in general terms and not prejudge the suitability of the Internet protocols to meet this need.

The Importance of the Internet

It would appear at this time that the Internet and its protocols represent the best approach for providing a general service for the support of emerging applications because of the effectiveness with which the Internet protocol serves as a bearer service and the overall architecture functions as an ODN. In the course of this project, the steering committee heard from a wide range of application developers in areas such as electronic commerce, information access, and business-to-business collaboration. In nearly all cases, the applications were based on one of two kinds of interfaces to the technology below. Either they were modeled on some mature service and used the existing service interface of that technology (such as video on demand over existing cable systems or fax over voice) or they were based on the features of the Internet. The steering committee heard repeatedly that the Internet standards were the basis on which new applications were being crafted, and even in cases in which the Internet was described as unsuitable, a careful exploration of the concerns usually suggested that the issue was not the standards themselves, but rather the existing public Internet as a delivery vehicle, with its current level of security, provisioning, and stability. The current volume of deployed devices using the Internet standards, together with the observed level of investment in Internet-related products and services, constitutes a unique foundation, one for which there is no alternative now or in any reasonable time frame. See Box 4.1.

Based on its assessment of industry trends, the steering committee thus concluded that the call for an open, technology-independent bearer service as a basis for emerging applications, as voiced in RTIF, was correct, and that a more concrete conclusion is now justified: the Internet standards are being widely used to enable new applications and are seen by a great majority of commercial players as the only viable option for an open, application-independent set of service interfaces at this time.

For this reason, the steering committee further concluded that specific attention should be paid to ensuring the viability of the Internet, in terms of both enhancing the standards to meet evolving application needs and making sure that networks based on these interfaces are deployed and made widely available as an environment for the innovation of new applications. The key topics to consider, then, are (1) what aspects of the

BOX 4.1
Commercial Importance of the Internet:
A Selection of Views

The commercialization of the Internet is already happening, with commercial users representing the largest user domain type registered in the United States. Participants in the January 1995 workshop and the May 1995 forum commented on the present and future importance of the Internet for their conduct of business. Some focused on the barriers to commercial use, such as needs for guarantees of security and intellectual property rights and the difficulty novice users experience in using applications on the Internet. Others noted that commercial services available today can meet these needs, indicating there may be at least a temporary mismatch of perceptions between providers and users. In the longer term, the Internet's sheer ability to build connections was seen as a powerful draw.

The Internet is not about technology fundamentally. It is a social phenomenon that is basically the world's largest interconnected set of computers. That is what makes the Internet have all the energy behind it and what gives it the power of the marketplace and interoperability at all kinds of levels.

　　　　　　　　　　　　　—Marty Tenenbaum, Enterprise Integration
　　　　　　　　　　　　　Technologies Corporation/CommerceNet

We want the ability to coordinate among the industries. Yet we need some push. We need some standardization to make interoperability, encryption, and a number of other things happen. We need culture change on the Internet from the information provider's standpoint, from the educator's standpoint, from the health care perspective. Our users need to better understand what we are trying to give them, and we need to better understand what they want, how they want it, and how they need to get it.

　　　　　　　　　　　　　—Cynthia Braddon, The McGraw-Hill Companies

The Internet excites a variety of people, but there are . . . a lot of people out there that are not going to be excited about the Internet in the next 10 years. . . . How do we get lower-level software for the part of the population that is not capable or is not interested in . . . sophisticated stuff? . . . How do we get all this aimed at all segments of society?

　　　　　　　　　　　　　—Joseph Donahue, Thomson Consumer Electronics Inc.

Not a lot of people, including me, had the nerve to raise our hands this morning when Bob Lucky asked the perhaps inappropriately phrased question about whether the Internet is the NII or not. But the truth of the matter is, if you have the Internet, you do not need much else to have the NII.

　　　　　　　　　　　　　—Andrew Lippman, Massachusetts Institute of Technology

---

BOX 4.2
The Architecture of the Internet

Most users of the Internet see it through experiencing its applications, most obviously the World Wide Web, but also the ubiquitous electronic mail, remote login, file transfer, and other applications. But from the perspective of the Internet designers, the essence of the Internet is not the applications, but rather the more basic functionality that makes the Internet a suitable place for those applications to operate. The structure of the Internet reflects two major design objectives: first, to support as many sorts of applications as possible, and second, to operate over as many sorts of network infrastructure as possible.

Although this may sound rather odd at first hearing, the Internet is more like a computer than a traditional network. The point is that most computers are designed to be general-purpose devices, capable of running a wide variety of applications—spreadsheets and word processors, databases and process control, and so on. Similarly, the Internet was designed to support a wide range of applications, including those that had not been conceived at the time the design was undertaken. The recent explosion of the World Wide Web, clearly not envisioned when the Internet was born, is a measure of the success of this ambition. In contrast, most traditional networks were designed to support a specific application, in particular telephony or video delivery.

At the same time that the Internet was intended to support a range of applications, it was also designed to utilize a range of network technologies: LANs, telephone trunks, wireless links, and so on. Over the last 20 years, it has evolved to operate over different underlying technologies with a wide range of speeds, distances, and error rates. It is organized to permit this adaptability as follows. It provides a set of basic functions, which all applications then use to obtain their network service. To

---

Internet have contributed to its apparent wide acceptance in the commercial world and (2) how the Internet will need to evolve and mature over the next decade to meet the growing needs of this sector. Box 4.2 discusses the organization of the protocols of the Internet and explains how its design allows for a general service to be constructed that takes advantage of the cost-reduced infrastructure that is engineered for the delivery of mature applications. The section titled "The Internet," included below in this chapter, further clarifies what the Internet really is and elaborates on some of its future directions.

The Coexistence of New and Mature Services

Experience with the Internet shows the power of a general bearer service as an environment in which new applications can come into existence. The sudden advent of the World Wide Web makes this point emphatically. However, advocacy of a network with bearer-service interface

permit the use of as wide a range of technology as possible, these services are defined not in terms of the detailed features of one technology, but rather in a very general way that does not depend on specifics such as bandwidth or latency. For each sort of infrastructure that is put into use, software is then written that translates the specific features of that infrastructure into the general, universal form of the service. The applications invoke that software, which in turn calls on the actual network technology.

This ability to operate over different sorts of network infrastructure is a key to the success of the Internet and its protocols. HFC, for example, is one possible infrastructure that might be used to extend the reach of the Internet to homes at higher speeds (see section in text below titled "Hybrid Fiber Coaxial Cable"). A number of products are now available that make it possible to carry the Internet protocols across this form of network technology. While the details of HFC differ from those for other network technologies, the Internet can operate in this context precisely because the details are hidden from the applications by the intervening software.

As discussed in the beginning of this chapter, the trend in the evolution of network infrastructure is that the infrastructure itself is separate from the services that are offered on it. The Internet is an example of this trend and an illustration of its power. In almost all cases, Internet service providers do not install separate infrastructure for their Internet service. They make use of existing facilities, such as long-distance trunks installed to support voice, "dark" fibers in metropolitan areas, copper pairs and cable systems for residential access, and so on. The only hardware items normally purchased and installed by an Internet service provider are the devices that connect the different infrastructures together, the routers, and, for providers that support dial-up access, the equipment to terminate these telephone calls. Most of the expenses for an Internet service provider are the costs of renting the underlying facilities and the costs associated with supporting the customer.

architecture, as called for in RTIF, raised in some industry players the concern that a more inclusive approach was being suggested, that is, that all communications services, including mature services such as telephony and television, should be migrated to this general architecture as an objective of the NII. This objective was not what was advocated in RTIF or in the material gathered for this project. Nor is it advocated in this report.

Voice (telephony) is a case in point. The standards specific to that application of course predate the Internet standards. The infrastructure and interface standards supporting the telephone system are mature and stable and have been engineered to provide very cost-effective delivery of the service. Meanwhile, the growth in technology to support voice communications over the Internet has caused some speculation about the transfer of voice traffic from the public switched telephone network to the Internet. There is no reason to migrate this service to a network such as the Internet that might be less cost-effective for voice, since it was not optimized for that purpose. The recent fad of voice communications and telephony over the Internet may suggest to some that the Internet is perhaps more rather than less cost-efficient than the existing telephone system. A more realistic conclusion is that voice over the Internet currently appears appealing due to differences in pricing (in part a reflection of regulatory circumstances), differences that must prove temporary if Internet telephony becomes a significant component of total telephone traffic.

It is critical to understand the following distinction: the Internet must be able to carry voice (and video), but it is not necessary, or indeed desirable, that all voice and video be carried on the Internet. Today, the Internet is only partially suited for carrying real-time voice, because traffic overloads can cause excessive delay in the delivery of voice packets, which disrupts the playback of the speech. Plans are now under way to evolve the Internet so that it can carry real-time voice streams with predictable delays. Voice, and other real-time traffic such as video, can then be used as a component of any multimedia applications that might emerge. Achieving this objective does not require that the Internet carry voice with the same efficiency as the telephone system, since the goal of the Internet is generality, not cost-reduced application solutions.

The Internet has shown clearly that an open and level playing field leads to vigorous innovation, and the steering committee believes that this opportunity for innovation should be open to anyone willing to offer a new service or attempt a new application. Since the eventual business structure of an unproven innovation is usually unclear, it seems reasonable by default to innovate in an open context, which the steering committee sees as maximizing the chance of success. The interface that needs to be open is the application-independent interface (the bearer service, or in specific terms the Internet protocol).

New physical infrastructure need not be deployed if, in 10 years, some now-emerging application has become so prevalent that economics justifies moving it to a new set of specialized service interfaces. Precisely because physical infrastructure is being engineered to be decoupled from service, it should be possible to build a new specialized service on the deployed infrastructure. None of this effort would interfere with the long-term viability of the general bearer service (or, in concrete terms, the Internet), which would continue to support both new services and those mature services that operate well there. Experience with the mechanisms of the Internet suggests that their use of bandwidth is sufficiently cost-effective for the services the Internet has spawned that so far there has been little pressure to move any applications off the Internet to more cost-reduced delivery services and interfaces.

CURRENT TECHNOLOGY—EVALUATING THE OPTIONS

The discussion above has alluded to a number of technologies of significant current relevance, such as hybrid fiber coaxial cable or the Internet. This section briefly reviews the key features of several important technologies and assesses the extent to which they address some of the concerns raised above, such as a capability for generality and flexibility.

Hybrid Fiber Coaxial Cable

Fiber-optic cable has an information-carrying capacity that is orders of magnitude greater than that of copper. In the long term, some time in the next century, ubiquitous deployment of fiber to every home and office would open up vast amounts of bandwidth to end users. (See the white paper by Paul Green for a complete discussion.) However, deployment of fiber requires a large investment to cover the costs not only of the fiber cable and associated optoelectronic equipment, but also of the labor and construction needed to lay physical cables through cities and suburban neighborhoods. Thus, although fiber has been deployed extensively in the backbone sections of telephone and cable television networks nationwide, it is only relatively recently that the access portions of these networks—the multitudes of separate links that connect end users to the networks and that account for most of the total mileage in the system— have begun to be upgraded to include fiber. Wireline access networks comprising a mix of fiber and copper elements are now being deployed in residential areas.

For such access networks, a very important technical approach—currently embraced by many cable providers and also being evaluated by telephone companies—is hybrid fiber coaxial cable (HFC; often abbreviated as hybrid fiber coax). This approach is best understood as an extension of current cable television infrastructure. In first-generation cable systems, a distribution system of coaxial cables and amplifiers fans out from the community head end to each house. In an HFC system, fiber-optic links connect the community head end to small neighborhoods, and the traditional cable technology is then used to fan out inside each neighborhood to reach individual homes. The advantage of this system is that the fiber replaces long cable runs that include many amplifiers, each of which represents a point of failure, a limit on capacity, and a potential source of signal degradation.

The expectation for HFC is that it will transform an existing cable plant dedicated to analog video delivery to a more general infrastructure capable of supporting a range of consumer services. The higher bandwidth capacity from the head end to each home will permit traditional analog video services and newer digital video services to coexist. Additionally, the reduced number of amplifiers and better noise characteristics of the HFC environment will permit practical use of the reverse-channel capacity of the system, which will thus allow for two-way services such as telephony and data transmission.

Although different vendors offer different specific technical features, the basic characteristics of planned HFC systems are well understood. Traditional, all-coaxial (coax) systems can carry no more than about 80 analog television channels. In most cable systems currently being upgraded to HFC, an additional 200 MHz of spectrum is available for digital services. The digital modulation technique most commonly contemplated for this context, called 256 QAM, yields a downstream digital capacity of 1.4 Gbps within this spectrum—enough to deliver multiple digitized video and other data streams to each user simultaneously.

Some assumptions about service penetration suggest how an HFC system could be used for delivery of digital services. A typical HFC network is expected to pass 500 homes per node—a neighborhood of homes served from a single fiber—of which about 300 might be customers of the system. If about 40 percent of those customers subscribe to the digital services (at some extra charge), then 120 homes are sharing the available bandwidth. If it is assumed that perhaps one-third of the subscribers might be using digital services at a given moment, then the likely peak load is 40 homes. Divided among 40 homes, the downstream capacity is about 35 Mbps per home, which is sufficient to support several video streams to each home.[2]

Given the considerable interest in what sort of data services might be possible with an HFC approach, it is useful to look at what can be achieved with current products. In the last year a number of devices called cable modems were offered to the cable industry that use one or more video channels in each direction to carry bidirectional data across coax and HFC systems (Robichaux, 1995b). At a current cost of $500 to $1,000 per consumer (a cost expected to drop to perhaps $200 with volume), they seem to represent a studied balance between provision of generality and controlled cost. Existing cable modems use a single analog television channel on the cable (6 MHz of bandwidth) to transmit about 27 Mbps of data downstream, which is almost three times the capacity of an Ethernet. (Commercial cable data modems available within 1 to 2 years will provide for 39 Mbps per channel based on 256 QAM.)

Traffic in the upstream direction uses the 5- to 40-MHz portion of the available spectrum, which is used today (if at all) by community access television for feeding video back to the head end. This part of the cable spectrum has generally been found to have problems of electrical noise but can be utilized if specific technical issues are attended to. In particular, a more robust, lower-efficiency modulation technique must be used, which yields an upstream bandwidth inside a single analog channel of perhaps 10 Mbps. Most cable data modems today divide this upstream capacity into smaller channels, either 1.5 Mbps (the same as a T1 telephone circuit) or 128 kbps (the same as the basic-rate ISDN telephone service). Another approach takes the full 10 Mbps and allocates it dynamically among all the potential users—much as an Ethernet LAN is operated. Thus today's cable data modems using one downstream channel and one upstream channel, can currently provide up to 27 Mbps downstream and up to 10 Mbps upstream.

This capacity can be shared by all the homes in a fiber neighborhood, typically 500 homes, noted above. However, to allow for increased demand, most HFC systems are being designed to permit eventual separation of neighborhoods into units as small as 100 homes, in which case the 27 Mbps downstream and the 10 Mbps upstream per channel (however subdivided) would be shared among no more than 100 potential customers. For video or other advanced services, it is reasonable to assume that only some of the potential customers would subscribe to the service and that of those, only some would be active. The resulting degree of sharing would be similar to what is experienced today on many corporate LANs such as Ethernet. In addition, more than one down and/or up channel could be allocated to data services, if there were sufficient demand or if different sorts of data services were to be provided on a single cable. While there is not yet a great deal of operational experience with these cable data modems, the prospect is that two-way data services over cable can be successfully deployed.

Deploying cable data services today requires that the cable system be upgraded at least by the addition of up-channel amplifiers and the use of fiber to serve a neighborhood of reasonable size. Even if the cable provider does not add the additional downstream amplifiers to activate the additional 200 MHz of capacity discussed above, it is still possible to deploy current-generation data modems without disrupting existing services. At least some of these cable modems transmit data toward the home using a frequency above that of all of the channels carried by current cable systems today. Data services thus can be added to an existing cable system without requiring the cable operator to give up any of its existing cable video offerings.

Current cable infrastructure can be upgraded at a fairly modest cost (estimated at perhaps $125 to $130 per house passed, on average) to yield the more advanced HFC system, which would give existing cable operators a short-term advantage (compared to new entrants, such as telephone companies) in the capability to move to a more general infrastructure. However, there was considerable discussion in the workshop, forum, and white papers about the degree to which cable HFC systems would actually provide sufficient bandwidth in a general form (as opposed to being tied to video delivery) that could serve as a practical infrastructure for emerging applications, or more specifically to support the Internet standards for this purpose.

Despite some disagreement, a reasonable conclusion is that although the HFC systems may or may not provide enough capacity to serve a fully developed market of as yet unknown applications, there is enough capacity to explore the marketplace and to let consumers who wish to lead the market purchase enough capacity to get started. It was the opinion of various of the facilities providers that if this point could be reached successfully, further investment to upgrade the capacity would not be an impediment. In fact, additional technical steps already exist to increase the capacity further. For example, as fiber is deployed further into the network and the number of homes per node decreases, an upper range of frequencies (such as 900 MHz to 1 GHz) could be made available for upstream traffic as well.[3] Chapter 3 discusses related issues of economics, including the appeal of incremental investment, in greater detail.

Fiber to the Curb

Hybrid fiber coax is not the only approach to bringing higher-bandwidth services to the home. "Fiber to the curb" (FTTC), an alternative that has been proposed for broadband access, is a term that could, of course, be applied to any technology that carries fiber to this point in the distribution network, with either twisted pair copper or coaxial cable reaching from the curb to the home. In some discussions, the term "FTTC" is used to describe a system for delivery of traditional telephone service and narrowband switched services. In other cases, FTTC is used to describe a system for the delivery of video and broadband services. FTTC systems designed for video are in general designed for advanced services, and not for distribution of analog television signals, since for analog video there are more economical points at which to terminate the fiber. Thus, FTTC systems are typically all-digital. Further, because most FTTC proposals envision services such as video on demand, the head end for the FTTC system often includes a high-capacity digital switch, which can route different video signals to different channels on the FTTC system. Cost estimates for FTTC systems may increase substantially if the cost of such a switch is included in the components, a factor that makes it difficult to compare the costs of HFC and FTTC systems.

A typical FTTC system might carry several hundred digital channels. The fiber carrying these signals would terminate at a small electronic unit, typically in a pedestal, which would serve 10 to 30 residences. The connection from the pedestal to the homes could be coaxial cable, twisted copper pairs, or both. Over such a short length of twisted pairs, coding schemes can carry a number of channels of video on copper wire, so that FTTC schemes could, in some cases, provide a means to reuse some of the existing copper wires in the telephone system.

The pedestal in FTTC systems is somewhat more complex than the fiber-to-coax converter in an HFC system, but the increased costs might be somewhat balanced by the option of cheaper equipment in the residence, since the very short wire runs permit use of a simpler coding scheme on the wire. However, a major cost issue for FTTC is powering the electronics in the pedestal. Running a power cable from the head end along with the fiber adds to the system cost. One proposal for using FTTC is to build an FTTC system alongside some other older system, such as a simple coaxial system, so that the coaxial cable can be used to carry power as well as to deliver basic analog video.

Beyond FTTC systems are systems that carry fiber all the way to the home. Several participants in the forum and workshop observed that the issue of fiber to the home is one of economics. As discussed in Chapter 5, it was predicted that this step might occur within 20 years. However, systems such as FTTC with coaxial cable to the home are capable of delivering very substantial data rates into the home, potentially hundreds of megabits per second, depending on the specific approach used. Thus a lack of fiber all the way to the home should not be equated with an inevitable bottleneck for bandwidth in the path.

Digital Services and the Telephone Infrastructure

Central to Alexander Graham Bell's invention of the telephone was the idea of analog transmission—that the voltage transmitted was to be proportional to the sound pressure at the microphone. Thus for almost a century the telephone plant was designed to transmit analog signals in a narrowband channel.

Beginning with the introduction of the T1 carrier circuit in the 1960s, the telephone plant has evolved to digital operation. Essentially all interoffice telephone networks are internally digital, designed around the notion of voice-sized (64,000 bps) chunks of capacity that are set up and taken down to form connections that last typically for many seconds. First the intracity links were digitized, followed by the switches, and then optical fiber made the digitization of the long-haul links economically possible in the span of only a few short years. Optical fiber has increased the capacity of the digital long-haul transmission system to the point that the cost, if computed as a cost per bit, is nearly free. Although there are obviously costs associated with the long-haul system, there seem to be few concerns that it can meet the capacity requirements of an evolving global information infrastructure.

The current standard for transmission of digital information over fiber is SONET (an acronym for Synchronous Optical NETwork). SONET is largely a tool of the telephone companies to provide capacity, both for data and for voice telephone traffic, whereby each voice telephone connection is granted a two-way, 64-kbps data stream. SONET uses the raw bit capacity of a fiber stream to create multiplexed substreams of synchronous data. Thus SONET turns a big pipe into a collection of smaller pipes, which are individually synchronized at specified bit rates. Long-distance fiber trunks are now utilizing the SONET standard, and in the metropolitan areas, the telephone companies have widely deployed SONET fiber rings.

Now only the "last mile" remains as the vestige of the analog telephone plant. But of course much of the economics of communications resides in this ubiquitous gap between the homes of the country and the reservoir of digital capacity in the network beyond. This part of the system is now being digitized for voice service through the use of a digital overlay known as digital loop carrier technology that enables a number of homes to share a single connection back to the central office by converting the analog signals from the telephones into digital streams, and then multiplexing the streams from the different homes together on the single connection at a point near the home. These digital loop carrier systems can be more economical than individual wire pairs to each home, but they complicate the problem of sufficient broadband access by allocating to each home only the equivalent of one voice channel of digital capacity. This constraint prevents the use of the copper pair to support higher data rates, a capability that telephone providers have sought for several years, in order to be able to support delivery of video or interactive data access.

Data Over the Telephone System

To provide data services, the telephone companies have over the last two decades evolved a series of changes and overlays to the access network. The simplest is of course the brute-force approach of a voiceband modem, which essentially turns a data stream into a voiceband analog signal that can be transmitted over the telephone network just like any other voice-like signal. Although modem technology has become very sophisticated and ubiquitous, it is limited by the voiceband capacity of the telephone network—ultimately something less than 64 kbps; currently available products enable 28.8-kbps data rates.

For the digital transmission of higher-speed data over the access loop, a number of approaches have been developed, most prominently integrated services digital network (ISDN) and asymmetric digital subscriber line (ADSL) technology. In either case a special modem is used on the customer premises to enable the transmission of digits directly into the network. For ISDN the rate is 128 kbps, full duplex, while for ADSL the rate is 1.5 Mbps from the network (up to 6 Mbps over shorter distances) and considerably less in the upstream direction. Both ISDN and ADSL solutions depend on the particular circumstances of an individual home, such as the distance to the central office, the presence of a digital subscriber line, and the amount of interference encountered.

ADSL was developed with a view toward the transmission of video signals over the existing access circuits. There are other forms of digital subscriber line technology as well, such as the symmetric high-bit-rate digital subscriber line (HDSL), which can transmit 1.5 or 2 Mbps over two pairs of copper wire for up to 18,000 feet. Broadband digital subscriber line (BDSL) technology, also under development, carries data downstream at rates of 12 Mbps to 52 Mbps and upstream at 1.5 Mbps to 3.1 Mbps over distances of a few thousand feet. These newer forms of digital subscriber line technology could be used over the installed copper wires, where distance and other characteristics permit, for interactive data access (such as connection to the Internet) and would provide higher data rates than does ISDN. For data services, the HDSL or BDSL path from the residence would be connected to a packet switch located either in the central office or remotely in the serving area, if necessary, to ensure that the copper runs were not too long. Equipment of this sort is now being tested in field trials.

Making effective use of access circuits is not the only problem to be solved if data are to be transmitted over the telephone system. It is also necessary to specify the format of the data, the signaling to be used to control the transmission, and all the other components of a transport system. This information is necessary so that switches within the telephone system can operate on this data. A number of proposals have been adopted by the telephone industry, with varying degrees of success, in the last two decades. These data communications standards relate to ISDN; X.25 and its newer incarnation, frame relay; switched multimegabit data service (SMDS); and asynchronous transfer mode (ATM) (see Table 4.1 for a concise description). These standards are not strictly comparable, in that the associated services are organized in somewhat different ways, but they all deal with the packaging and handling of data by both the end terminals and the network itself.

Internet service, which is also defined by data communication standards, has not yet been offered widely by the telephone providers, although several are now marketing it, or have declared their intention to

TABLE 4.1 Data Communications Service Standards Adopted by the Telephone Industry

Standard	Speed	Type
Integrated services digital network (ISDN)	128 kbps basic rate, 1.5 Mbps primary rate	Connection-oriented[a] streams
Frame relay	Up to 1.5 Mbps	Virtual private lines, connection-oriented[a]
Switched multimegabit data services (SMDS)	From 1.2 Mbps to 34 Mbps	Public addressing, connectionless packets[b]
Asynchronous transfer mode (ATM)	155 Mbps (other rates available)	Small, fixed-size packets, connection-oriented[a]

[a]"Connection-oriented" means that the call route is prearranged, as in today's voice telephone call, so that a packet (or cell) carries only an indication of the connection with which it is associated.

[b]"Connectionless" means that each packet contains the routing address, like an envelope in the postal system.

do so. Internet service is different from the services listed above in that its delivery is less directly tied to a set of hardware technologies. Thus, from the perspective of a telephone provider, the Internet is a service that would operate on top of one of the services listed above.

While ISDN was originally defined as a switched service fully capable of carrying data across the entire telephone system, today it is important to the information infrastructure primarily as a fast method for accessing private data networks and the Internet. As mentioned above in the discussion of digital options for access circuits, it may be thought of simply as a "better modem." To support Internet access, the customer establishes an ISDN connection from the end point to some Internet access packet switch and then sends Internet Protocol (IP) packets over the ISDN connection.

Frame relay represents a way to provide a virtual private network among a number of sites, such as a closed corporate network. The term "virtual" has been used to describe these networks because, while they appear to the user as a set of private connections among the sites, there are no separate circuits that have been allocated from the telephone infrastructure to support them. Frame relay is a packet service, and the packets of various frame relay subscribers are mixed together across the underlying trunks. This statistical multiplexing, typical of services that are called virtual, provides a much lower cost service, at the risk of some uncertainty about instantaneous capacity. Such uncertainty about allocation of capacity does not seem to be a serious issue for many users, however, since frame relay is proving popular in the marketplace.

SMDS is another packet service like frame relay, but it differs in that it does not involve preestablished paths among a set of sites. Instead, it can be used as a public network, in which any site can send to any other by putting the proper address on the packet. In this respect SMDS is somewhat similar to the Internet protocols. However, its addresses are in a different format (they resemble telephone numbers), and SMDS can also be configured to provide a closed user group, similar to the service provided by frame relay.

Whereas ISDN, frame relay, SMDS, and the Internet are overlay services designed to deliver data access over the existing telephone infrastructure, ATM represents a radical rethinking of the network itself. ATM has grown from a mere descriptor of payload within what was previously called "broadband ISDN" to a force of its own that uniquely has gained support from both the computer and telecommunications industries. Since ATM will probably be an important building block for the networks of the future, it is explained in some detail below.

Asynchronous Transfer Mode

The aim of ATM is to provide a flexible format for handling a mix of future traffic—on the one hand, streams of high-speed, real-time information like video, and, on the other, packetized, non-real-time information like electronic mail. ATM represents one attempt to handle both kinds of traffic efficiently based on a technical compromise—small packets or "cells" with a fixed length of 48 bytes, and a connection-oriented approach built around "virtual channels" and "virtual paths" so that routes for packets are preestablished and packets within a given connection experience similar delays on their trips through the network. The design goal for ATM is to optimize network cost and speed by adopting a single compromise for all applications. Thus ATM is seen as flexible, powerful, economical, and particularly suited for multimedia applications.

ATM is being commercialized on two major fronts. Telecommunications carriers are preparing to use it as a backbone infrastructure for flexible provisioning of the multimedia services of the future. Meanwhile, the computer industry has adapted ATM to the needs of high-speed LANs. The two industries have joined in forming an independent standards body, the ATM Forum, which has been focusing on formulating "adaptation layers" for ATM that specialize its operation for particular classes of application.

If ATM is to serve as the common building block for digital services in the telecommunications industry, it must be able to provide effective support for the Internet protocol, since most data networks today communicate through the networks using IP. To accomplish this, the IP packets must be broken up into the smaller ATM cells so that the relatively large IP packets can "ride on top of" the small and nimble ATM cells. Next, the connectionless addressing of the IP must be converted to the connection-oriented ATM system; i.e., a "call" must be established for the IP packet's route via ATM. Third, the congestion control and bandwidth allocation mechanisms of ATM and the Internet protocols must be made to work together. These issues are not trivial, and much work is currently being done to resolve the efficiency of Internet transport through an ATM system. But if these issues can be resolved, both ATM and the Internet protocols should benefit, since the telecommunications industry will acquire a new technology that it can deploy for high-speed data transfer, and the Internet will acquire a new and advanced infrastructure over which it can operate.

The potential benefits of Internet-based networking over an ATM infrastructure are illustrated in the white paper by Gregory Bothun et al. The paper discusses operational trials in Oregon and Colorado, where an ATM-switched network running IP was used to dramatically increase the capacity of university networks. Because the new infrastructure supported IP, university users did not have to abandon their existing protocol structure. Moreover, this approach facilitated collaboration with other institutions, particularly local K-12 schools, whose networks were not based on ATM but did support IP. As Bothun et al. point out,

> One might assume that high-end transport options would preclude the participation of secondary schools; however, this did not prove to be the case. The use of IP-based networking provided the ability to cost-effectively bring secondary schools into the networked environment. . . . With the central dominance of IP-based routers, telecommunications transport became a transparent commodity to be mixed and matched based on cost-performance analyses for each individual location.

Local Area Networks

The last few years have seen major advances in the performance and cost-effectiveness of network technology for the local area, ranging from the work group to the multibuilding campus. Indeed, there was very little discussion of this technology area in the white papers or the forum, largely because it does not seem to represent any serious impediments to progress.

In terms of performance, the major advances have been to increase speeds. ATM local area network (LAN) technology with 155-Mbps host interfaces has now entered the marketplace. In parallel, standards have been defined for Ethernet operation at 100 Mbps, and host interface cards for this option are now also on the market. The faster Ethernet is seen by many in industry as the next generation of faster LAN, since the interface cards are now priced at not much above the cost of a premium 10-Mbps Ethernet interface only a year ago.

A closely related advance has occurred in hubs, the points at which the cables from hosts are connected, which now include a range of products with different levels of performance (at, of course, different costs). Higher-performance hubs incorporate switching among the interface ports, which means that separate pairs of hosts can communicate at once without interfering with each other, in contrast to the earlier hubs in which a packet from only one host could be handled at any one time. ATM has always been based on switching at the hub, but both 10- and 100-Mbps Ethernet now also offer switching as a product option.

Wireless

Wireless communication offers a number of options for local networking as well as for advancing access to the information infrastructure. This section discusses wireless in the telephony and data transmission applications. Trends in over-the-air broadcast, and the impact on the broadcast industry, are discussed in the next section.

Wireless is being used to address two problems in network operation. The first is mobility, the ability of the user to move around while being connected. Mobile users are now increasingly evident, ranging from agents at rental car return facilities and roving checkout clerks in shopping areas to traveling office workers in locations lacking access to wireline devices. The other role of wireless is to reduce the cost and complexity of deploying new services. Some of the new video distribution services clearly illustrate the latter objective, whereas cellular telephony seems to illustrate the former—but perhaps the latter as well, since in some developing countries cellular is seen as a cheaper technology to deploy for general telephony.

Current trends in wireless telephony suggest that there will be rapid changes and advances in the market. The providers of advanced cellular services and personal communication service (PCS) believe that their market will be demand driven, as Chapter 5 indicates. The recent Federal Communications Commission (FCC) auctions of spectrum for PCS and the evolving standards for cellular telephones both suggest a substantial industry investment, which should lead to increased product availability in a very few years. Indeed, since the FCC licenses mandate a schedule of

BOX 4.3
Personal Communication Service Licensing Parameters

Narrowband[1]

Nationwide: (50 states, D.C., American Samoa, Guam, Northern Mariana Islands, Puerto Rico, U.S. Virgin Islands, generally)

• Base stations must provide coverage to a composite area of 750,000 square kilometers, or serve 37.5 percent of the U.S. population, within 5 years of the date that an initial license is granted.

• Base stations must provide coverage to a composite area of 1,500,000 square kilometers, or serve 75 percent of the U.S. population within 10 years of the date that an initial license is granted.

Regional: (5 regions: Northeast, South, Midwest, Central, West)

• Base stations must provide coverage to a composite area of 150,000 square kilometers, or serve 37.5 percent of the service area population, within 5 years of the date that an initial license is granted.

• Base stations must provide coverage to a composite area of 300,000 square kilometers, or serve 75 percent of the service area population, within 10 years of the date that an initial license is granted.

Major Trading Areas (MTAs): 47

• Base stations must provide coverage to a composite area of 75,000 square kilometers, or 25 percent of the geographic area, or serve 37.5 percent of the population of the service area, within 5 years of the date that an initial license is granted.

transmitter installation for PCS, the time frame of new facilities deployment is more or less predictable (see Box 4.3). In most cases, the FCC licensing parameters have 5- and 10-year penetration targets, with the 10-year target representing substantial (50 percent to 75 percent) penetration.

Much of the interest in wide area wireless has been in cellular telephony and narrowband services such as paging. This focus reflects the relative maturity of those markets, which permits somewhat better business planning. It also reflects the fact that, given current technology options, installing wireless infrastructure that meets more general service requirements such as higher-speed interactive data access is rather more

- Base stations must provide coverage to a composite area of 150,000 square kilometers, or 50 percent of the geographic area, or serve 75 percent of the population of the service area, within 10 years of the date that an initial license is granted.

Basic Trading Areas (BTAs): 487

- Must construct at least one base station and provide service within 1 year of the date that an initial license is granted.

Broadband[2]

30-MHz Blocks

- Must provide a signal level sufficient to provide adequate service to at least one-third of the population in the licensed area within 5 years of being licensed, and two-thirds of the population in the licensed area within 10 years of being licensed (population may be defined according to 1990 or 2000 census).

10-MHz Blocks

- Must provide a signal level sufficient to provide adequate service to at least one-quarter of the population in the licensed area within 5 years of being licensed, or make a showing of substantial service in the licensed area within 5 years of being licensed (as based on 1990 or 2000 census).

---

[1]Narrowband: 901-902 MHz; 930-931 MHz; 940-941 MHz
[2]Broadband: 1850-1890 MHz; 1930-1970 MHz; 2130-2150 MHz; 2180-2200 MHz

SOURCE: MTAs and BTAs based on *Rand McNally 1992 Commercial Atlas and Marketing Guide,* 123rd Edition, BTA/MTA map; exceptions as noted in FCC rules (47 CFR 24.102; CFR, 1994).

costly. The perceived costliness of more general wireless infrastructure naturally suggests that deployment decisions in this sector will tend toward more targeted solutions. In fact, a major part of the wireless investment over the next few years will be in real estate and in the construction of antenna towers. These towers probably will permit the installation of several different radio systems, so that in terms of tower construction, the wireless industry is also building an infrastructure of potential generality. (Note, however, that some options for cellular and PCS systems involve relatively small cell sizes and small antenna structures that do not need towers.)

Although the options for higher-speed wireless data transmission are less fully developed, the possibilities are quite exciting. The cost of radios that operate at higher regions of the radio spectrum has declined rapidly—only a few years ago, producing an inexpensive radio operating above 1 GHz was considered challenging, whereas now one can purchase, for a few hundred dollars per station, wireless LAN technology that operates at 5.8 GHz. This technical advance opens up a large range of spectrum for consumer devices. Other products are available that offer short-range LAN emulation and point-to-point data communications over a few miles at data rates of up to LAN speeds (a few megabits per second) and at prices of a few thousand dollars or less. These sorts of devices, which are available from five or ten vendors and are entering the market for workstation interconnection, show some of the potential for wireless.[4]

Most of the current products for interconnecting workstations operate in unlicensed FCC bands at about 900 MHz or 2.4 GHz. Both of these bands have power limits for unlicensed operation that restrict the range and speed of service. Devices that operate at about a megabit per second have a range of a few hundred feet, and devices that operate at lower speeds, 100 kbps or less, can blanket a region with a radius of perhaps half a mile. These technical limitations mean that devices currently on the market do not have the capacity to provide full access to the residential market, which would be better served by a device with a data rate of a few megabits per second and a service radius of a few miles. However, if current products indicate the state of the technology, it would seem possible to build a higher-capacity device if the spectrum were available under suitable conditions for transmitter power and information coding. The recent proposal to the FCC from Apple for an "NII band" around the 5-GHz portion of the spectrum, potentially supporting applications over 10-km distances at about 24 Mbps, had the objective of serving this purpose (see Apple, 1995).

Noted elsewhere in this report is the possibility that the forces of competition and the motivations of private industry for investment may limit the interoperability of emerging telecommunications infrastructure. Next-generation cellular standards in the United States offer a possible example of such an outcome. Differences of opinion about the relative merits of two emerging approaches to PCS, together with the pressures for the rapid introduction of products into the high-demand market, have resulted in two digital cellular standards being brought to the U.S. market, one based on time division and one based on code division. This outcome, while allowing different providers to explore different approaches, suggests that a consumer will not be able to purchase a single digital cellular telephone and use it for roaming to all other digital systems within the United States.[5] Some consumer dissatisfaction with this situation has already been expressed.

In contrast, more active involvement by the government in Europe has essentially led to the selection of a single digital standard for next-generation cellular telephony (Global System for Mobile Communications; GSM), which will permit the use of a single device almost anywhere within Europe and in many other parts of the world. This stronger participation by government in technology creation perhaps helps European citizens and European industry, but the European standard has also been criticized for using spectrum less efficiently, which may add to long-term costs. The European standard has also been criticized for disrupting the operation of hearing aids.

Broadcasting[6]

The terrestrial broadcast system of today was designed for one specific purpose, the delivery of entertainment video. However, broadcasting represents another example of the current trend to separate the specifics of the infrastructure from the set of higher-level services being offered and to push into more general technology. Since the major investment of the broadcaster is in the tower and the operation of the transmitter, any use of a television channel that offers new service has a low incremental cost.

The essential first step in providing new types of services to consumers is the transition to digital standards for video transmission. The development of standards for digital television signals can permit four channels at the same resolution to be transmitted in the space where one was carried before. These new digital channels represent an asset that can be used to provide additional traditional television channels, or perhaps deflected into some new service. This development will give consumers a much larger selection of programs. In particular, many niche markets may now be served economically, catering to every consumer taste. The broadcasting industry is clearly assessing its options, taking into account the current regulatory situation.

Digital terrestrial broadcasting is also necessary to implement high-definition television (HDTV) and advanced television broadcast and cable service. Standards for these services may be approved by the FCC in the coming year (Andrews, 1995b). Broadcasters will be able to profit from the sale and transmission of many types of program- and nonprogram-related digital data, in addition to the HDTV and multiprogram stream standard television services. HDTV will start as a prime-time service in part because prime-time programming is already shot mostly on HDTV 35-mm film. In other parts of the day, standard digital 525-line television will be broadcast, with four program streams filling the standard channel in place of one, through the use of digital compression.

A consequence of the digital conversion is a plethora of standards for representing the television picture. At least three important standards are required for digital transmission of video:

- *The resolution of the picture on the screen.* The HDTV standard defines a higher resolution and a different ratio of height to width than does the standard definition television (SDTV) standard, which yields a picture more similar to the NTSC picture of today.
- *The compression technique for encoding the picture.* For this purpose, the industry is converging on the MPEG-2 standard (named after the standards-developing Motion Picture Experts Group; see Plantec, 1995), but there are variations within the standard (called the profile and the level) that determine the picture quality, the efficiency of the compression, and the cost of the decoder.
- *The method of transmitting the compressed digital signal.* Different transmission methods will be used depending on whether or not there is a limitation to the power of the transmitter, and, in consequence, on how "noisy" the reception is.

The different industries concerned with delivery of video—terrestrial broadcast, cable, and satellite—have in some cases settled on different options for these standards. Cable systems generally are not limited in transmitter power, and they have very good noise characteristics. The current proposals for digital transmission across cable systems thus tend toward schemes that can pack as much digital information as possible into an existing analog video channel. The scheme currently preferred, called 64-QAM, can fit 27 Mbps of data into a 6-MHz analog channel. Terrestrial broadcast standards, which must take into account worse noise conditions, are currently using a more robust scheme, called 8-VSB, that fits 19 Mbps of data into the same channel. In contrast, satellite television broadcast, because of the extreme limits on power and resultant poor noise conditions, uses a very robust but bandwidth-consuming scheme, called QPSK, that uses four analog video channels to carry 27 Mbps of data. The different industries have also, at present, tended to adopt different profiles and levels of the MPEG-2 standard, again because the options represent different trade-offs in bandwidth, quality, and cost.[7]

To deal with this range of formats, the nature of the television will have to change. It is technically possible to build a television that can decode multiple standards, but this adds to the cost of the device. The alternative is to provide the consumer with a set-top device specific to the method being used to deliver the signal. The television itself would then become a monitor, with many of the advanced features in the set-top box. Such a change in the terrestrial broadcast industry would represent a major transition, since today the design of all televisions (as mandated by the FCC) permits the reception of over-the-air broadcast without a translation box. However, it seems inevitable that such boxes will exist, if only to permit the analog NTSC televisions of today to receive the digital signals soon to come.

Research today is addressing the question of building televisions that can, at least to some extent, decode multiple standards at a reasonable cost. An HDTV decoder for a lower-resolution SDTV television can be built at a cost only slightly above that for an SDTV decoder and will permit reception of HDTV on an SDTV television. Building an MPEG decoder for the more complex "main profile" requires additional memory in the device, a requirement that could add $40 to $50 to the cost of the decoder at today's prices for memory (Reed, 1995). Receivers capable of dealing with both QAM and VSB should reasonably be built at a cost only slightly higher than the cost of a single dedicated decoder (see the white paper by Jill Boyce et al.). But the final arrangement of modules and components in the digital television of the future is far from clear.

Finally, systems are emerging for the wireless transmission of video signals in a low-power broadcasting mode. Multichannel multipoint distribution service (MMDS), also known as wireless cable, uses low-power microwave signals sent from a central tower to customer equipment. Depending on the set of licenses available for channels in any particular area, up to 33 analog channels may be available. Use of digital compressed encoding can further increase the number of channels that can be broadcast. Pacific Telesis recently announced its intention to offer 100 channels of digital video over MMDS in southern California. A more recent technology using a smaller cellular structure at a higher transmission frequency (28 GHz) is local multipoint distribution service (LMDS). This service, still in the experimental stage, might offer two sets of 50 channels each. These wireless approaches may provide an interim way for telephone companies, broadcasters, and other players interested in video delivery to compete with current cable providers without building a complete hybrid fiber coaxial cable or fiber-to-the-curb infrastructure.

The NII is intended to provide for interactivity between the consumer and the program provider. Currently, the capability for interactive response to terrestrial broadcasts is provided by the telephone. However, because more than half of all television households receive their broadcast signal via cable, these households will be able to interact with the program provider using the return channel on the digital cable system. The potential of MMDS and LMDS for two-way interactivity is less clear and might rely on basic telephone service for low-data-rate upstream communications. In the next 5 years, it is expected that cellular telephone service and PCS will be widely deployed, providing yet another means of low-data-rate interactive response to the program provider.

Satellite

Satellites have long played a role in the backbone segment of long-distance communications networks. A variety of satellite technologies also exists for end-user access to communications services. In the business communications market, very small aperture terminal (VSAT) systems are used by firms such as hotels, department store chains, and car dealerships to conduct data communications between a central office and remote sites, at variable data rates depending on the nature of the system; some have sufficient capacity to support video transmission. VSAT systems offer two-way communications, although data rates are frequently slower from remote sites toward the center than in the outbound direction. The remote site receivers use an approximately 1.8-meter dish, and signals are carried by satellites in geosynchronous orbit above the earth's equator. Hughes Communications has announced (and discussed at the January 1995 workshop) plans to build a geosynchronous satellite system, Spaceway, which would allow end users access to the Internet, online information services, and other applications at speeds of up to 400 kbps, using a 24-inch transmitter/receiver dish. The system is expected to be aimed at both consumer and business markets.

Geosynchronous satellites also support one-way broadcast services to consumers, primarily video entertainment. Satellite systems operating in the C and Ku[8] bands of the frequency spectrum were developed for television networks to distribute programming to their affiliates for terrestrial broadcast. However, rooftop and backyard satellite receivers, with dishes of up to 10 feet in diameter, are an alternative to terrestrial broadcast and cable television for many users. C-band systems can receive approximately 150 unscrambled analog signals and another 100 scrambled channels. In the past 2 years, two direct broadcast satellite systems based on digital standards have become available, Primestar and RCA's Direct Satellite System. These services carry a package of free and pay television channels and support higher-quality video and sound than do analog systems (Samuels, 1995).

Both voice and data systems depending on networks of satellites in low earth orbit have been announced by several firms in the past few years. One of the higher-capacity systems envisioned is Teledesic, which by the year 2001 is expected to incorporate 840 satellites and provide full telephone, high-speed data (up to 2 Mbps), and interactive video services, accessible worldwide (OTA, 1995; Brodsky, 1995).

Power Industry as Infrastructure Provider

Electric utilities invest in replacing wires on a regular basis, since wires are hit by lightning, and thus carry a risk of failure over time. The industry has observed that the incremental cost of including a fiber-optic cable inside its ground wires is very low, which naturally suggests that investment in fiber represents a good risk as a basis for entering into new business opportunities. Because it does not carry an electrical current, fiber is a natural means to transport control signals through a utility's power distribution grid. In addition, deployment of fiber communications networks reaching into customer premises would enable utilities to reduce their power-generation costs by offering demand management services such as automated, remote control of air conditioning, lighting, and heating systems. Reducing customers' energy usage would reduce overall power demand and enable utilities to delay investing in new power-generation facilities.

As discussed in the white paper by John Cavallini et al., only a very small fraction of the capacity of a fiber network that reached into customer premises would be needed to support energy services. Remaining capacity could be resold or used to support the utility's entry into additional lines of business, such as telephony or entertainment distribution. Utilities currently face choices about how and where to invest in making these infrastructures general-purpose. Technical, regulatory, and economic factors that are as yet undetermined will influence the form a multipurpose utility-owned communications network might take, but the prospect appears feasible in principle.

The Internet

To understand the Internet, one must distinguish its two aspects. First, there is "the Internet," usually written with a capital "I," which is the actual collection of links and switches that make up the current public network. This, and the applications that run over it such as the World Wide Web, are the aspects that have excited the public and press.

The other aspect of the Internet is the set of documents that define its protocols and standards. These standards, which are printed in the document series called the Internet Requests for Comment, define how networks that are part of the Internet can interconnect, and they guide the development of the software that is needed for any machine to attach to the Internet.

But the public Internet is not the only use for these protocols and standards. Anyone can purchase the necessary network technology and connect a number of computers into an internet (with a lower case "i").

And there are probably thousands of such internets, since many businesses today run private corporate networks that support the Internet protocols (as well as others).[9] Over the last 5 years, privately constructed networks have by far exceeded the public Internet in driving the demand for packet routers and related products.

Change and Growth

The continued and rapid growth of the public Internet is a well-known phenomenon. But the growth of the Internet is reflected in more than the rate of new deployment. The protocols, too, are changing in response to evolving needs. The Internet standards should not be thought of as frozen for all time. Indeed, a major part of the success of the Internet has been its ability to change as new technologies and service requirements emerge. At the present time, the explosive growth of the public Internet has forced a redesign of the central protocol—the Internet protocol (IP) itself—to produce a new version called IPv6. IP defines that very central service that ties the range of applications to the range of network infrastructures. One example of a change forced by growth is the need to increase the size of the Internet addresses used to identify the computers attached to the network. If the Internet continues to grow as predicted, there will not be enough addresses available to name all the devices that will be attached. A different address format with room for longer addresses is thus a central part of IPv6. Other features, too, such as increased security and automatic configuration (so-called "plug-and-play" attachment to the Internet) are being added to the next generation of IP. This advance to IPv6 will be difficult to accomplish, since the IP is now implemented and installed in millions of computers worldwide. The success or failure of the migration to IPv6 will be a measure of the Internet's ability to continue to grow and evolve.

Other changes relate to new application services. For example, multicast, which is the ability to send a single message and have it reach a number of recipients with high efficiency, is now being added to IP. This capability, together with the coming support for real-time services such as audio and video, permits the development of a wide range of new applications, such as multiway teleconferences, provision of audio and video information on the World Wide Web, and broadcast of specialty audio and television sources (Berners-Lee et al., 1994; Eriksson, 1994). For example, live audio feeds from the U.S. House of Representatives and and U.S. Senate floor are now available as an experiment across the Internet.

One of the ways that the design of the Internet allows for change and evolution is that as much as possible, the functions of the Internet are implemented in the end nodes, the attached computers, rather then in the core of the network, the routers and the infrastructure. First, as discussed above, having fewer dependencies on the infrastructure permits the use of a broader range of infrastructure. But perhaps more importantly, if functions and services are implemented on the end node, they can be changed or replaced without having to modify the internals of the network. In particular, creating a new application on the Internet requires only that appropriate software be distributed to interested users, and does not require making changes to the router code.[10] Thus, users can experiment with new applications at will.

The limitation of pushing function to the edge of the network is that the minimal end node suitable for attachment to the Internet must have a certain amount of processing power. The alternative, in which the network contains more of the functions, permits the end node to be cheaper. Indeed, it will be a while until an Internet-style end node can be manufactured for the cost of a cheap telephone (see Chapter 2). But for networks such as the Internet that attempt to deliver a general set of services, there is no evidence today that overall costs can be reduced by shifting function into the center of the network. With the trend toward increased functionality and programmability, even for more specialized devices such as telephones and televisions, it is reasonable to predict that soon even very simple and inexpensive devices will contain the functions necessary to implement access to the Internet.

The Internet phenomenon is tied as much to the increasing power of the processing chip as to the advent of higher-capacity communications links such as optical fibers. The ability of the user to purchase inexpensive end-node devices, of course, is basic to the Internet's existence. But it is also the processor that permits the construction within the network of cost-effective routers and other devices that realize the Internet, such as name servers or data caches. The power and flexibility of programmable devices influence the economics, the functions, and the future of the Internet.

Of course, to many, the Internet phenomenon is not fibers or silicon, but people. The Internet, by its open architecture, has permitted a great number of individuals to conceive and try out innovative ideas, and some of these, like the World Wide Web, have taken root and become a basic part of the success of the Internet. The process by which Internet standards are set reflects this philosophy of open involvement. The Internet Engineering Task Force meets three times a year to debate and set standards. It is open to any who want to come, and attendance at meetings has topped 1,000. The Internet is not constrained by an over-arching vision of what it should become (although such visions are certainly offered and do serve as guides); it flourishes by the bottom-up enhancement that arises when people propose ideas, demonstrate that they work, and offer them to the community for debate and standardization. This process has worked well for the last 20 years. How well it will continue to work, given the increasing commercial pressures on the standards-setting process and the increasing size and visibility of the Internet and its design community, remains to be seen (see Box 4.4).[11]

Transport Infrastructure to Information Infrastructure

For its first 20 years, the designers of the Internet were concerned with the basic problem of moving data between machines, in the context of computers and network facilities with differing characteristics. At this level, the data being moved are viewed as simple strings of bits or bytes. The format of the information is viewed as a higher-level problem. Of course, the Internet standards included a description of how those bytes were to be formatted for critical applications such as electronic mail. But the central problem was the basic one of getting these bits across the wires to the recipient.

At this time, the emphasis of the Internet developers has expanded. While considerable efforts are still being made on the lower layers of the standards—to incorporate new infrastructure elements such as ATM, or to add new delivery modes such as real time, and to deal with critical issues such as scale and management—new problems now being addressed relate to the format and meaning of the bits, in other words, the task of turning the bits into real information.

The World Wide Web provides a good example of some of the issues. Central to the success of the Web is a standard that describes the encoding of information so that it can be displayed as a Web page. This standard, called HTML (an abbreviation for Hypertext Mark-up Language), allows the creator of information to control the presentation of the material on the page (its size and style, for example) and to specify how the text, graphics, images, and other media modes will be combined on the screen of the user. In fact, although the basic HTML format is very simple (most users who can deal with a word processor can create a Web page with an hour or so of training), it enables the creation of rather complex information objects, such as forms on a Web server that can be filled out by the user. It is this standard for presentation of information that has made possible the construction of different "Web browsers"—the user interface software for interacting with the information on the Web, and has made it possible for so many providers of information to format that information for use there.

But, in fact, there is a need for a variety of information formats on the Internet. Even for the simple task of formatting information for display and printing, a range of standards exist. As the white paper by Stephen

BOX 4.4
What Will Happen to the Internet?

The Internet has undone what Columbus discovered 500 years ago: It has made the earth flat once again. Maybe it has even made it a bit like a shallow bowl, where every being can "see" every other with relative ease. Broadcast radio and television have made it such that most humans can sense remotely what others are doing; but the Internet allows for the two-way communication that spurs evolution.

The question is, Will the Internet collapse of its own disorganized weight, get regulated to death, or shrug off all attempts to control it and simply take over the earth? In biological terms these alternatives can be likened to cancer, drugs, and green slime.

What are the main factors that will determine the outcome of the struggle to "grow" the Internet in a reasonable way? I see a handful of such factors:

- *The "media hype" factor.* By the time this gets published, I expect that the Internet will have been the subject of a Geraldo or Oprah expose.
- *The "build-a-better-one" factor.* The Internet was originally designed to assume very little about the underlying data transport facilities. This assumption has stood the test of time—the mail goes through, files get transferred, and the Mosaic browser roams the planet in search of interesting information. The number of addresses (potential subscribers) has grown so fast that there is a move afoot to add the capability for many more subscribers. However, the desire to add more and more functionality to the base service threatens to create a design that only an airplane designer could love.
- *The "common-good" factor.* Talk about "data have-nots" and social imperatives pose the prospect of new rules, but legislating universal data access will kill it before it builds enough of a natural market to drive down prices through volume and competition. When it is cheap enough, data access will be ubiquitous. The other, more intractable problem is that on the Internet, local is global. Anything I do in California can be observed and interacted with by persons in Hong Kong or Sao Paolo or Toledo. Whose rules of censorship, taxes, and prices should apply?
- *The "elephant-view" factor.* The Internet is a vast opportunity space. There are many suppliers of solutions at every layer of the data communications infrastructure. And they all work like the devil to enhance their local benefits. This results in a gradual blurring of the nice clean architectural model that we started with and creates short-term disruption in the marketplace while competitors try to respond to new approaches.
- *The "trust-it-to-luck" factor.* There is a large contingent of Internet pioneers who say "leave it alone." Don't regulate it, don't tax it, don't improve it except to allow it to take on more customers. Just let it evolve. It is not everything it could be, but it is great for what it is: a cheap way of allowing anyone to share digital information with anyone else. To those who wish to make it serve particular niche needs, they say, go build those facilities on the base system, but do not make all the rest of us have to pay your overhead.

—Daniel Lynch, Interop Company and Cybercash Inc.

Zilles and Richard Cohn observes, in some cases an author of information may want to specify its format totally—controlling the layout and appearance of each page exactly. A document format standard such as Portable Document Format can be used for this purpose. The Web's HTML represents a middle ground in which the creator and the viewer both have some control over the format. At the other end of the spectrum, permitting the user maximum flexibility in reformatting and reprocessing information is enabled by database representations such as SQL (Structured Query Language), for example, that are concerned not with display formats but with capturing the semantics of the information so that programs can process them. The current trend, consistent with the approach taken in the Internet to deal with multiple standards, is for all of these to coexist, permitting the creator to impose as much or as little format control as is warranted for any particular document.

Looking at the Internet today, one sees tremendous innovation in these areas, just as there was in the past concerning the basic issues of bit transport. Examples of current standardization efforts include "namespaces" and formats of information objects, protocols for electronic commerce, and a framework for managing multimedia conference sessions.

Over the next few years, this increased attention to higher-level information architecture issues will have an impact on the "inside" of the network, the routers and internal services. For example, some Internet service providers are planning to deploy computers with large disk arrays at central points within the Internet to store popular information (e.g., Web pages and related files such as images) close to the user, so that it can be delivered on demand without having to be fetched from across the globe. This sort of enhancement will increase the apparent responsiveness of the network and at the same time reduce the load on the wide-area trunks. It represents another example of how the increasing processing power that becomes available can be used to enhance the performance of the network, independent of advances in network infrastructure.

Open Interfaces and Open Standards

The Internet is perhaps an extreme example of a system that is open; in fact it is open in a number of ways. First, all of its standards and specifications are available for free, and without any restriction on use. The meetings at which standards are set are open to all.[12] Second, one objective of the design of the standards is to make it as easy as possible for networks within the Internet—both public networks of Internet service providers and private networks of corporations, institutions, and individual—to connect together. Thus the Internet is open to providers as well as users. Third, its internal structure is organized to be as open as possible to new applications. For example, some of its traditional features, such as the software that ensures ordered, reliable delivery of data (the protocol called TCP), are not mandatory, but can be bypassed if this better suits the needs of an application.[13] This openness has made the Internet an environment conducive to the innovation of new applications.

STANDARDS AND INNOVATION IN THE MARKETPLACE

It is important not to underestimate the total number of standards that collectively define the existing personal computer (PC) marketplace, the Internet, the telephone system, or the video delivery infrastructure. Standards describe low-level electrical and mechanical interfaces (e.g., the video plug on the back of a television or the Ethernet plug on the back of a computer). They define how external modules plug into a PC. They define the *protocols*, or agreements for interaction between computers connected to a common network. They define how functions are partitioned up among different parts of a system, as in the relationship between the television and the decoder now being defined by the FCC.[14] They define the representation of information, in circumstances as diverse as the format of a television signal broadcast over the air and a Web page delivered over the Internet.

Corresponding to the volume of standards is the range of standards-setting activity. The United States has more than 400 private standards-developing organizations. Most are organized around a given industry, profession, or academic discipline. They include professional and technical societies, industry associations, and open-membership organizations. Among the most active U.S. information technology standards developers are the Institute of Electrical and Electronics Engineers, a professional society; the Information Technology Industry Council, which administers information processing standards development in Committee X3; and the Alliance for Telecommunications Industry Solutions (ATIS), coordinator of Committee T1 for telecommunication standards. Inputs from domestic standards activities by such organizations to international standards organizations (discussed below) are coordinated by the American National Standards Institute.

Standard interfaces allow new products related to information infrastructure to interoperate with each other and with existing products. They are therefore essential for new markets to develop. However, differences in how standards are set can be found among industries, and the approach to standards setting may affect progress in the multiindustry, multitechnology world of the NII. Consider historic differences between the telecommunications and computer industries.

The telecommunications industry has depended on a variety of national and international standards organizations. The International Tele-communications Union (ITU) is the primary telecommunications standards organization at the international level. As a United Nations treaty organization, its members are governments. The ITU sets thousands of standards for telecommunications services and equipment and for their interoperability across interfaces, as well as allocating radio-frequency spectrum. U.S. representation at the ITU is coordinated by the State Department, with participation by other public agencies and private industry. Since AT&T's divestiture, domestic U.S. telecommunications standards have generally been developed by industry-led formal standards organizations, such as ATIS, mentioned above. All of these organizations seek to produce formal "de jure" standards through a process of consensus in technical committees. Standards for some kinds of equipment and services must be approved by the FCC, sometimes adding months or years to the process.

To a much greater extent than the telecommunications industry, the modern computer industry has relied on the marketplace for creating "de facto" standards. In such a system, companies' fortunes depend to a significant extent on their ability either to create de facto standards or to supply products rapidly that conform to emerging de facto standards. In the computer industry, this trend has been driven by market competition, the rapid pace of computer technology change, and the "bandwagon" effect that leads consumers to adopt technologies that appear to be emerging as widespread standards rather than risk being left unable to interoperate with other users and systems.[15]

In practice, standards development exists within a continuum.[16] Many computer industry standards are formalized in national and international standards organizations, such as the International Organization for Standardization—although these standards frequently lag the de facto processes of the market. There are also a multitude of "hybrid" systems. For example, it was the combination of market forces and formal standards committees that created many of the LAN standards currently in use. The emergence of standards consortia in both the computer and telecommunications industries reflects a compromise between the slower pace of consensus standards setting in formal organizations and the chaos of the market. If different consortia produce different standards, however, the fundamental problem of reaching a standard remains.[17] No matter what the method, real and meaningful standards are essential to mass deployment of technology. Anything less is immaterial; standards mean volume!

Neither system of developing standards is perfect. De jure standards creation, while it may be more orderly, tends to be slow and is not immune to political pressures. Furthermore, it may not result in a common standard—witness the regional differences in ISDN deployment. De facto standards, while they may emerge more rapidly, can result in a period of market chaos that delays mass deployment—and the marketplace also sometimes fails to produce a single, dominant standard.[18] They may also lead to antitrust pressures, as experienced by both IBM and Microsoft.

Both formal and market-driven standards setting can favor established major players, but for different reasons. In the case of de jure standards, the long delay in settling on standards allows the established major companies to adapt to the new technology capability and provides for formal representation of users as well as producers. De facto standards, on the other hand, require market power, and the established major players have it. Thus, they can benefit, but only if they can move rapidly.

The process of setting standards for the Internet is an interesting and important example of the balance of concerns. The Internet standards are somewhat between de jure and de facto. While the Internet standards body (the Internet Engineering Task Force; IETF) has not been endorsed by any national or international standards body,[19] it operates with open membership and defined processes for setting standards, and it attempts to avoid domination by any industry sector or large market players. It has been praised for producing standards that work, because it looks for implementation experience as part of its review process. It has also been criticized for the slowness of its processes and for what some see as a somewhat disorderly approach to consensus building.

It is worth noting that some of the important standards in wide use over the Internet, including the standards for the World Wide Web, were not developed formally through the IETF process. Instead, they were proposed by other groups, discussed informally at IETF meetings, distributed on-line over the Internet, and then accepted by industry without further IETF action. Although this partial bypass of the formal IETF processes worries some observers, there can be no argument with the success of the World Wide Web in achieving rapid market penetration. It remains to be seen how IETF and informal Internet standards-setting processes will evolve and function in the future.[20]

There is strong private sector motivation for effective standards setting. Many participants at the forum and workshop said in effect that while the government should act to facilitate effective standards setting, it must not create roadblocks to such efforts by imposing government-dictated standards processes.[21] Government use of private, voluntary standards in its own procurement, however, can be supportive.[22]

The process of setting standards is only one part of the delay in getting a new idea to market. If the idea requires software that is interoperable on a number of different computing platforms, the sequence of steps today to push a new innovation into the marketplace is to propose the new idea, have it discussed and accepted by a standards body, and then have it implemented by some party on all the relevant computers. A brute-force way of bypassing this process is for one single industry player to write the necessary code for all the relevant computers, as Netscape did for its Web browser. Netscape coded, and gave away in order to create the market, three versions of its Web browser—for Windows, for the Macintosh, and for Unix. One drawback to this approach is the large effort required by one industry player. An additional drawback is that the person responsible for each computer needs to retrieve and install the software package.

An idea now being proposed to avoid these drawbacks is to define a high-level computer language and a means for automatic distribution and execution of programs written in this language. Under this scheme, an interpreter for such a language would be installed on all the relevant computers. Once this step was taken, a new application could be written in this language and immediately transferred automatically to any prepared computer. This would permit a new innovation to be implemented exactly once and then deployed essentially instantly across the network to interested parties. An example of such a scheme is the proposal for the Java language from Sun Microsystems. Sun has implemented an interpreter for the Java language, called HotJava, which can be incorporated into almost any computer. Netscape and Microsoft have announced that they will put an interpreter for Java into their Web browsers. Such developments will permit new applications to be written in Java, downloaded over the Web, and executed by any computer running most of the popular browsers.

This set of ideas, if successful, could have a substantial impact on the process of innovation, by speeding up evolution and reducing implementation costs in areas where it is relevant. David Messerschimtt of the University of California at Berkeley observed:

> [O]ne of the key attributes of the NII should be dynamic application deployment; we should be able to deploy new applications on the infrastructure without the sort of community-of-interest problems and standardization problems associated, say, with users having to go out to their local software store and buy the appropriate applications. . . . [It] should be possible to deploy applications dynamically over the network itself, which basically means download the software descriptions of applications over the network.

This set of ideas could also permit the construction of new sorts of applications. For example, programs could be sent to remote machines to perform searches on information there. Thus, remote program execution could be a means to implement intelligent agents on the network. More speculatively, these ideas might change the distribution of function within the network. Clearly, remote interpretation of programs exploits the increased processing power of the PC of today. But some have speculated that this approach, by downloading on demand only the required software into a PC, could reduce the complexity and cost of that PC by eliminating some of the requirement for disk space and memory. This shift might help ameliorate the economic challenge of providing NII access for the less affluent. However, many are skeptical that this shift of processing power back from the end node and into the network, which runs counter to the recent history of the computer industry, will prove effective. Specifically, it would require increased bandwidth in the subscriber access path, which seems difficult to justify economically. There is no clear conclusion to this debate today.

MANAGEMENT AND CONTROL OF THE INFRASTRUCTURE

The aspect of the information infrastructure that is most exciting to the user is the service interface that defines what the network can provide to the user—how fast the network will operate, what sorts of services it can support, and so on. Perhaps understandably, these issues received the most attention at the workshop and forum. Equally important as networks grow bigger, however, are the issues of management and control. At the January 1995 workshop, Mahal Mohan of AT&T commented on the "tremendous number of numbering, switching, overall administration, [and] service-provider-to-service-provider compensation" details involved in supporting network-based services, details, he lamented, that "tend to get overlooked in just counting out the bandwidth of what is coming to the home and who owns it."

The issues of control and management for the Internet are particularly instructive. The Internet grew with a very decentralized model of control. There is no central point of oversight or administration. This model was part of the early success of the Internet; it allowed it to grow in a very autonomous manner. However, as the Internet grows larger and, at the same time, expectations for the quality and stability of the service increase, there are those who believe that changes are needed in the approach to Internet management and control. In the 1994 to 1995 period, there were a number of reports of errors (usually human errors) in the operation of the Internet routing protocols that have caused routing failures, so that information is misdirected and fails to reach its destination. The protocols and controls in place today may not be adequate to prevent these sorts of failures, which can only grow more common as the number of networks and humans involved in the Internet continues to grow.

At the forum, Howard Frank of the Advanced Research Projects Agency expressed surprise at having heard "no discussion at all about the management structures, information management technologies, help services," and so on. He observed that progress in these areas is necessary so that "an internet can evolve from a rather chaotic, independent, loose collection of things to a managed system of the quality of the telephone system, which will allow us to go from a few percent to the 50 percent mark."

A white paper by David Clark of the Massachusetts Institute of Technology argues that the Internet and the infrastructure over which it runs, which were totally separated in the early days of the Internet, must now come together in some ways to facilitate better management and control. Talking about maturing services such as the Internet, Clark observes:

> If the service proves mature, there will be a migration of the service "into" the infrastructure, so that it becomes more visible to the infrastructure providers and can be better managed and supported.
>
> This is what is happening with the Internet today. The Internet, which started as an overlay on top of point-to-point telephone circuits, is now becoming of commercial interest to the providers as a supported service. A key question for the future is how the Internet can better integrate itself into the underlying technology, so that it can become better managed and operated, without losing the fundamental flexibility that has made it succeed. The central change will be in the area of network management, including issues such as accounting, fault detection and recovery, usage measurement, and so on. These issues have not been emphasized in many of the discussions to this point, and they deserve separate consideration in their own right.

Milo Medin of @Home called for approaches such as distributed caching to "avoid vaporizing the Internet" due to excess traffic, yet there is no mechanism to encourage or enforce such prudent practice.

Any change in the overall approach to Internet management and control will require the development of an overall architecture or model for the new approach. This sort of major redesign is very difficult to contemplate in the Internet today, due to the large installed base of equipment and the bottom-up approach of the standards process. Whether and how to evolve the management and control model of the Internet thus represents a major point of concern for the future.

At the same time that some are calling for more regimented approaches to Internet management and control, others argue that the Internet style of control is preferable to the model that more closely derives from the traditions of the telephone company. The current ATM standards have been criticized by some for this reason. The signaling and control systems being developed come from a heritage in the telecommunications industry that, while a reasonable model when it was first adopted, may be coming under increasing strain. The Internet community has developed a different technical approach to signaling and control, which may prove to be simpler while more robust. Instead of building complex mechanisms to ensure that any fault inside the network can be locally detected and corrected, the end nodes attached to the network periodically repeat their service requests. These periodic re-requests for service reinstate the needed information at any points inside the network that have lost track of this service request due to a transient failure. It is thus the case that there is still a significant set of technical disagreements and uncertainties about the best approach to network management and operation, both for the maturing Internet and for the next generation of technologies for the mature services such as voice and video.

An issue that is now receiving considerable attention is pricing and cost recovery in the Internet (see Chapter 3 for more discussion). In the past, the Internet has been paid for on a subscription or fixed-fee basis. There is now considerable debate as to whether some forms of usage-based charging are appropriate or necessary. The white paper by Robert Powers et al. notes the need to balance recovery of consumed service with the cost of implementing the billing mechanism. Since billing systems and their use have costs, it is an open question whether telephony-style billing is the right model. The answer no doubt depends on the type of applications that users will demand. Electronic mail places rather small demands on the network, but video conferencing is quite different. Pricing is relevant to network technologists not only also because of issues relating to implementing accounting and billing systems, but also because pricing influences how (and how much) networks are used. These incentive effects interact with the network architecture to affect the performance as well as the profitability of networks.[23]

NOTES

1.   Andrew Lippman of the Massachusetts Institute of Technology observed that industry has not been good at predicting what applications will prevail and should thus engineer for the unexpected, and not focus on the specific application of today.

2.   Different assumptions about market penetration and traffic load would obviously change these results.

3.   Time Warner has demonstrated the feasibility of such a system in trials in Orlando.

4.   The Wireless Information Networks Forum (WINForum), an industry association, petitioned the FCC in May 1995 to set aside additional spectrum for wireless local area networking at higher data rates than current options allow.

The proposed allocation would support high-speed LANs at 20 Mbps, sufficient for multimedia applications. See WINForum (1995).

5.   All digital cellular phones are expected to be able to be used with traditional analog facilities, which will remain in place for the foreseeable future. However, the added complexity of a device that can support multiple standards may add to its cost, especially in the short run.

6.   Material for this section was taken from Henderson (1995) and from Reed (1995).

7.   A further variation is whether fixed- or variable-rate video encoding is used. A variable-rate encoding can permit better representation of complex scenes within a program, at the cost of a higher peak rate. However, other sorts of digital information can be transmitted in the instants that the full channel capacity is not needed for the video. In one recent experiment, a 50-second commercial provided enough unused capacity to transmit 60 megabytes of data.

8.   Ka band frequencies are also in high demand as companies rush to offer satellite video-conferencing and computer networking. Using this band, systems such as Hughes' Spaceway could offer "bandwidth on demand" where "today's 24-minute download from the Internet would take less than 4 seconds at a cost no higher than today's rates." See Cole (1995), OTA (1995), and Markoff (1995).

9.   Some corporate networks should properly be thought of as being part of the public Internet, since they are directly connected and exchange packets. However, many corporate networks, if connected at all to the public Internet, exchange only specific and limited applications such as electronic mail.

10.   This statement is not accurate in every instance; certain enhancements to the Internet such as support for audio and video will require upgrades to the router code itself.

11.   The CSTB (1994b) report *Realizing the Information Future* includes an expanded discussion of the pressures and concerns now arising in the Internet standards process.

12.   Internet standards are discussed and set by the Internet Engineering Task Force (IETF) and its working groups, which collectively meet three times a year. In addition, much work is carried out on the Internet itself. For information, see the Web page of the IETF at http://www.ietf.org.

13.   This situation prevails with real-time transport of audio and video, where quick delivery is more important that 100 percent reliable delivery.

14.   See the 1991 Cable Act (P.L. 98-549), amending 47 USC Sec. 544. It required that "[w]ithin one year after October 5, 1992, the Commission shall prescribe regulations which establish minimum technical standards relating to cable systems' technical operation and signal quality. The Commission shall update such standards periodically to reflect improvements in technology. A franchising authority may require as part of a franchise (including a modification, renewal, or transfer thereof) provisions for the enforcement of the standards prescribed under this subsection. A franchising authority may apply to the Commission for a waiver to impose standards that are more stringent than the standards prescribed by the Commission under this subsection." These efforts have been codified at the FCC as Section 15.115 "TV interface devices, including cable

system terminal devices" and Section 68.110 "Compatibility of the telephone network and terminal equipment."

15. IBM System 360 and Microsoft MS-DOS and Windows are the classic examples.

16. Government-mandated regulations and procurement specifications constitute a third category of standards. Agencies at all levels of government set regulatory standards for products and processes in order to protect health, safety, and the environment. They also produce specifications for public procurement of goods and services. The *Federal Register* regularly publishes requests for comments on standards proposed by federal agencies. Some of these are developed by agencies, while others originate as voluntary standards set in the private sector and are adopted by reference in the text of regulations and specifications.

17. A very broad consortium, known as the Information Infrastructure Standards Panel (IISP) and spearheaded by the American National Standards Institute, has attempted since mid-1994 to bring together a large number and variety of organizations and entitites concerned with standards relating to the national and global information infrastructure. In late November 1995, the IISP issued a list of 35 "standards needs," ranging across such areas as reliability, quality of service, provision of protections (e.g., security), specific types of interfaces, and data formatting (see Lefkin, 1995). It is premature to judge the outcome of this effort, although anecdotal reports from some parties familiar with it have noted the difficulty in cross-industry forums of achieving results with sufficient focus and specificity to constitute an advance from the basis in disparate, separate standards-developing activities.

18. An example is AM stereo, in which the FCC forbore from picking a standard; none ever emerged because no market could develop in the absence of a standard, and no standard could develop in the absence of a market.

19. Recently, through the auspices of the Internet Society, the IETF has been establishing liaison with organizations such as the ITU. But sanctioning of the IETF and its standards by other formal standards bodies has not been a factor in the success of those standards. Market acceptance has been the key issue.

20. In the case of the World Wide Web, a consortium of industry and academic partners has been organized at the Massachusetts Institute of Technology with the goal of furthering the standards for the Web. It is an attempt to create a neutral body especially organized to deal with the very rapid advances and strong industrial tensions present in the Web architecture. Whether it represents a cooperative complement to the IETF or an explicit rejection of the IETF processes remains to be seen.

21. A recent National Research Council (1995) study examined standards development in multiple industries. It concluded that the relatively decentralized, private-sector-led U.S. standards-setting process, while messy and chaotic, is generally the most effective way to set standards in a market economy.

22. Federal selection of standards for the government's own systems is a topic that has been considered by the Technology Policy Working Group. Its December 1995 draft report calls for a process that "minimizes the number of required standards for the Federal Government's purchasing of NII products and services, limiting them to those that relate to cross-agency interoperability" (TPWG, 1995b,

p. i). It notes that "there is already existing government policy which covers the preference and advantages to government selection of voluntary standards (e.g., consensus standards). This policy is contained in OMB Circular No. A-119 Revised 10/20/93, 'Federal Participation in the Development and Use of Voluntary Standards'" (p. 14).

23.   The interaction between pricing and architecture was the focus of a special interdisciplinary panel at the 1995 Telecommunications Policy Research Conference (September 30–October 2, Solomons, Maryland). Entitled "Architecture and Economic Policy: Lessons from the Internet," the panel featured papers prepared jointly by network technologists and economists, which were revised for spring 1995 publication in the journal *Telecommunications Policy*.

5

Technology Choices:
What Are the Providers Deploying?

INTRODUCTION

Predicting the future of technology deployment is an inexact under-taking, given the many uncertainties in technical developments, market forecasts, and regulatory actions. However, an assessment of current plans and trends is a good starting point for identifying a range of possibilities. This chapter presents a variety of information about current levels of deployment in the key areas of network technology and infrastructure. It also reviews the main infrastructure provider industries' announced plans for new deployment over the next several years, as revealed in white papers contributed as part of the NII 2000 project, comments at the workshop and forum, and trade and market-research publications. (Announced deployment plans, of course, are not necessarily firm commitments; they may change, as did those of many firms during the course of this project. However, every attempt has been made to present information that is as up to date as possible.)

This chapter represents, in part, a response to the Technology Policy Working Group (TPWG) request for a "road map" of technology deployment over the next 5 to 7 years. The material included here answers the TPWG's call for a synthesis of projections; however, there are no available data that reliably support precise forecasts of specific deployment events by specific dates. The steering committee has attempted to identify the boundary conditions of future deployment and some potential signals indicating major turning points, or forks in the road, which should be monitored as indicators of change in the next several years. Table 5.1 presents the steering committee's broad conclusions about the technological capabilities—with respect to end-user access to services—of infrastructure that is likely to be deployed and available in the next 5 to 7 years. Some aspects of nomadicity, and of hardware and software technologies that enable information infrastructure, are implicit in table entries, but these topics are not fully summarized in the table. The remainder of the chapter provides supporting evidence and analysis.

The discussion assumes a very basic familiarity with several important information infrastructure technologies, such as hybrid fiber coaxial cable (hybrid fiber coax; HFC) architectures for residential broadband (high-data-rate) communications, integrated services digital network (ISDN) and other digital telephone services, wireless voice and data services, and broadcast television. Chapter 4 introduces these technologies in brief, discussing key issues underlying technical debates about deployment (for example, the capabilities of likely architectures for fiber-optic networks in residential areas). This chapter focuses on what is being deployed today, what plans have been announced, and what the overall capabilities of anticipated information infrastructure components will be. The decision to invest in deployment of infrastructure depends, of course, on an expectation of demand for services over that infrastructure. Accordingly, in addition to addressing deployment—the supply of infrastructure—this chapter also presents selected data on both current and projected demand for information infrastructure-related services. These data are drawn from a range of published government and private sources. Other economic and regulatory issues that affect investment prospects and timing of deployment are considered more fully in Chapters 3 and 6.

This chapter divides the topic of infrastructure into several broad categories: (1) infrastructure of wireline telephone carriers, including both the local access component and the backbone (long-distance) component; (2) data communications services carried over the wireline infrastructure; (3) wireline infrastructures for advanced services to the home being deployed by cable television and telephone companies; (4) on-line information services and Internet access; (5) wireless services, such as cellular telephony, personal communication service (PCS), and wireless data; and (6) broadcast services, including terrestrial and satellite television broadcasting and multichannel multipoint distribution service (MMDS, or wireless cable). These distinctions do not reflect industry boundaries as clearly as they once did, as restrictions on lines of business erode and mergers and alliances occur among the firms offering these services. Nevertheless, distinctions in the technological capabilities of these types of infrastructure remain important, and projections of their deployment, however speculative, are necessary for an understanding of the NII's capacity to support current and future applications.

More material is provided on telephony than on cable or miscellaneous wireless technologies. Consistent with available materials is the expectation that telephony will continue to be the dominant source of two-way bandwidth for homes and small businesses in the near-term period of interest. In a perfect world, comparable material and analysis would be presented on the full range of information infrastructure applications and services; however, their speculative nature and relative invisibility in the aggregate, as reflected in available data sets, precluded such a presentation.

WIRELINE TELEPHONY

Summary and Forecasts

The local access infrastructure in 5 to 7 years (the primary time scale on which the steering committee focused) will be based on digital switching. This infrastructure will support basic voice-grade, circuit-switched telephone service ("plain old" telephone service, or POTS), with enhancements such as caller identification and call forwarding. POTS will grow slowly relative to more advanced access services. However, because of its current overwhelming dominance, POTS will still be the primary telephone service.

The principal role of ISDN will be as an access method to data networks, transporting packets to and from the remote business or residence. While ISDN will be available virtually everywhere in the Unites States, its deployment rate (actual sales of service to customers) is uncertain. Low-cost customer premise equipment for ISDN will become available in the next 1 to 2 years, both for the client side (adapter cards) and the remote access (points of presence (POP), local area network (LAN)) side. However, service installation costs coupled with very high monthly service costs will limit residential and small-office deployment. Rapid deployment of ISDN can happen, but only if the price of service approaches that of POTS. It is not clear at this time what factors will drive telephone companies to lower prices, although competition from alternative access services (such as cable and wireless data) could lead to such an outcome.

Long-distance and interoffice telephone infrastructure will be fiber-based with sufficient bandwidth to meet anticipated demands. In the local access infrastructure, because of the high cost of deploying new fiber cables, fiber availability at the customer's premises will continue to be limited to business users in high-density districts—where more users and traffic volume can be served by each fiber deployed. (Telephone com-

TABLE 5.1 Infrastructure Capabilities for End-User Access Within 5 to 7 Years

Capability	Residential Telephony: Traditional Analog Voice Facilities	Residential Telephony: ISDN	Residential Advanced Services, Cable and Telephony: HFC, FTTC
Data rates to and from the end point	Low—not far above currently available 28.8-kbps data rates	Moderate— 128 kbps	Moderate to high— downstream digital broadcast of 100s of TV channels; two-way data transmission via cable modem at 100s of kbps to 10s of Mbps
Bidirectionality (downstream and upstream bandwidth)	Symmetrical	Symmetrical	Asymmetrical, but upstream capacity will be adequate for many interactive services and is extensible with incremental investments
Continuous operation (connection is "always on"—e.g., enabling e-mail delivery to the user at any time)	User must dial in (or be called) to connect to the network; circuits are generally available when demanded	User must dial in or be called; call set up is rapid enough that operation is effectively continuous if either end can initiate the call	Data and video services—yes; voice telephony—see traditional analog voice facilities
Real-time multimedia access (full-motion video)	No	Limited— adequate for tele-conferencing	Yes—but asymmetrical, pending investment in upstream capacity (see above)

NOTE: For definitions of the abbreviations used in this table, see Appendix G, p. 278.

Business Wide Area Networking: Frame Relay, SMDS, ATM	Wireless: Terrestrial Cellular, PCS, Mobile Data, Wireless LANs	Satellite Voice and Data: VSAT, LEO	Terrestrial and Satellite Broadcast: ATV, LMDS, DBS
High—1.5 Mbps to 155 Mbps and higher	Mobile—low, 10 to 20 kbps; LANs—moderate, 100s of kbps to current wire-based LAN speeds	Moderate to high—400 kbps (Spaceway) to 2 Mpbs (Teledesic gateway service)	Moderate to high—digital broadcast of 100s of video channels; data broadcast currently at 100s of kbps
Symmetrical	Depends on system	Depends on system	Upstream channel is through another medium, such as wireline or wireless telephony
Yes	Some services require dial-in; others provide continuous operation	Some services require dial-in; others provide continuous operation	Yes, if television receiver is turned on
Yes	Highest-bandwidth wireless LANs can support multimedia; other wireless services cannot	No (exception— higher-capacity LEO satellites, such as those in the Teledesic system)	Yes, but downstream only

pany deployment of hybrid fiber and copper infrastructures capable of supporting broadband services in residential neighborhoods is discussed separately in this chapter, in the section titled "Cable Television and Telephony: Advanced Services to the Home.")

Local Access and the Larger System

The public switched telephone network is the most broadly deployed two-way (nonbroadcast) component of the national information infrastructure (NII). It is an evolving infrastructure; however, starting from such a large base, system-wide changes will take time to implement. Projections of future NII deployment may reasonably start, therefore, with analysis of the present telephone infrastructure.

The local operating companies, or local exchange carriers (LECs), represent the access portion of the telephone network. More than 1,300 companies provide local telephone service in the United States; most are far smaller than the regional Bell operating companies (RBOCs). They provide local service to end users and sell access to their network to interexchange carriers (IXCs) that offer direct-dialed long-distance service.[1] The seven RBOCs and GTE together account for most of the local exchange market. Historically, these firms have held a monopoly on end users' access to telephone communications within their respective service areas, although competitive access providers (discussed below in this section) have a growing share in many markets. The other major part of the telephone network is represented by the long-distance companies, or IXCs. There are about 450 IXCs, most of which resell capacity purchased from other, facilities-owning carriers; the three largest are AT&T, MCI, and Sprint. Their networks form backbones carrying traffic between separate local areas.

The physical infrastructure of the local exchange consists of access lines, switches, and trunks. Access lines connect end users at homes, businesses, and other locations to the telephone network; they constitute the portion of the network known as the local loop. Switches and interoffice trunk lines direct and carry communications across the network. Communications that leave the local telephone company's service area must pass over facilities owned by long-distance carriers and terminate on facilities owned by other firms, such as other LECs and wireless (primarily cellular) carriers. (See Chapter 4 discussion of technology trends in telephone infrastructure, as well as the white papers by J.C. Redmond et al. and Stewart Personick.)

According to the Federal Communications Commission's (FCC's) *Statistics of Communications Common Carriers* (1994, Table 2.5), all U.S. LECs combined (a larger group than in the *Infrastructure* report cited below) serve 147.9 million access lines. About 40 million switched circuits (30 percent) and virtually all dedicated, leased circuits are business and institutional access lines; many of these connect to sites with multiple users on a private exchange, each with a unique telephone number. Therefore, the total number of telephones attached to the network is significantly greater than 147.9 million.

The types of services that may be carried over the physical telephone infrastructure depend not only on the bandwidth and transmission quality (absence of errors) in the links, but also on the type of encoding and switching. The ongoing transition from analog to digital switching in the telephone system is important both for improving the quality of basic voice service (POTS) and as a prerequisite for many services beyond POTS. A 1995 FCC report (Kraushaar, 1995b), *Infrastructure of the Local Operating Companies Aggregated to the Holding Company Level*, presents a detailed view of recent deployment of infrastructure—specifically, lines and switches—by the RBOCs and GTE (see Table 5.2). Together, these firms account for over 90 percent of the nation's total access lines. According to the report, which includes data through the end of 1993, digital switching has steadily become predominant within the local network: 66 percent of access lines are served by digital switches, 33 percent by analog stored program control switches, and 1 percent by electromechanical switches.

The North American Telecommunications Association (NATA) projects a continued increase in the proportion of access lines served by digital switches. By 1996, NATA forecasts a total of 201 million access lines. Of these, 82 percent will be served by digital switches, 18 percent by analog switches, and less than 1 percent by electromechanical switches (NATA, 1995, p. 66).

Integrated Services Digital Network

The copper portion of the local plant traditionally carries one voice circuit to and from the customer premises per twisted pair of copper wires, using analog transmission. However, all-digital transmission technologies such as ISDN are extending the capacity of the copper plant. (Asymmetric digital subscriber line (ADSL) technology can increase copper's capacity even further; see Chapter 4. Development of the technology is continuing, but no large-scale deployments by any carrier have yet been announced.) The FCC's report (Kraushaar, 1995b) indicates that the theoretically available, total ISDN access line capacity (basic or primary rate) at central office switches is more than 42 million. This capacity represents the maximum number of lines that could be served by the telephone carriers' current ISDN-capable switches—digital switches with

TABLE 5.2 Infrastructure of the Local Operating Companies, 1991 to 1993

	1991	1992	1993
Switches (incl. local, tandem, hosts, and remotes)	16,400	16,700	18,529
Total access lines served (millions)[a]	123.0	125.8	131.4
Percent of access lines served by:			
Digital switches	52.6	58.7	66.3
Analog switches	44.6	39.7	32.5
Electromechanical switches	2.7	1.6	1.1
ISDN-capable switches	964	1,437	2,173
Total ISDN access line capacity (millions)	21.3	29.8	42.1
ISDN basic rate interfaces equipped[b]	298,176	491,430	587,229
ISDN primary rate interfaces equipped[b]	1,730	3,147	5,814
Local loop copper terminations in central office (thousands)[b]	208,381	209,059	215,578
Local loop fiber terminations in central office (thousands)[b]	277.7	576.7	620.2

[a]Includes both residential and business access lines.
[b]Interfaces equipped at the central office, whether or not circuit is in use.

SOURCE: Kraushaar (1995b).

the necessary software control to support ISDN.[2] The current sales of ISDN services, however, are far below the theoretical capacity in the switches, at approximately 400,000 to 500,000 lines (Wildstrom, 1995).

To serve new ISDN customers, the telephone carrier must have ISDN-capable switches, which must in turn be equipped with per-line terminating equipment. The latter is an investment that can be made incrementally, in response to (or anticipation of) customer demand; it is not necessary for the carrier to equip the entire network for ISDN at once. Typically, more interfaces are equipped at the central office than are actually in use; the FCC estimates that installation of interfaces at the central office leads sale of services and actual subscriber use by 12 to 18 months. The number of ISDN basic rate interfaces equipped with the necessary line connections in the central offices at the end of 1993 (the year for which the most recent FCC data are available) was 587,229. (The FCC's estimated 18-month margin is therefore consistent with the estimated 1995 ISDN subscribership of 400,000 to 500,000.) The number of higher-capacity, primary rate interfaces equipped in the central offices was 5,814 in 1993. The majority of basic rate interfaces and all primary rate interfaces in use are currently serving business or other institutional customers, rather than home users (Kraushaar, 1995b, p. 26; FCC, 1994, Table 2.10).

According to the white paper by Stewart Personick, ISDN availability will continue to expand. Through 1996, availability will range from 53 percent of the NYNEX service area to 86 percent of the Pacific Telesis area. NATA cites forecasts by Dataquest that the number of basic rate interface ISDN lines in service will increase to 1.1 million in 1998, at an average annual growth rate of 47.1 percent. The level of investment needed to achieve this growth is uncertain; however, Personick's white paper estimates that deploying the switching capacity, line-termination equipment, and related systems in the central offices to meet demand for ISDN (and other, higher-capacity services) will represent a total investment on the part of LECs in the billions of dollars.

As noted above, the sales of ISDN services to date are far smaller than what could be supported by the theoretical availability of ISDN in the telephone system. Growth in demand will be stimulated by several factors. One important source of demand for ISDN is as an access technology for connecting remote users (such as workers in homes and small offices) to router-based networks, such as workplace LANs or on-line services; for low-volume users, this will be cheaper than leasing a dedicated circuit. For example, deployment of ISDN connections by on-line service providers is beginning to take place, in anticipation of subscribers using ISDN to access their services. CompuServe recently announced plans for local ISDN access in 10 cities, supplementing current ISDN access via an 800 number. Prodigy and America Online officials indicate that they are focusing on bringing their subscribers up to 28.8-kbps modem access (Hayes, 1995).

Another factor in the growth of demand for ISDN is the lower costs for customer-premise equipment needed to take advantage of ISDN. Investment in customer equipment, such as adapters for connecting personal computers (PCs) to ISDN lines, is the responsibility of the end user; increases in volume production, standardization, and improvements in the price-performance ratio of computer equipment will continue to bring this cost down rapidly in the next several years. (ISDN line adapter prices fell from $2,000 in 1994 to less than $500 in 1995; see Wildstrom, 1995.) However, the prices that telephone carriers charge for ISDN service are not declining nearly as rapidly as customer equipment prices, and ISDN remains significantly more expensive than POTS. Until this gap is narrowed, it appears unlikely that the market for ISDN will grow rapidly. Substantial competition from alternative access providers, such as cable television systems and wireless networks, is one factor that could accelerate ISDN price decreases.

Access lines with higher capacity than POTS and ISDN are available to customers from telephone companies and capacity resellers, in the form of leased, dedicated lines to customers. These customers are primarily at businesses and other institutional locations where volume of use justifies the expense of the connection. The circuits, which may be copper or fiber (although new deployments today are usually fiber), generally carry digitized voice and/or data. Common increments of capacity are 56 kbps, 1.5 Mbps (T1 or DS1), and 45 Mbps (DS3), at successively higher prices per connection but successively lower prices per unit of capacity. Deployment of the data services that can be carried over these circuits, such as frame relay and asynchronous transfer mode (ATM), are discussed in the section "Data Communications" below in this chapter.

Telephone Industry Fiber Deployment

Fiber deployment is a significant indicator of advancing telecommunication technology. Fiber represents both the capacity to carry new, higher-bandwidth applications (such as digitized video) and the reengineering of the infrastructure to carry basic telephone service with lower costs and higher quality and reliability. Long-distance carriers told the steering committee that for the next 5 to 7 years, they will continue to have sufficient bandwidth to meet the nation's demand for voice telephony, data, and video communications. The backbones of their networks will be optoelectronically switched, over fiber lines; all-optical switching, however, will still be under development and will be far from substantial deployment. The white paper by Robert Powers et al. notes that the bit rates achievable through a given fiber have grown from 405 Mbps in 1983 to 2.4 Gbps today, with an anticipated leap to 40 Gpbs by 2000, using wave-division multiplexing. The authors calculate that by 1996 or 1997 it should be possible for a fiber pair to carry over 600,000 voice circuits, eliminating concerns about bottlenecks in the long-distance portion of the telephone network "for the foreseeable future."

In the local exchange, fiber is widely deployed between central offices; however, only a small fraction of total local-loop plant is fiber-based (see, for example, the white paper by Mahal Mohan). The FCC's annual *Fiber Deployment Update: End of Year 1994* (the most recent edition available; see Kraushaar, 1995a) presents detailed data on current fiber deployment by major IXCs and the Bell, GTE, Contel, and United local operating companies. The IXCs have deployed 101,861 miles of fiber cable, while local operating companies have deployed 257,734 miles of fiber cable. There is an average of 25 to 35 separate strands of fiber per cable. The capacity of this infrastructure, as noted by Powers et al., may be subject to approximately 16-fold increases with higher-speed optoelectronics by the end of the decade. Even with present technology, the capacity of the IXCs' fiber could be increased substantially by activating deployed fiber that is currently unutilized ("dark" fiber).[3] Dark fiber is currently about 50 percent of the total for AT&T and about 44 percent for Sprint. The percentage of lit or activated fiber for local operating companies ranges from 26 percent for SBC (formerly Southwestern Bell) to 60 percent for GTE.

The FCC reports that 94 percent of channels in the LECs' local loop plant terminate at the central office on copper and 6 percent on fiber (Kraushaar, 1995b). Four of the seven Bell operating companies reported data distinguishing the number of fiber miles in the subscriber plant (local loop) from total plant. For NYNEX, Pacific Telesis, SBC, and U S West, subscriber plant fiber miles are 52 percent of total fiber miles (Kraushaar, 1995a). Most fiber deployment in the local loop is in the portion closest to the central office; most lines change over to copper before reaching the end user (crossing the "last mile" to customer premises). However, the number of fiber lines reaching the customer (mainly in the form of dedicated circuits leased to businesses) is growing rapidly. The number of subscriber services terminated on fiber at the customer premises at the 1.5-Mbps (DS1) rate at the end of 1993 was 148,286, up from 37,029 in 1989 (an average annual growth rate of 140 percent).[4] The white paper by J.C. Redmond et al. cites forecasts of the number of dedicated access lines as reaching more than 3 million DS1 lines and about 1 million higher-rate, DS3 lines by 2002. Of these lines, virtually all new deployments will be on fiber to the customer premises (possibly excluding a final, short segment close to the customer, depending on the architecture used).

Digital access lines are used for both voice and data applications. However, data communications are the primary source of the rapid growth in the demand for these lines. A Yankee Group survey of Fortune 500 firms' telecommunications managers reports, for example, that 8 percent of these firms are now using dedicated 1.5-Mbps lines for data communications. By 1999, 24 percent expect to do so, and 5 percent will be using 45-Mbps lines for data (Yankee Group, 1995b).

Kraushaar (1995a) also discusses fiber deployment by competitive local exchange carriers (COMPLECs), also known as competitive access providers.[5] The report considers only facilities-based carriers, not capacity resellers. The report includes firms such as Metropolitan Fiber Systems, Teleport Communications Group, and competitive access systems owned by Time Warner Communications, which is also one of the largest U.S. cable television firms. Fiber owned by the COMPLECs listed in the report (not an exhaustive list, but including the major firms) comprises 9,304 miles of cables. (Each cable contains, on average, from 20 to 200 individual fibers.) This total mileage reflects a 63 percent average annual growth rate from 1990 to 1994. The two largest systems, Metropolitan

Fiber and Teleport, serve 2,670 and 1,560 buildings, respectively. Most of the COMPLECs' business today is in one of two categories: access for business and other institutional customers to an IXC (bypassing the dominant local carrier) or linking an IXC's local points of presence. (Data are unavailable to suggest how long it might be before COMPLECs reach significant penetration in residential areas; currently, this penetration is virtually zero.) According to the white paper by Gail Garfield Schwartz and Paul Cain, COMPLECs are deploying fiber faster than incumbent carriers in the 50 to 60 metropolitan markets where they are active. These deployments are principally in Synchronous Optical NETwork (SONET) rings, supporting advanced, broadband data, voice, and video services.[6]

Fiber deployment will continue to grow from the base described in this section. (Fiber in the residential access networks will be an additional driver of this deployment, as this chapter's section on advanced services to the home discusses.) One forecast of the speed of overall fiber deployment is given in a recent Frost & Sullivan report (1995) on fiber-optic equipment and related products. (Costs for fiber cable and equipment are only a fraction of the total investment cost of deploying fiber networks; the majority is labor and installation. However, equipment expenditures are a reasonable indicator of rates of overall deployment.) The report projects that the U.S. market for fiber-optic products (such as fiber cable, optical couplers, and optoelectronics equipment) in local telecommunications systems will more than triple, from $761 million in 1994 to nearly $2.5 billion by 2000, a 21 percent compound annual growth rate. This market was only $74 million in 1990. In 1994, local telephone systems accounted for three-fourths of the U.S. fiber-optics market; cable television companies were 17 percent of the market, and COMPLECs were 6 percent.

Demand for Telephone Services

Telephone carriers finance a large proportion of their investments in infrastructure out of the revenues they receive for services. The FCC reports that toll service revenues of long-distance carriers totaled $61.5 billion in 1993. (AT&T long-distance revenues were $35.7 billion; MCI, $10.9 billion; Sprint, $6.1 billion; and LDDS Communications, $1.1 billion.) Local exchange carriers (RBOCs and others) totaled an additional $13.8 billion in toll-calling (long-distance) revenues within their service areas (FCC, 1994, Table 1.4).

More detailed information is available for carriers that are required to make annual reports to the FCC—the major local exchange carriers and AT&T's long-distance unit, AT&T Communications. AT&T Communications' total operating revenues, consisting almost entirely of long-distance network services revenues, were $35.7 billion in 1993; this included $3.6 billion in long-distance private network revenues, of which $2.4 billion was from digital private networks (FCC, 1994, Table 2.9). (The next section discusses the breakdown between voice and data services across the telephone carriers' networks.) AT&T Communications' largest expense item was $13.4 billion for local network access (necessary to connect to end users), paid almost entirely to LECs. LECs that report data to the FCC, including the seven RBOCs and GTE, had $90.2 billion in total revenues: $41.7 billion in basic local service revenues; $27.3 billion in network access revenues; $13.0 billion in long-distance revenues (including $1.1 billion from private networks, of which $0.3 billion was from digital private networks); and $9.3 billion in miscellaneous revenues, including directory and billing revenues. Using slightly different definitions, the Yankee Group reported RBOC revenues for 1993 as follows (1995a): $35.7 billion from local service, $9.8 billion from long-distance service, $20.3 billion from network access, and $17.9 billion from other services (equipment, publishing, cellular, others).

International calling is growing at a much faster rate than is any other area of voice telecommunications (or other mature NII services, such as broadcasting). Two significant demand factors are (1) calling by recent immigrants to the United States to relatives in their country of origin and (2) the increasing usefulness of the network due to the wiring up of the rest of the world (reflecting an economic factor known as the network externality). The FCC reported total net revenue from international services for all long-distance carriers as having grown from $1.8 billion in 1984 to $2.9 billion in 1988, and accelerating to reach $7.8 billion in 1993 (FCC, 1994, Table 4.6).

DATA COMMUNICATIONS

Summary and Forecasts

The business sector is making major investments in data communications. Within the decade, most employees who work in offices will have a PC attached to a corporate network, which will in turn be connected to the public switched network (e.g., through an Internet connection). High levels of network penetration will extend beyond the large corporation to the small business and the remote office. Total corporate investment in networking is difficult to estimate, since it includes capital expenses (for such items as interface cards, LANs, routers, and modems) and salaries for staff, as well as payments to telephone carriers and other firms for network services. However, businesses' annual investment for basic infrastructure and support is probably more than $10 billion. With a projected 75 million networked corporate PCs by the turn of the century, business networking is a very important part of the national information infrastructure.

Despite this high level of investment, payments explicitly for data communication services account for only a small share of telephone carriers' revenues. However, such payments underrepresent actual revenues for carrying data, because data frequently move over circuits that mix voice and data and count as voice circuits in telephone industry statistics. More broadly, these telephone carrier revenues underrepresent the total economic and societal importance of data communication as a component of the nation's information infrastructure.

There are two important, current trends in corporate data networking. The first is a shift away from networks built on dedicated circuits and toward switched services provided by carriers, such as frame relay. This trend is driven by the inherent cost efficiency of bandwidth-sharing packet-switched services and is not likely to reverse. The second is the trend toward attachment to the Internet. While many corporations have private corporate networks, they also see a need to attach to the Internet as a means of access to a public data network. The increasing use of the Internet Protocol (IP) technical standard within private corporate networks increases the potential for interconnecting these networks to the Internet.

The applications supported by the very large business infrastructure will generate significant demand for network access. However, much of this access will be realized, at least for the next few years, over low- to medium-speed links such as dial-up via modem, ISDN, and lower-speed frame relay. The extent to which this demand for access will eventually require investment in substantially higher capacity within the public network infrastructure than is necessary to meet demands for voice and lower-capacity data communications depends on the advent of new, higher-bandwidth applications such as video.

Several technologies are being deployed within the public switched network to support higher-capacity data services and mixed services (voice, data, and video). Some providers believe that ATM will be the dominant technology in the public switched network by the turn of the century, while others believe that frame-based services such as frame relay and Internet will provide an effective data communications infrastructure. The spread of applications that demand more bandwidth and the deployment of increased capacity in the network to support them are, of course, mutually dependent. A significant indicator to monitor in the next few years is whether new bandwidth-intensive applications such as video succeed in penetrating the market.

Data Services Provided by Telephone Carriers

According to a recent Yankee Group report (1995a), explicit data services (those for data only, not voice and data combined) represent less than 1 percent of total RBOC revenues. Most data communications, however, travel over the telephone network by means of services that are also used for voice and cannot technically be distinguished as either voice or data from the carrier's point of view. For example, fax and modem data are encoded and transmitted as analog signals over analog voice circuits; digital circuits, such as ISDN and dedicated high-speed lines, frequently carry both voice and data. Estimates vary concerning the percentage of telephone network traffic actually accounted for by data. Pacific Bell President David Dorman recently estimated that at some time in 1995, data (including fax and modem) would pass voice to represent more than 50 percent of the traffic the telephone industry carries.[7] Dorman noted that voice traffic is growing at 2 percent annually from a large base, whereas data traffic has been growing at 30 percent annually.

The Yankee Group survey of large businesses found a lower percentage of data services relative to voice services than that given in the above estimate (Yankee Group, 1995a). However, the survey found that the need for data services is growing. In 1994, outside network services expenses for 200 managers of large corporate networks were 61 percent for voice and 36 percent for data. The group estimated that by 1996 the proportion will be 54 percent for voice and 40 percent for data. It also estimated that levels of data traffic will increase by 39 percent, which suggests that most users expect price decreases for a given usage level. In addition, the survey responses indicated that an overall shift is in progress from dedicated circuits to switched services, implying greater reliance on telephone-carrier-provided network management and related services. Between 1994 and 1996, the type of service relied on is projected to change as shown in Table 5.3.

The explicit data services listed in Table 5.3 are growing rapidly, but from a small current base, and will therefore continue to represent a small share of telephone industry revenues. The Yankee Group (1995a) reported that the 1994 frame-relay services market was $356 million and that the market for switched multimegabit data service (SMDS; another public packet-switched service) was $22 million. Another Yankee Group survey (1995b) found that 22 percent of Fortune 500 companies will be using frame relay for access to remote corporate locations by 1996. A study by the Vertical Systems Group estimated that the current base of U.S. frame-relay customers (mainly businesses) is under 1,000 but will grow to approximately 8,000 by 1997.[8] The study estimated that each customer links together an average of about 20 separate sites, leading to

TABLE 5.3 Reliance on Various Kinds of Data Services, 1994 and Projected for 1996

Data Service	Percentage	
	1994	1996 (projected)
Private line	76	51
Frame relay	2	20
X.25 packet networks	10	6
Switched services (ISDN and others)	12	11
ATM	—	9

SOURCE: Yankee Group (1995a).

significant demand for frame-relay equipment—an estimated 1997 market of nearly $500 million for service provider equipment, $200 million for private network switches, and over $300 million for access equipment. (This equal distribution between service provider and customer equipment expenses illustrates the importance of capital investment by customers, as opposed to providers, as the next section elaborates.)

As discussed in Chapter 4, ATM is an emerging technology intended for local- and wide-area networking (including both privately deployed networks and networks purchased from telephone carriers) and eventually for voice, data, and multimedia services throughout the public telephone system. ATM is one possible avenue for meeting business networking needs. Consulting firm CIMI Corp. projects ATM switch deployment for wide area networks (WANs) as growing from an installed base of 1,136 ATM ports in 1995 to 64,815 ports in 1999, a 175 percent annual growth rate (Wallace, 1995). As projected in the white paper by Redmond et al., ATM switches will be dominant in the telephone network after 2000, possibly reaching 100 percent deployment by about 2015.

The Internet is also meeting business networking needs, and the two technologies will in fact coexist as Internet service providers (ISPs) build their networks atop the telephone infrastructure, which may include ATM and other data services. Internet service providers constitute a small but rapidly growing segment of the marketplace. A recent assessment of the market by securities firm Cowen & Company concluded that the total revenues for ISPs were $288 million in 1995 (Cowen & Company, 1995). This figure includes revenues for the firms dedicated to Internet access, such as PSI, Netcom, and UUNet, as well as for the Internet services provided by LECs, IXCs and others. They are estimated to serve 1.2 million customers. These data make clear that the on-line service providers such as America Online, Prodigy, and CompuServe are currently much larger than the other ISPs, since they serve an estimated 11.3 million customers (Arlen, 1996, p. 1). (See also the section "On-line Services and Internet Access for Consumers.") However, Cowen & Company predicted that the relative importance of Internet service providers will increase for individual access, and by 1998, they will approach on-line services in size, with 8 million to 11 million users and revenues of $2.7 billion.

Cowen & Company (1995) further noted that the current pattern for ISPs is rapid growth and investment, leading to limited current profits. Cowen & Company estimated that the combined ISPs are installing 1,000 points of presence in the public switched network in 1995, which will require a hardware investment of $150 million. This level of investment should lead to full market penetration by 2000, after which levels of investment will be driven only by increases in demand. The total investment that these players will make suggests that casual entry into wide area Internet service is not to be expected. However, at least one other company, @Home, is planning to construct a new, wide area Internet infrastructure in the next few years (see the section "Cable Television and Telephony: Advanced Services to the Home").

Cowen & Company estimated that by the year 2000, there will be 200 million users on the Internet worldwide, with 100 million connected through corporate or institutional links and up to half connected by individual access links. They estimated that as many as 1 million corporations will be connected to the Internet. This projection is consistent with another conclusion from a Cowen/Datamation survey cited in the above report (Cowen & Company, 1995), in which telecommunications managers indicated that 62 percent of corporate networks are connected to the Internet in some manner and that there are plans for an additional 21 percent to attach.

Business Networking

Business networking includes interconnection of LANs across wide areas (in WANs), as well as remote access (connection of remote sites, small offices, mobile workers, and telecommuters to corporate networks). Business networking is leading not only to increased sales by carriers and third-party providers of data services such as frame relay and Internet access, but also to a rapidly growing investment in data communications infrastructure by business customers themselves. In contrast to residential networking, in which the capital investment by the consumer is minimal and the facilities provider makes the major up-front investment, the networking of a corporation involves considerable customer investment in equipment. This includes network interface cards for computers, site

TABLE 5.4 Projected Growth in Workplace PC Connections to LANs in the United States, 1995 to 1999

Installed Base	Users (millions)				
	1995	1996	1997	1998	1999
LAN interfaces	48	58	67	72	75
PCs	59	68	75	78	80

SOURCE: Data from IDC (1995d,f).

wiring, packet switches and routers, and software, as well as other elements. These investments may, in fact, greatly exceed corporations' expenditures to LECs and other outside parties for network services.

Most networked PCs in corporations today are connected to LANs that are in turn interconnected across the public network infrastructure. Thus, the number of PCs connected to the public network is much greater than the number of discrete connections to the network. Most of the corporate network costs are capital investment and internal staffing; the amount of revenues flowing into the LEC and similar providers is therefore not a direct measure of the level of corporate investment. International Data Corporation predicts that the LAN market will be saturated by 1998 in the United States and Europe, with over 90 percent of PCs connected to LANs (IDC, 1995d,f). (This study factors out PCs in the consumer market.) IDC projects growth in workplace PCs connected to LANs in the United States as shown in Table 5.4 and investment in LAN hardware as shown in Table 5.5.

The data in Table 5.5 indicate an investment rate in hardware for corporate data networks of slightly more than $5 billion per year in each of the next few years. This number is the estimate only for specific key technologies and is certain to be an underestimate of total hardware expense. It also does not address the issues of staffing and charges for metropolitan area networks and WANs. It seems reasonable to estimate that total corporate investment in data networking will exceed $10 billion per year. Telephone companies would receive only a small part of this spending and thus will continue to perceive explicit data services as having a smaller impact on their business than the economy-wide magnitude of investments in networking would seem to indicate.

Another perspective on network penetration in the installed computer base comes from IDC interviews with 15,000 information systems executives and 8,000 consumers worldwide (IDC, 1995b). In the United States today, only 19 percent of small businesses (those with under 99

TABLE 5.5 Annual Business Investment in LAN Hardware in the United States, 1995 to 1999

	Dollars (millions)				
	1995	1996	1997	1998	1999
Ethernet	1055	1086	971	794	602
Token Ring	532	446	351	304	236
High speed	—	n/a	n/a	n/a	1,000
LAN hubs	2,135	2,239	2,064	1,897	1,725
Routers	1,546	1,743	1,830	1,814	1,756
Total	5,268				5,319

NOTE: —, negligible; n/a, not available

SOURCE: IDC (1995f).

TABLE 5.6 Percentage of Business Sites with a LAN

Sector	Small Firms (under 99 employees)	Large Firms (100 or more employees)
Banking	48	98
Other finance	27	84
Discrete manufacturing	30	83
Process manufacturing	26	81
Health care	30	77
Transportation/communications/utilities	38	94
Retail/wholesale	15	75
Business services	40	91
Education	60	93
Federal government	—	95
Other	34	85

SOURCE: IDC (1995b).

employees) have a LAN, whereas 80 percent of large businesses do. These numbers vary strongly by sector, as Table 5.6 shows. Over one-third of sites with more than 10 employees had a LAN (Table 5.7).

Most of the PCs at sites with a LAN are connected to it. The percentage ranges from 80 percent of PCs connected for small sites to 71.5 percent for larger sites. (Because small businesses have a lower LAN penetration, the total percentage of PCs on a LAN for small sites is only 30 percent, whereas overall for large business it is 70 percent.)

TABLE 5.7 Percentage of Business Sites with
a LAN in Relation to Size of Site

Number of Employees at Site	Percentage of Sites with LAN
1-9	14.3
10-19	37.1
20-49	37.1
50-99	46
100-199	75.4
200-499	77.1
500-999	85.9
1,000+	89

SOURCE: IDC (1995b).

IDC data indicate a tremendous penetration of LANs into businesses by 1999, with even small companies having aggressive network plans projected to be operational by that time (IDC, 1995d,f). By 2000, it is reasonable to conclude that almost all corporate users will have easy access to a PC, and a very high percentage of these will not only be on a LAN, but will also be attached via a router to some form of WAN—such as a private network, the Internet, or both. The year 2000 may be too soon to predict saturation of external network access, but it is clearly predicted as the time for saturation of the LAN interface market.

Small office, home office, and mobile workers connect to their main workplace LAN through remote access. Most such workers do not have enough data traffic demand to justify a dedicated circuit for connection and thus will choose to connect via one of three options: analog modems over POTS, ISDN, or frame relay. According to a report from Infonetics Research, based on a survey of 144 companies, there are about 300,000 remote offices in the United States (Infonetics Research, 1994). Among these, 67 percent have some form of remote access, a number that Infonetics predicts will climb to 96 percent by 1998. Expenditures in the remote-access market (including software, remote access servers, communications boards for dial-up access, hubs, modems, and routers) were $490 million in 1994 and are forecast to reach $2.2 billion by 1997. Over 90 percent of the users achieve their network connection using a dial-up modem; however, 90 percent said that they would prefer to attach via a router (thus serving a cluster of networked machines) rather than a single workstation. In 1994, 50 percent of remote offices had a LAN. By 1998, 20 percent of users may move from a dial-up modem to ISDN or frame relay. In the surveyed companies, the Internet protocol suite was used in 90 percent of the cases, with IPX (Novell) being used in 70 percent. This suggests both the current commercial importance of the Internet protocols and the need for multiprotocol support.

The computer modem market has accelerated rapidly in the past few years, in part because many personal computers now are shipped with modems installed. IDC estimates that in 1994, shipments of modems rose dramatically, from 5.9 million to 10.1 million units.[9] The majority of new modem sales are devices conforming to the V.32 *bis* and V.34 standards, the fastest currently available; according to Dataquest, sales of these modems reached almost $1 billion in 1994, a 78 percent increase from the previous year (Hertz, 1995). IDC projects that the market for V.34 modems will grow very rapidly, from 255,000 units in 1994 to 7,650,000 units in 1998 (Hertz, 1995). The development of the PC Card (formerly known as PCMCIA) standard has facilitated modem sales for portable computers (as well as some PC Card-supporting desktop computers); 528,000 PC Card modems were sold in 1993, the first full year of production. Because many portable computers are used by mobile workers, they are particularly relevant to the issue of remote access to corporate networks.

In the context of the current 147.9 million total telephone access lines, it is likely that the number of data access circuits for LAN interconnection and remote access will continue to be dwarfed by voice circuits in 1999. However, behind these data connections will be 75 million networked workplace PCs and their users, as well as home-office and mobile PCs. In terms of end points (the information appliance), and taking into account the amount of time a typical user spends in front of a computer as opposed to a telephone, the two are likely similar in terms of economic and social importance, if not in revenues to the service providers. Should highly bandwidth-intensive applications, such as desktop video conferencing and various forms of multimedia, become widespread in the business environment, business networking may become high enough in volume to stimulate accelerated investment by telephone companies and third-party network service providers (such as Internet access providers) in ATM, Internet (TCP/IP), and other switching technologies.

CABLE TELEVISION AND TELEPHONY: ADVANCED SERVICES TO THE HOME

Summary and Forecasts

Access architectures providing substantial broadband services to residences (including home-based businesses) are being deployed. However, the cable and telephone companies find themselves in different circumstances at present, which substantially influences the rate and nature of deployment. Cable firms have a clear technology path to follow, upgrading their existing coaxial cable (coax) networks to a hybrid fiber coax (HFC) mode. This approach offers a short-term cost advantage over telephone companies and others, and cable firms will substantially complete this process in the next few years. The use of this infrastructure for advanced entertainment services, telephony, and data services will increase incrementally, as regulation and business viability dictate.

Future deployment of broadband networks by telephone local exchange carriers (LECs), by contrast, appears more variable and uncertain, because without existing coax networks, LECs face higher installation costs in providing a broadband infrastructure. At the same time, because they are not constrained by an existing coax deployment, LECs have more technical options, such as HFC versus the more advanced fiber-to-the-curb architecture, either of which can be supplemented with ISDN and ADSL at the network's margins to support reuse of existing copper plant for data and possibly video services. LECs also have several wireless options for competition for video delivery, as discussed in the subsection "Wireless Cable."

The two-way communication capacity available to users in the home with HFC is likely to be sufficient within the next 5 to 7 years not only for delivery of interactive entertainment with limited, upstream, point-and-click commands, but also for relatively more bandwidth-intensive purposes such as provision of on-line services, Internet access, file transfer, and remote access to workplace LANs. Whether the upstream capacity will be deployed to support even higher-bandwidth services such as video conferencing or uploading of multimedia files to public file servers (e.g., acting as multimedia publishers from the home) will depend on many factors, including demand for these services, outcomes of market trials in progress, emergence of a viable business model for provider cost recovery, software and hardware standards, mass-market economics leading to lower-priced access devices (set-top boxes, PC interfaces), and crucial regulatory concerns discussed in Chapter 6.

Ultimately, ubiquitous deployment of fiber to businesses and homes would solve most access and bandwidth issues. The massive investment required implies that this level of deployment will not be reached for at least 20 years. However, the ability of cable, telephone, and other providers to deploy infrastructure for advanced services incrementally will enable the business case for deployment to be explored and refined over time.

Advanced Cable and Telephone Services to the Home

Cable television (analog video broadcast over terrestrial cables) and basic voice telephony are both almost universally accessible from U.S. homes. In March 1994, 94 percent of households had telephone service (FCC, 1994, Table 8.1). The television penetration rate was higher, at 97 percent. Most U.S. homes are now passed by, and thus have the choice of accessing, a cable television service; about 62 percent of houses with a television subscribe to cable (Veronis, Suhler, 1995, p. 313; McConville, 1995).

Cable and telephone companies are in various stages of experimentation and deployment of new infrastructure to support high-bandwidth communications to and from the home. The common element in these architectures is the deployment of fiber optics in much of the network. Cable companies are upgrading their existing coaxial cable networks to hybrid networks with fiber in the center of the network and coax at the periphery. Besides deploying fiber, cable firms are beginning to invest in new electronics and switching capacity that can support two-way services. Telephone companies already have networks in place that are highly optimized for two-way communications. However, their networks reach individual homes with copper wires, which have much less capacity than the cable systems' coax. Some telephone companies are deploying HFC systems in parts of their service areas, while others are evaluating architectures that bring fiber closer to the home and rely on twisted pairs and advanced digital transmission schemes to bridge the last gap to the home. (See Chapter 4 for a more detailed examination of HFC technology trends.)

Most RBOCs have announced plans for substantial investment to upgrade their networks. As of early 1995, these included, for example, Pacific Telesis, $16 billion over 7 years; Bell Atlantic, $11 billion; U S West, $10 billion; and Southern New England Telephone, $4.4 billion (Arnst et al., 1995, p. 96). Much of this investment will go toward deployment of fiber access networks with fiber reaching from the central office toward, but not entirely to, the home. Analysts with the investment firm of Bear Stearns predict that LEC investments in fiber deployment within the local loop will ultimately surpass cable company investments (Friedman, 1994, p. 137).

There have been, however, several setbacks in telephone company broadband deployment in the past year. Box 5.1 presents several major telephone and cable companies' reported plans for deploying hybrid fiber networks.

Delays and rollbacks in video trials by several telephone companies may be motivated by factors such as uncertainty over consumer demand for interactive video; anticipated changes in telecommunications regulation that could alter the terms under which telephone companies might compete in video delivery; pursuit of alternative opportunities for offer-

---

BOX 5.1
Major Companies' Plans for Deployment of Hybrid Fiber Networks

Telephone Carriers

• *Ameritech* has applied to deliver video via hybrid fiber coaxial cable (HFC) to 1.2 million customers in several cities within its region (discussed in detail in the white paper by Joel Engel). The systems would be separate from Ameritech's telephone network, would be regulated under cable television rules (as opposed to the video dial-tone rules under which other telephone companies have applied to carry video services), and at least initially would not carry telephone traffic.

• *Bell Atlantic* applied to provide video services in specified communities over architectures combining fiber (in a fiber-to-the-curb architecture) and twisted pair (using asymmetric digital subscriber line in the latter segment). Bell Atlantic planned to pass up to 8 million homes in its region by 2000 with video dial-tone. However, some filings were withdrawn in the spring of 1995, implying at least delay.

• *BellSouth* applied for an HFC trial in Atlanta, with telephony and interactive services.

• *GTE* plans to pass 7 million homes by 2003 with HFC, starting with analog video broadcasting to 1 million customers by 1996; later upgrades would add digital broadcast and interactive services.

• *NYNEX* has in progress in New York City an HFC video trial offering interactive services to 50 customers.

• *Pacific Bell* planned to pass 5 million homes by 2000 and has HFC networks under construction in four major cities. However, in September 1995 it announced that deployments would be scaled back to encompass only some parts of the San Francisco Bay area, while in Southern California it would invest instead in multichannel multipoint distribution service (wireless cable).

---

ing video entertainment services, such as wireless cable; and recent advances in technology, such as improvements in ADSL and digital video switching, which could render obsolete their initial plans for HFC networks and lead to alternative approaches combining fiber and twisted pairs, such as fiber to the curb (FTTC).

Early trials with interactive video entertainment appear to be leading to a decreased emphasis on these services as the main source of demand motivating investment in residential infrastructures.[10] Information services, Internet access, telecommuting, and financial services are some other areas of demand that could motivate investment in residential ar-

- *SBC Communications* (formerly Southwestern Bell) has applied to conduct a trial using fiber-to-the-curb architecture in Richardson, Texas.

- *Southern New England Telephone* plans to conduct an all-analog video dial-tone trial in Connecticut over a network passing 150,000 homes. It canceled original plans to use digital technology in this trial, in response to slower-than-anticipated availability of mature digital technologies.

- *U S West* is using HFC for a video trial in Omaha, Nebraska, with 50,000 subscribers. It applied to deploy HFC-based video dial-tone services in several other cities but withdrew this application in the spring of 1995.

Cable Operators

- *Tele-Communications Inc.* plans to convert 90 percent of its 11 million cable subscribers to HFC by 1996. It has a video-on-demand trial in progress in Littleton, Colorado, and planned to conduct an HFC telephony trial with Teleport in Arlington Heights, Illinois in 1995. It plans to market mobile telephone service nationwide through its alliance with Sprint, Cox Cable, and Comcast.

- *Time Warner Cable* plans to pass 15 million homes with HFC by 1998 (the white paper by Wendell Bailey and James Chiddix gives additional details). Time Warner has a broad interactive-services trial under way in Orlando, Florida, and has become a competitive local exchange carrier in Rochester, New York, providing a number of apartment buildings with telephone service over its HFC cable plant. All system upgrades include deployment of amplifiers in the upstream direction, enabling two-way data and other services.

SOURCE: This information is drawn from white papers contributed to the NII 2000 project by Joel Engel; Wendell Bailey and James Chiddix; and J.C. Redmond et al. Information is also drawn from trade and other publications; see Brightman (1994), p. 42; Cauley (1995a,c); *Communications Daily* (1995b); Lindstrom (1995a,c); McCarthy (1995); and *Wall Street Journal* (1995d).

chitectures with two-way (upstream as well as downstream) capabilities. Cable modems, which can carry data services to and from the home over a cable television system, are already available from a range of manufacturers, including LANcity, General Instrument, Motorola, Scientific-Atlanta, Intel, and Zenith (Lindstrom, 1995b; *Communications Daily*, 1995c). These modems offer data rates of up to 40 Mbps in the downstream direction and 100 kbps to 10 Mbps upstream; LANcity, for example, offers symmetrical 10-Mbps communications. Current plans are for modems to be sold to cable operators, which will rent them to subscribers.

At the May forum, Milo Medin discussed @Home's plans in the next several years to connect residential customers to on-line services and the Internet through cable systems, including Tele-Communications Inc., at data rates much higher than those of POTS or ISDN. Use of these modems depends on two-way capacity in the cable network, which is enabled by amplifiers in the upstream direction on the coax portion of the cable plant. Cable industry representatives told the steering committee that this capacity will become available in most cable systems as part of their upgrades to HFC over the next few years (see the white paper by Wendell Bailey and James Chiddix). In addition, according to equipment manufacturer Scientific-Atlanta, current sales of cable-system devices designed to provide return-path signals are approximately equal to sales of forward-path units, indicating that operators are installing full two-way plant.[11]

ON-LINE SERVICES AND
INTERNET ACCESS FOR CONSUMERS

Summary and Forecasts

On-line services include consumer services such as news, entertainment, social interaction, education, and on-line banking, as well as business information services such as market research, technical information, and patent and trademark data, among others. In addition, on-line and Internet access services represent an intermediate level of infrastructure, built upon (and stimulating demand for) lower-level infrastructure such as telephony. They serve in turn as bases on which specialized consumer, business, educational, government, and other types of services can be offered. On-line services and Internet access for consumers represent significant sources of demand for a range of commercial, education, entertainment, and other services. Their growth may also stimulate deployment by telephone carriers, cable operators, and other infrastructure providers in the next 5 to 7 years. (Internet access for business networking purposes is discussed separately, in the section above on data communications.)

On-line Services and Internet Access

Business information services are a significant U.S. industry. The investment firm of Veronis, Suhler & Associates forecasts growth from $29 billion (1994) to $39 billion (1999) in business spending for marketing, financial, credit, payroll, product and price, legal, technical, and other business information (Veronis, Suhler, 1995, p. 296). Half of these business services are currently delivered in electronic form (one-fourth on line and one-fourth electronic or CD-ROM databases) and half in print form (directories, newsletters, and so on; see Veronis, Suhler, 1994, p. 253). A forecast of the relative sizes of the print and electronic segments of the business information market is not available from this source; however, even assuming that electronic, interactive media remain no more than half of the total business information services market, business users would appear to be a significant market for interactive information services in the next several years. In fact, the growing penetration of LANs in the workplace, combined with improved information search and retrieval software, has the potential to put business-information access in the hands of workers in their offices, as opposed to information retrieval specialists in corporate libraries. This will stimulate an expansion of the electronic share of the business information services market.

According to a market review by SIMBA Information Inc., consumer-oriented on-line services receive lower revenues per subscriber, on average, than do business-oriented services (such as Lexis/Nexis, Dow Jones News/Retrieval, and Reuters); however, consumer on-line services have more subscribers than do business information services and are growing much more rapidly (SIMBA, 1995). As of the end of 1995, on-line services reached 11.3 million subscribers, a 15 percent increase over the preceding 3 months (Arlen, 1996, p. 1). America Online is the largest, with 4.5 million subscribers. The other leading services are CompuServe, with 4.0 million subscribers; Prodigy, 1.6 million; Microsoft Network, 600,000; e-World, 126,000; and Delphi Internet, 125,000. These six services account for 97 percent of subscribers, as estimated by Arlen (1996).

Veronis, Suhler & Associates estimated 1994 revenues for on-line services and consumer Internet access (distinct from business internet-working across the Internet, discussed in the data communications section above) at $1.4 billion, with a customer base of 4.7 million households (Veronis, Suhler, 1995, pp. 310 and 313). This represents about half of all households with both a PC and a modem. The report projects compounded growth in this market of 33 percent per year, to $6.1 billion by 1999. The projected growth is in response to improvements in services, content, and software tools for navigating the Internet; increasing penetration of PCs and modems; and the assumption that by 1999, 90 percent of households with a PC and a modem will subscribe to Internet access and/or on-line services.

Veronis, Suhler & Associates predict that access to on-line information and other services will increasingly take place over the Internet. Many content providers will establish their own presence on the World Wide Web, bypassing traditional on-line services such as America Online, CompuServe, and Prodigy, which will in turn expand their businesses of providing Internet access to individuals. (They will thus compete with some Internet service providers, such as Netcom, that serve both corporate and individual customers, as discussed in the section above on data communications.) Both on-line services and content sources available on the Web will stimulate new demand for Internet access among consumers, small office and home office users, and business users (within the last group, mainly those who do not already have Internet access as a consequence of their business networking requirements).

The relative success of consumer services offered through third parties, such as on-line services, compared to the success of services offered directly over the Internet will be an indicator of change in this market. One early sign may be evident in the fact that in October 1995, Pacific Telesis and Times Mirror dissolved a partnership aimed at creating an on-line information and home shopping service. The firms cited as the main reason for changing their plans the Internet's rapid growth and their expectation that businesses will pursue direct relationships with home customers over the Internet (Lippman, 1995).

WIRELESS AND BROADCAST INFRASTRUCTURE

Over the course of the NII 2000 project, including the January 1995 workshop and May 1995 forum, the steering committee received a range of inputs concerning projected capabilities of wireless and broadcast technologies to support emerging voice, data, and other NII services. The potential for many of these services appears significant, as the discussion of technology trends in Chapter 4 makes clear. However, very little input was received supporting specific forecasts of deployment of these technologies. The following material primarily reflects a variety of information drawn from market research literature and from trade and other publications.

Summary and Forecasts

The role of wireless will evolve over the next 5 to 7 years, with numerous changes in the technological and regulatory contexts. This section considers a number of very different technologies, including cellular telephony, wireless data networking, and terrestrial and satellite broadcasting. Most of the business sectors represented here, other than terrestrial television broadcasting, are rather new and have a less concrete perspective on their business model than do the more mature industries of wireline video and telephony. These new businesses therefore face a higher degree of experimentation and redefinition in the next several years.

Decreasing costs and new availability of spectrum suggest that there may be a major expansion of wireless telephony. In addition to terrestrial cellular and personal communication service (PCS) offerings, there have been applications for satellite-based telephone services that would add further to the competitive offerings. Additionally, demand for wireless telephony could be stimulated if it could be used for cost-effective data access at reasonable bandwidth; the large-scale viability of this application remains to be proven.

There are many proposed plans and visions about the use of wireless in support of data communications. Wireless LANs have been on the market for several years, and even though demand for these products has not accelerated dramatically, they suggest what the cost and potential of wireless data might be. Wireless as a component of nomadic computing is an application that stimulates much speculation but that has not yet entered the market to a significant degree. These services might emerge over the next 5 to 7 years, subject to regulatory decisions, emergence of technical standards, and a viable business model. Wireless has also been proposed as an alternative to wireline for residential, educational, and small business data access. This application also seems viable from a technical perspective but depends on the allocation of spectrum and the setting of standards. Prices for early offerings for wireless data seem competitive with wireline offerings under some circumstances. These areas may emerge, but are not likely to mature, in the next 5 to 7 years.

A number of new video delivery offerings have begun to emerge, and some will mature over the next 5 to 7 years. Direct broadcast satellite distribution of digital video signals has entered the market more quickly than anticipated and is viewed by some as potentially growing to represent a real source of competition to terrestrial broadcasting and cable video delivery. Provision of terrestrial wireless cable services is viewed with increasing interest by telephone carriers and others as a way to compete with existing cable systems without making large investments in a new, broadband wireline infrastructure. Traditional television broadcasters will begin converting to digital broadcasting within the next several years, although uncertainty about market demand and the need for products to support both analog and digital standards during the transition suggest that a fast transition is unlikely.

Wireless Telephony

Demand for wireless voice telephony services, almost entirely for mobile users, is projected to grow significantly. Decreasing costs of service, due in part to advances in the performance of hardware available at a given cost and new digital standards, are increasing demand for existing cellular services. In addition, the rollout of PCS over the next several

TABLE 5.8 Mobile Communications Subscribers, 1993 and Projected for 1998

	Users (in millions)	
	1993	1998 (projected)
Cellular		
Analog	16	22
Digital	0	13
Paging	16	26
Mobile data	1	7
Personal communication service (PCS)	0	2
Personal digital assistants (PDAs)	0	2
Total	33	72

SOURCE: NATA (1995).

years will create up to six new choices for mobile users throughout the United States, beyond the two now available in most places. The resulting competition is expected to stimulate demand for wireless voice communications. NATA's annual market review for 1995 projects growth in the number of mobile communications subscribers through 1998 as shown in Table 5.8 (NATA, 1995, pp. 133 and 136).

The Personal Communications Industry Association (PCIA) produced a rather different forecast in its 1995 survey of members (see the white paper by Mary Madigan). PCIA members anticipate, by the year 2000, combined demand for new PCS, cellular, paging, and narrowband PCS of almost 118 million subscriptions. This forecast for 2000 includes 15 million digital broadband PCS customers, with revenues of $8.8 billion (mainly voice services, 7 percent from data services); 50 million cellular subscribers (up from 23.2 million in 1994), of which 30 percent will be business users, with total revenues of $26 billion; and over 50 million narrowband PCS subscriptions (mainly business users), including advanced voice paging, two-way acknowledgment paging, and one-way and two-way messaging.

The white paper by Robert Roche of the Cellular Telecommunications Industry Association (CTIA) cites projections for demand that are somewhat more modest than PCIA's. CTIA anticipates cellular subscribership in 2006 in the range of 38.2 million to 55.1 million.

One factor that could stimulate demand for wireless telephony is increased wireline local-access prices that LECs could be forced to change, if the substantial network access revenues they receive from IXCs (quantified in the "Demand for Telephone Services" section above in this chapter) should decrease. Regulatory changes could drive down these network access charges, as could a shift of IXCs toward other, competing ways of accessing their customers—including wireless local access networks. AT&T's purchase of the largest cellular telephone service, McCaw Communications, represents such a shift.

However, deployment of infrastructure to meet growing demand for wireless may prove challenging. The white paper by Roche projects an enormous increase in the number of cellular and PCS antennas and base stations. For example, PCS will have six licensees per area, as opposed to just two for cellular. Although new digital technologies will enable switches to carry more callers, the higher frequencies of PCS mandate smaller cell sizes and thus more cells to achieve geographic coverage. Both Roche and Madigan note in separate white papers that delays and uncertainty in antenna siting, which is subject to regulation by local governments, will complicate this deployment.

CTIA has analyzed the anticipated costs of deploying nationwide PCS networks. Assuming $500,000 per switch, with one switch per basic trading area (of which there are 493 nationwide) and two per major trading area (102 nationwide); another $100,000 for the electronics in each cell site within each trading area, not counting the costs for real estate and for local permits; and four to six separate PCS networks, it can be anticipated that a $20 billion to $40 billion investment will be needed to deploy PCS voice networks nationwide.[12]

However, some vendors such as QualComm are developing digital microcell technologies that may make new wireless networks much cheaper than CTIA's estimates indicate. Microcells enable greater use of frequencies than do larger cells, raising the system capacity. As a result, microcell systems could eventually lower capital costs for wireless PCS, per circuit available in the total system, far below those for current cellular systems.[13]

A standards issue remains for digital cellular communications. Wireless carriers have chosen competing standards for digital cellular service in their operating areas. Time-division multiple access (TDMA) systems have the lead in the market, with more than 500,000 customers in the United States; but some carriers have chosen code-division multiple access (CDMA) because of its more efficient use of spectrum. CDMA is supported by Alltel, Ameritech, Bell Atlantic/NYNEX, Sprint, and AirTouch/U S West; TDMA is supported by AT&T/McCaw, BellSouth, Rogers Cantel, and SBC Communications (Poppel and Marino, 1995, p. 34). Global System for Mobile Communications (GSM) has been chosen as the digital standard in Europe and many other parts of the world. Although it is technically feasible for handsets to incorporate more than one standard, thus enabling them to operate in different locations as the user travels, the additional hardware adds significant expense.[14]

Wireless Data Networking

BIS Strategic Decisions Inc. forecasts that the number of users of data on wireless networks will grow from 500,000 in 1994 to 9.9 million by 2000 (*Wireless Messaging Report*, 1995b). The distribution of users of data services available on these networks is shown in Table 5.9.

As noted in the section above on data communications, one source of demand for wireless data services is the portable computer with a wireless data modem installed. A perspective on nomadic computing is given by IDC's estimates of the market for portable PCs (IDC, 1995e). Sales of portables are projected to grow at twice the rate of sales in the overall desktop PC market, from an installed base of 27 million in 1995 to 50 million in 1999. Wireless is seen, however, as a small component of these networked PCs. IDC does not estimate the installed base in this case, but it does estimate that the annual shipments of wireless-equipped portable PCs will grow from about 100,000 units in 1995 to 2.7 million in 1999.

IDC predicts only a modest market for wireless LAN adapters—devices used to connect computers to wireless LANs—from 422,000 units in 1995 to 1.2 million by 1999, with an installed base of 4.2 million in 1999. Revenues of $204 million in 1995 are projected to grow to $385 million in 1999. IDC concludes that when wireless standards emerge, lower prices and increased shipments will follow (IDC, 1995e).

The first nationwide mobile data services were packet radio networks—ARDIS (Advanced Radio Data Information Service) and RAM Mobile Data. These services provide low-speed communications at rates

TABLE 5.9 Distribution of Users of Various Wireless Data Services, 1994 and 2000

	Percentage of User Pool	
Service	1994	2000 (projected)
Narrowband PCS (paging, etc.)	0	26
Cellular and broadband PCS	70	54
Dedicated data	14	10
Specialized mobile radio	2	4
Satellite	14	6

SOURCE: *Wireless Messaging Report* (1995b).

of approximately 2.4 to 9.6 kbps (Brodsky, 1995). Somewhat higher-capacity data networks are under development by the start-up ventures Metricom and Tetherless Access Ltd. Metricom's product is a rapidly deployable network, operating in a portion of the spectrum allocated by the FCC for unlicensed wireless data networking; it consists of a mesh of poletop radios configured in a self-routing (not centrally switched) network, resulting in relatively low cost. Data throughput for end users is modest, up to 35 kbps, with flat-rate, unlimited-usage pricing. Tetherless Access offers the wireless equivalent of a 56-kbps private digital line; its advantage is the ability to deploy rapidly, without the need for stringing new cables. Although these services may not mature in the next 5 to 7 years, they offer opportunities for individuals to use advanced applications through wireless networking in locations where broadband service is either unavailable or prohibitively priced.

Cellular telephone services are primarily circuit-switched, although cellular digital packet data (CDPD) standards are gaining acceptance and CDPD service was available in 19 markets as of February 1995 (Brodsky, 1995). CDPD is based on the Internet protocol suite (TCP/IP) and is thus well suited for Internet connection.

None of the above systems offers the data communication rates available over wired systems with services such as ISDN. In the longer term, however, satellite systems may make higher capacities available for mobile users of both voice and data communications. For example, Teledesic (founded by Bill Gates and Craig McCaw) plans to offer globally available, high-bandwidth digital communications starting in 2001, with access at data rates of up to 2 Mbps (OTA, 1995; Brodsky, 1995). The investment cost for the network of 840 low-earth-orbit (LEO) satellites is estimated at $9 billion. Teledesic and similar LEO satellite-based communications networks represent a somewhat longer-term component of the nation's information infrastructure than do others outlined in this chapter; their potential to reach maturity is difficult to predict, given their high up-front investment requirements for an unproven service.[15] However, one federal study predicted that in the next 10 years, at least two of the various proposed LEO systems are likely to be deployed and operational (Asker, 1995). Thus, while LEO systems are unlikely to reach significant levels of deployment in the next 5 to 7 years, they could have significant impact further in the future.

Spectrum availability is clearly a limiting factor for data and other wireless communications, and so FCC spectrum policies are a central determinant of wireless infrastructure deployment. Two proposals to the FCC, both filed in May 1995, illustrate what could be done with additional spectrum. Apple Computer filed a petition for an "NII Band": 300 MHz of spectrum in the 5-GHz range for the purpose of unlicensed wireless data communications. Apple claims this would support data rates up to 24 Mbps over 10- to 15-km distances (Apple, 1995). The Wireless Information Networks Forum (WINForum) petitioned for 250 MHz of spectrum in approximately the same frequency range, also for wireless data communications at about 20 Mbps (WINForum, 1995). Both technologies could support applications such as wireless local area networking and wireless access to wireline networks. If approved by the FCC, and if standards were settled and hardware manufacturers could produce equipment at reasonable cost, wireless could be a highly capable form of data communication infrastructure. In addition, because physical wire does not have to be laid, any wireless network has the potential to be deployed much more quickly and cheaply than competing wireline broadband services. On November 2, 1995, the director of the National Telecommunications and Information Administration (NTIA) recommended to the FCC that it initiate proceedings for these services; it remains to be seen what result proposals such as these may have.[16]

Terrestrial and Satellite Broadcast Television

Legislation to reform telecommunications regulation has been under consideration by both houses of the U.S. Congress. One of the changes proposed would allow television broadcasters to use part of their licensed spectrum, including that which was originally set aside for high-definition television, to provide supplemental digital services. According to investment analysts with Bear Stearns, digital television broadcasters could use this excess capacity to enter digital wireless businesses such as fax transmission, two-way paging, and dispatching. However, large investments would be required were they to offer higher-capacity interactive products and services (Friedman, 1994, p. 125).

Wireless Cable

Multichannel multipoint distribution service (MMDS), also known as wireless cable, is a competitor for wireline cable television distribution. The capacity of MMDS is less than that of traditional cable, with only about 25 to 40 channels. (However, digital technologies may increase this capacity many times.) Where wired infrastructure is lacking, deploying a new MMDS system is competitive with new cable plant, at about $1.5 million to $3 million per head end and $450 to $550 per subscriber. As a result, the primary market for current analog MMDS is value-conscious customers. Bear Stearns analysts project 5.5 million subscribers by 2000. MMDS operators currently offer limited interactive services using the telephone network as the return channel (the subscriber calls the central office). One provider, American Telecasting, demonstrated a completely wireless interactive technology in 1993 (Friedman, 1994, pp. 148-149).

As several telephone companies have delayed deployment of HFC and FTTC infrastructures, some, such as Pacific Telesis, have shown an increasing interest in entering the wireless cable market through deployment of new systems or purchase and upgrade of existing systems. Wireless cable represents a means for entering the video distribution market more quickly and inexpensively than by deploying all-new cable infrastructures. The recent contract for Thomson Consumer Electronics to provide 1 million wireless set-top boxes to Tele-TV, a consortium of LECs, indicates the substantial volume of likely telephone company entry into this market (*Cable Regulation Digest*, 1995).

Direct Broadcast Satellite

With the advent of new digital direct broadcast satellite (DBS) systems (see Chapter 4), sales to consumers of satellite products have accelerated more rapidly than expected. DBS subscriptions are growing at a rate of 25,000 per week (*Communications Daily*, 1995a). Sales of receivers for the newest DBS service, Primestar and RCA's Digital Satellite System, topped first-year sales of color televisions and video cassette recorders; according to the Electronic Industries Association (EIA), they represent the most successful new product in the history of consumer electronics (*Communications Daily*, 1995d). An EIA survey found that more than 590,000 Digital Satellite System receivers were sold in the first year of availability, with 1995 sales forecast in the range from 1.2 million to 1.5 million units.

NOTES

1. See FCC (1994), p. vi. The Federal Communications Commission maintains detailed information about the current infrastructure; however, it does not make forecasts in this area.

2. This total includes lines that are routed to the switches from other central offices through foreign exchange services.

3. Because most of the cost to deploy fiber is labor and installation (e.g., digging trenches), most firms lay more fiber than they need to meet current demand, in anticipation of activating, or "lighting," the dark fiber in the future.

4. Note that these totals exclude trials, as well as all fiber deployment by competitive local exchange carriers (COMPLECs). See Kraushaar (1995b).

5. COMPLECs typically serve business customers, for at least two reasons: (1) businesses represent high-volume, high-value customers; and (2) deployment of new infrastructure in concentrated business areas of communities is much less costly than deployment in lower-density areas.

6.   The FCC reports that a typical deployment consists of a fiber ring containing from 20 to 200 strands, with ends connected at a hub station. Each customer is therefore served by two redundant routes to the hub.

7.   See EDGE (1995). Note also that data traffic on the Internet has been growing far more rapidly, as noted in Chapter 4; however, it begins from a small base compared to data traffic on public and private networks overall.

8.   See *PC Week*, Oct. 17, 1994, p. A10.

9.   Demand for modems is driven not only by the need for remote access to corporate networks by workers in the home and on the road, but also by applications such as on-line services and Internet access (IDC, 1995c).

10.   This theme was raised by several participants in the forum. For discussion of early results of trials, see Schwartz (1995).

11.   Robert Luff, chief technical officer of Scientific-Atlanta, quoted in *Communications Daily* (1995e).

12.   Preliminary data provided to NRC staff by CTIA, June 1995.

13.   By one estimate, the cost could be $14 per circuit, as opposed to $5,555 per circuit using current, analog cellular technology. Assumptions in this estimate include cell site spacing of 20,000 feet versus PCS base station (port) spacing of 1,000 feet and 180 channels per cell or a PCS port. The cost per PCS base station is estimated to be far less than that for a cellular base station, at approximately $2,500 instead of $1 million; the PCS system would use many more stations, and the cost per available circuit in the total system would be much lower. See Cox (1995), p. 31.

14.   Research and development related to incorporating multiple cellular standards in software, which would reduce the cost of handsets, are in progress and may help alleviate this burden within several years. See OTA (1995), pp. 84-86.

15.   See OTA (1995), pp. 78-79. For example, the bond rating for the Iridium project, a planned LEO satellite-based voice telephony service, was recently downgraded, leading the company to revise its efforts to raise through external debt the $4.7 billion expected to be needed to deploy its 66-satellite system. The firm now plans to raise funds internally. See *Communications Daily*, September 21, 1995, p. 5.

16.   The NTIA, part of the U.S. Department of Commerce, is the executive branch agency with responsibility for telecommunications policy and management of radio spectrum for government uses. See *Telecommunications Reports* (1995j).

6

Public Policy and Private Action

INTRODUCTION

The evolution of the national information infrastructure (NII) poses a number of problems, alternative solutions, and opportunities for private and public parties. With an emphasis on gathering private sector perspectives, this project did not set out to define appropriate roles for government. Contributors to the forum made clear that there is hardly a consensus among representatives of various industries about the role of government. Across the range of issues relating to information infrastructure there is evidence of imperfect performance both in markets and by government. Therefore, the serious debate and commentary center on what imperfect government actions to remedy imperfect markets are justified. The workshop, forum, and set of white papers developed for the NII 2000 project, like the steering committee, mirror society in presenting divergent perspectives.

Regardless of political sentiments about its role in general, government at all levels will inevitably be a major player. Government agencies—at state and federal levels—participate in almost every information-related role pursued by the private sector—publisher, user, network manager, innovator. Governments have additional responsibilities by virtue of their constitutional obligations—as arbiter, regulator, convener, and even leader in the interest of equity and an efficient, productive society. The federal government has unique responsibilities with respect to the transnational issues arising in the global information infrastructure

(GII) and advancing the national technology base through support for research and development.[1]   Support for research and development (R&D) can help to increase the options,[2] lower the costs, and enhance the capabilities of technologies that can be brought to the NII marketplace.

Given the preponderance of private investment and the uncertainty surrounding information infrastructure markets, many people point to the importance of reducing government constraints on private decisions and investment. The big task for government, they would note, is careful but determined deregulation of telecommunications services. A second task is the studied avoidance of new regulations in response to problems arising in the new uses of technology. The concern is not only to avoid constraining competition, but also to minimize the kinds of actions to manipulate the system that telecommunications regulation has unintentionally fostered. As Robert Crandall of the Brookings Institution observed, "Once regulation becomes a system for politically redistributing income, and cross-subsidizing one service out of another, it becomes very difficult to allow competition and the entry of new technologies."[3]   Participants in this project pointed to both telecommunications regulation, per se, and the Modified Final Judgment decree arising from the AT&T Corporation antitrust suit as forces constraining entry.[4]   Although those inputs centered on existing telephone and cable businesses, other comments related to the challenge of how to foster entrepreneurialism, development of new information infrastructure industries, and market entry by smaller and nontraditional players. As Quincy Rodgers of General Instrument observed, smaller players have fewer resources, limiting their ability to enter certain markets successfully. Technological innovation and competition should be encouraged together, he and others argued, leaving to the marketplace the determination of which technologies deliver value to customers.[5]

Many others ask, How can so many industries and so many users expect to acquire enough shared knowledge to create consensus unless some legitimate public body, not competing in commercial markets, is willing to take a leadership role aimed at orderly evolution of the NII? Governments, perhaps uniquely, can try to encourage all parties (their own agencies included) to address cross-cutting issues cooperatively and constructively. The challenge is to effect government leadership that keeps options open, encourages innovation, and allows markets to work.

Whether the government role is seen as something to be minimized or something to be leveraged, it will reflect two realities. First, the intertwining of public and private investments and activities shaping the NII implies that consultation between government and private sector institutions will have to be effective at the operational as well as the strategic or policy level. This interaction will have to reflect the fact that public and private investment and activity together are dominated by private sector elements. Second, the NII—and the GII of which it is a part—is an incredibly complex economic and technological system. Simply understanding its behavior is a major task; finding appropriate tools for addressing gaps and bottlenecks requires a level of knowledge of system behavior that no one industrial sector (or governmental unit) is likely to have. Examination of these two realities in turn is furthered by understanding how the Internet has gained in significance in both contexts.

Public-Private Engagement

The high level of collaboration among its suppliers and users—and the associated roles of public and private institutions—makes information infrastructure a hybrid of the principles guiding other (and not unrelated) forms of public infrastructure, including traditional public utilities and education, which present contrasting mixtures of public and private roles.[6] The Internet provides a powerful illustration. It developed out of the mission responsibilities of several federal agencies plus state and regional interests in both feeder and backbone networks. The Internet has demonstrated that some commonality of vision can make a decentralized process more efficient and effective.[7] However, there was no grand plan; the "bottom-up" character of the development, typical of most technology-driven changes that occur in a competitive environment, engendered vitality and legitimacy.

The Internet developed largely as a result of research conducted in many institutions across the country and regional needs to interconnect state and private institutions and sources of information. The NSFNET, a principal Internet backbone commissioned by the National Science Foundation (NSF) and operated under cooperative agreement by a joint venture among IBM, MCI, and the nonprofit Merit Inc., was a proving ground for cooperation among government, industry, and academia in the planning, development, and operation of information infrastructure.[8] Public and private research and investment have supported the creation of collections of valuable information as well as services to make them available. Thus the Internet illustrates government investment as a catalyst to private investment in both the demand and the supply sides of information infrastructure. For a discussion of emerging prospects, see "Government as User and Service Provider" below.

Unresolved is the appropriate role of government in assuring operational integrity of an NII that is increasingly diverse in its components, service offerings, and management. See observations from David Messerschmitt of the University of California at Berkeley in Box 6.1. In an Internet that is not a critical system for its users, anecdotal evidence of operational

---

BOX 6.1
Network Control and Management

If we really have a goal of a national information infrastructure that incorporates some existing networks, such as the Internet, telephone networks, et cetera, [it will combine] existing networks [having] existing control structures (e.g., Signaling System 7 in the telephone network). The Internet does not have such a structure. But it is developing it for the purposes of providing quality-of-service guarantees. The question I have is, how are we going to develop some kind of standards or some way to ensure that all of these different pieces of this overall infrastructure interoperate at the control or signaling level? We tend to talk about standards in terms of [examples such as] MPEG, which involves the actual signals going through at one time. But how are these networks going to control each other? When I have to access a Mosaic server across the Internet from a TCI-run cable TV system, how does the addressing and quality of service information get transferred from the cable system to the Internet in some organized fashion?

—David Messerschmitt, University of California at Berkeley

---

failures may not be a cause for alarm and may even be a transient phenomenon, although it is also a cautionary indicator for the nation's information infrastructure in general, since mature infrastructure must be reliable. These operational failures also raise questions about whether some minimal common institutional structure or mechanisms for governance are needed to preserve system integrity, availability, and so on.

Finally, the Internet also provides a vehicle for exploring the costs, benefits, and alternatives for equitable access to information infrastructure and associated services.[9] See Box 6.2. Attorney Allan Arlow, Tora Bikson of the RAND Corporation, Richard Friedman of the University of Wisconsin Medical School, Allen Hammond of New York Law School, and other contributors expressed concern about the prospect of "information have nots," acknowledging that some segments of the population are not sharing—as a function of market forces alone—in the widening deployment of advanced services and sophisticated information appliances.[10] The Internet, and more limited government service programs (e.g., Social Security) and commercial programs using dedicated or specialized systems, offer the opportunity for some experience through library- and school-based access and kiosks (with public terminals) that provide access in various public spaces (Jackson, 1995). They show both the potential for and limitations of public access arrangements, with limitations including the level of access achieved, the public nature—and therefore limited personal privacy afforded—of the access, and the limited ease of use and thus the training requirements.

BOX 6.2
Universal Service

Yesterday the term universal service did not differentiate between access and the service itself, because for a phone call the phone and the service were essentially the same thing. Now, or in the future, we are talking about two different things. One is equitable, if not universal, access to the network so that everybody can touch the network, even if that means walking to a library. A separate issue is whatever subsidy is appropriate to make sure that the people that "we the public" want to have certain services, have those services.

—Robert Powers, MCI Telecommunications Inc.

You cannot have an NII if you do not hook most of the people in the United States into it. At least you cannot have an affordable NII. . . . Nothing is more universal in the United States than television: 98 percent of all homes have television; 96 percent of all homes have telephones; 63 percent of all homes have cable. Good access to the American home depends on television.

—James McKinney, Advanced Television Systems Committee

Paying customers should be the largest contributor at first: educated middle- and upper-income individuals who are driving the use of technology today. Second, there should be free access to schools, libraries, and other public facilities providing basic access and exposure to the network infrastructure, which will build demand for the future. And finally, universality, the end goal, is not possible without a revenue stream to attract and hold investment.

—Michael Greenbaum, Bell Atlantic Corporation

Over the near-term (5- to 7-year) horizon of this project, public and institutional access may be the only access available to some segments of the population, given the constraints on expanding the quantity and quality of bandwidth capacity serving residences and small businesses. Because for many public access remains a second-best option compared to personal systems (e.g., telephones, televisions, and computers in residences),[11] it is an area that warrants explicit monitoring and assessment, on behalf of those who cannot afford their own personal computers. Public access should be the focus of a testbed or other type of experimental program to explore technical, cost-sharing, and other dimensions of the issue.

NII Systems Issues

The central NII systems issue relates to promotion of an overall architectural concept (see Box 6.3), something that many participants endorse in principle but find difficult to attain in practice. The steering committee endorses the ideal of architectural convergence while noting the pragmatic and not inconsistent expectation for multiple approaches. It distinguishes the question of objectives from that of process.

The process of developing NII architecture is not a neat one. At the forum Howard Frank of the Advanced Research Projects Agency (ARPA) asked explicitly, "Do you see any kind of process that could bring a convergence of architectural concepts?" The confounding of technological and business strategies makes a clean answer to that question elusive. One element of such a process that emerged from the NII 2000 project is vision-setting discussions and forums, in which a central challenge is to remain apolitical. *Realizing the Information Future* (CSTB, 1994b) argued for the benefit of a common architectural framework, and the many briefings and presentations associated with that report's dissemination furthered discussion within individual industry and technical communities. Complementary public discussions have taken place over the past 2 years under a number of different auspices.[12] The NII 2000 project built on that stream and emphasized cross-sectoral and cross-industry interaction. It also carried forward a leadership-via-convening approach that can foster development of common understanding and provide for interaction among disparate parties (multiple provider industries or providers and users). Such discussions can have an impact on the development of architecture without interfering with particular deployment activities, because interoperability can be achieved at a higher level in the architecture than that represented by the facilities that dominate investment decisions.

A more active process revolves around the surging interest in experimentation with Internet applications, which have provided practical, hands-on exposure to open architecture and internetworking. They may also be more broadly visible than the market trials of more closed systems ongoing among cable, telephone, and other companies. Accordingly, attention to the Internet grew over the course of the project, raising questions about what, if anything, the government should do to help the Internet evolve in the context of commercial operation, other than to transfer its management institutions carefully from government support to user (or investor) funding. Any further process, presumably, should tip the business case toward a common architectural framework. The message of the NII 2000 project is that such a business case may emerge over time. How quickly and whether it can or should be accelerated remain subject to debate, with the notable exception of R&D (see "Technology Development Through R&D"), on the importance of which there were affirmation and consensus despite the project's emphasis on downstream deployment.

BOX 6.3
Architecture

Where does the NII fall on the continuum ranging from the decentralized model with all intelligence residing in the terminal, spanning the Internet model and the ability to develop and deploy new applications very quickly, . . . to the centralized model, which includes the old telephone system? . . . *Is it possible to have a single model for the NII on this sort of continuum?* . . . Is there one network, or is there instead an internetwork of at least several types of networks that are organized according to quite different paradigms?

I think that in some respects we are talking past each other, because some very different types of applications are being discussed. The two fundamental types of applications are (1) those that depend on database access, including information retrieval and many of the entertainment applications that involve accessing a central reserve of information (entertainment video, for example), and (2) communications—between two computers, two people, or between the computers of people. For applications based on database access, full connectivity is less critical, as can be seen in the case of companies like America Online and CompuServe that have made a business out of users subscribing to only one of these services. On the other hand, an application like Mosaic running on the Internet illustrates the value of full connectivity of users to a database. . . .

Is full, logical connectivity required within a national information infrastructure? If so, then interoperability, standards, and other associated issues become much more difficult to deal with. A related question is, Are we going to have a common infrastructure for both types of generic applications, database access, and communications, or are we going to have a proliferation of separate infrastructures for these two kinds of applications? If we have communications infrastructure that provides for full connectivity between users, then we inherently have simultaneously infrastructure that also serves for database access applications. . . .

It is not necessary that all near-term deployment provide all the capabilities represented in a strategic vision. Indeed, one critical aspect of such a vision is that it should be easy and cost-effective to add new technologies and capabilities to the NII as unanticipated applications and user needs emerge. If this flexibility is achieved, it is only necessary that near-term investments be compatible with a long-term strategic vision, and hence not preclude future possibilities or force later disinvestment and widespread replacement of infrastructure.

If people can access the Internet over their cable system and it is providing what they want, then over time the bandwidth of that Internet pipeline will grow, and the bandwidth of everything else will shrink, and gradually people will move toward the solution they like. That is a market force. *Perhaps the Internet or its extension could serve [the necessary] function—which is not the task of bringing together many different things, but rather the process of starting with what we have and extending it in the direction we want to go.*

—David Messerschmitt, University of California at Berkeley

Discussion among contributors from a range of telecommunications and content industries illustrated how many factors intertwine to complicate movement toward a more open architecture, as examined in Chapters 3 and 4. For example, Edward Horowitz, whose company, Viacom Inc., has left the cable business to focus on content generation and marketing, commented on the importance to content providers of unconstrained access by customers and complained about service providers as bottlenecks. Bell Communication Research's Padmanabhan Srinagesh, who has been studying the economics of internetworking, suggested that "there might be a trade-off between encouraging competition at the lower levels, at the level of bits in the networks, versus having an open architecture where the people who provide the bits also provide a standardized open interface that other people can use to compete with them for end users." But the National Cable Television Association's Wendell Bailey observed that the cable industry was built on control of content, albeit in an environment of local monopoly franchises: "We relish, as an industry, our right to be an editor."

Content publishers and customers may prefer the convenience of maximal openness, but conduit owners express concern that an obligation to carry any kind of content reduces them to common carriers and may therefore constrain their potential to generate profits through selection and differentiation. At the same time, if they are not common carriers they assume a heavy legal obligation with respect to the content they provide, even it they did not originate it. Perceptions of how common carriage has fared in conventional telecommunications contribute to reservations (relating to profitability, potential regulation, and business development prospects) expressed by some about the business implications of open architectures. Another source of concern is uncertainty about how the market will evolve to support competition based on ownership of facilities and/or service supply—what forms of industry structure will be sustainable?

As noted in Chapter 3, there were those at the forum who expressed concern about what might happen in telecommunications and information service markets if prices became chaotic. Others worry that open competition in an industry so bound to its fixed costs will produce effects akin to those experienced in the airline industry following deregulation. The low consumer prices that "price wars" might bring would be welcomed by many, but an industry shakeout and reconcentration might follow, which could either sustain or slow investment in deployment. One telephone company representative said that "there would be many starters but few finishers." See Box 6.4.

While the steering committee heard a number of concerns about the possibility of closed systems hindering the development of the NII, it

---

BOX 6.4
Competition's Darker Side?

In the long run, [technological and associated cost trends may give rise to] an industry with chronic excess capacity. An industry like that is very susceptible to price wars. If there are two or more broadband wires to the house providing essentially the same service, both economic theory and practical experience suggest that price is going to get competed down to marginal cost, leaving the producers with no way to cover their fixed investments in infrastructure. The result is bankruptcy, financial distress, et cetera. So here are a few scenarios.

One is to just let it happen. The problem is cutthroat competition and financial distress. After two or three repetitions, firms start losing interest in investing in the market, because there is no way to recover their infrastructure investment. They drop out, only a few major players remain, and local or maybe even national monopolies result.

Well, what about monopolies? Monopoly provision is better than no provision at all. Local monopolies, such as the local telephone service, the cable TV service, and so on can provide broadband service on a city-by-city basis. The problem is that you get the usual monopoly distortions in terms of excessive pricing, lack of innovation, and maybe even worse, the dreaded "R" word: the cause for regulation.

The third scenario is the "killer app" scenario, in which a very high bandwidth application becomes very popular and the revenues from selling the transport for such a "killer app" are sufficient to cover the infrastructure investment. But what is that application? As we have heard today [at the forum], nobody knows what the "killer app" is—two-way video, interactive virtual reality. . . . There is not going to be a market there if people aren't willing to go for the applications. So it is the usual chicken-and-egg problem.

Finally, the last scenario is vertical integration with the content providers. That seems to be the most popular solution. . . . But if the market for transport becomes very competitive in the future—if transport is a commodity business—then the money is going to have to flow the other way. The content will have to cross-subsidize the transport. Then the content is what is paid for, and the transport is thrown in for free; it is just a cost of delivering the content. A question is, Will the content providers really stick to their joint ventures once they have competing transport providers clamoring for their business? That remains to be seen.

—Hal Varian, University of California at Berkeley

---

finds little reason for concern that closed systems will represent an issue that will require policy intervention, beyond traditional tools of competition policy such as antitrust. The position of most developers is that new applications will come into existence over the Internet, an open system, and that an application, if initially created in an open form, has a natural resistance to being bundled. In support of this tendency, the steering committee notes the success of the Internet itself, the evolutionary path by which the on-line service providers have become Internet access providers, and the trends toward open systems and open protocols in general. If the open form is robust in terms of functions and institutions, it will survive. If it is not, that form should not be sustained by policy unless there is a compelling national need. Research, however, can produce results that may make open systems more attractive (e.g., by lowering perceived costs), potentially accelerating their implementation.

Thus, the steering committee concluded that the government in particular need not and should not make any presumption that it must protect the open nature of mature products, but that it should move to foster an open, innovative environment in which new services and applications can occur. This approach includes encouraging the deployment of communications infrastructure that is general and flexible, removing regulatory barriers to innovation (for example, making spectrum for experiments easily and predictably available)[13] and competition, and continuing to foster the success of the Internet through R&D and use in the delivery of public services.

DEFINING ROLES FOR GOVERNMENT

The large volume of descriptive material and statements of opinion elicited at the workshop and the forum and in the white papers provide some insights into current and potential roles of government (at all levels) in policy making. They fall primarily into the following categories:

1. Regulation and other rule-setting influences on market entry and conduct;
2. Direct government use of and experimentation with information infrastructure in the delivery of public services; and
3. Exploration of systems issues and fostering of technology development through research and development to create options, standards to choose among the options, and systems-level consensus to guide the choice of standards.

Three other government roles that cut across or influence the above three policy areas include attention to international aspects (trade, regulation, and interconnection and interoperation), data and analysis relating to infrastructure trends, and convening of different parties and sectors. These areas are discussed in turn in the following sections.

Regulation, Rules, and Norms

Complete examination of issues related to regulation was beyond the scope of this project, but the body of inputs (see Box 6.5) underscored the

BOX 6.5
Regulation and Market Roles

Do the conditions exist in the regulatory environment that make it possible for every player sitting at this table to risk its capital on relatively equivalent terms?

—Gail Garfield Schwartz, Teleport Communications Group

Monopolies [established by regulation] become powerful forces for creating hostages in government and lead to the retardation of technological development. Those monopolies have led to a slowdown in television's introduction and spread in the 1950s, a substantial slowdown in cable television's introduction and spread in the 1960s and 1970s, and a substantial slowdown through regulation of the development of wireless communication systems in the 1970s, 1980s, and even into the 1990s.

—Robert Crandall, Brookings Institution

If a phone company today attempts to upgrade to ADSL [asymmetric digital subscriber line], it cannot do so until somebody on M Street has said that is a good idea. If a UHF station in Los Angeles says, look, we are tired of sending *I Love Lucy* to the masses, we want to take our 6 megahertz and use it for two-way digital paging, they may not do so at all. If they wish to take their 6 megahertz 24 hours a day and slice it into fragments of 5 minutes and sell it to all comers, that is illegal as well. . . . Nextel created a cellular network largely by understanding process, buying up radio dispatch licenses, and then getting them dezoned.

—Peter Huber, Manhattan Institute for Policy Research

In some states, cable operators are common carriers. So it is not a model that I would reject out of hand. . . . Because, in the 500-channel world, it is hard to see how you really are a lot different from a common carrier.

—Wendell Bailey, National Cable Television Association

The federal government should not go in and try to preempt the local governments. It could and should establish some overarching guidelines for acquiring sites so that it will at least facilitate the process. For PCS [personal communication service], we have build-out requirements. We cannot afford to sit around too long and try to get sites. We spent a lot of money to get the licenses. So there needs to be some help. There is certainly a sensitivity, however, at the local level that you cannot just have the federal government saying that the wireless entity can put up a tower or a base station anywhere it wants.

—Mary Madigan, Personal Communications Industry Association

[T]he problems can include . . . the actual absence of a process for handling the permitting. In some locations there are actual prohibitions where people say, "not within the jurisdiction here," but at the same time they want the service. Some, unfortunately, are viewing this as an opportunity to make a bonanza: "We want seven percent of your gross revenues, plus we want some fee per site." Some have even actually gone so far as to say, "if you want to locate it in certain areas, you can deploy as many as you like, but you have to pay this fee, and no more than two people per antenna," which is absurd.

—Robert Roche, Cellular Telecommunications Industry Association

TABLE 6.1   Regulation and Shareholder Value: An Organizing
Framework

	Earnings	Growth	Risk
Federal Communications Commission	Price caps/rate of return Earnings ceiling/sharing Productivity target Consumer dividends Investment targets	Rate restructuring "Streamlined" regulation New service approval	Rate structures Depreciation charges New entry New service approval
State Public Utility Commissions	Incentive regulation Intra-LATA entry Regulatory lag Earnings attribution	Usage-sensitive rates New service offerings Service "restructuring"	Rate "rebalancing" Universal service Carrier of last resort Rate averaging Intra-LATA entry/pricing
U.S. Congress	Tax policies National information infrastructure Noncompensated service require- ments	Line-of-business restraints Mergers and acquisitions	Noncompensated service require- ments
Department of Justice/ Judiciary	Line-of-business restraints	Line-of-business restraints	Line-of-business restraints

SOURCE: Darby Associates (1995) as published in *Communications Business & Finance*.

negative influence of regulation on innovation and markets and therefore
deployment. See Table 6.1 for an overview of regulation as a source of
business risk. State and local regulation stimulated considerable commentary from contributors, reflecting its influence on residential broadband service choices (including cable-telephone competition) and its dis-
proportionate impact on emerging wireless services—for which basic
facilities are being built—and on state and local infrastructure initiatives.[14]

   In brief, many deployment decisions and activities are proceeding
independently of regulatory decision making or are based on best guesses
as to likely developments in telecommunications reform.[15] The proliferation of Internet-related activities—Web servers and applications, security
services that support commercial transactions over the Web, the formation and growth of Internet access providers, and so on—illustrates an
unregulated venue for growth. By contrast, contentious disagreement

among the Federal Communications Commission, telephone and cable companies, and the courts on the regulatory treatment of video delivery services underscores the way complex interactions among technology, business, and regulatory conditions shape investments. The recent moratorium on filings relating to video delivery services under 47 USC Sec. 214, which requires plans to be articulated months or years in advance of deployment, reflects those disagreements. So, too, does litigation relating to the Cable Communications Policy Act of 1984 (P.L. 98-549), which prevented telephone carriers from providing video programming within their region; a U.S. Circuit Court of Appeals ruled this ban unconstitutional, and the Supreme Court will decide the issue in 1996.[16,17] The wireless phenomenon drives some[18] to call for action ranging from greater reduction to total elimination of spectrum regulation. Speaking more generally, only one participant, Viacom's Edward Horowitz, suggested that there was an intermediate position between regulating or deregulating, achievable by "sunset" provisions.

Protecting the NII: Ethics and Mechanisms

Contributors to the NII 2000 project articulated concerns about privacy, intellectual property, free speech, ethical conduct, and, in particular, security, but given the scope of the project these issues did not receive a great deal of attention.[19] The discussions of plans for and progress toward deployment, especially in the context of the relatively insecure Internet, suggest that these concerns have not been showstoppers—although they may have altered the form or emphasis of decisions about deployment or use. Thus, Robert Crandall cautioned that some of the rhetoric on these issues may be a red herring. See Box 6.6.

Ethical and behavioral norms provide the context in which various services and mechanisms will evolve. Despite little experience to date, many commented on the uncertain implications of linking up a very large and very diverse set of people with access to a wide and powerful set of information resources and computing tools. The positive aspect of this trend is the possibility of bringing together and meeting the needs of various communities of interest. The negative aspect was acknowledged by some, such as Milo Medin of @Home, who remarked that "the network itself is bringing people far closer than they used to be. And that level of interaction between people is going to cause friction in addition to these communities of interest." The changing environment, possibilities, and scope of interactions led Lois McCoy of the National Institute for Urban Search and Rescue to propose a need for a "Bill of Rights,"[20] a logical extension of the articulation of privacy principles and security tenets undertaken by the IITF and codes of ethics generated by a variety

---

BOX 6.6
Intellectual Property Protection in Perspective

Robert Crandall of the Brookings Institution expressed skepticism during the forum concerning the point "that perhaps it is exposures to civil suits and the failure to resolve all the difficult questions involved in intellectual property protection that may be slowing down the development of the NII. I don't know that we have any evidence of that at this point. We just went through an attempt to revise tort liability laws and federalize it in the U.S. Congress. One of the reasons that it didn't proceed any farther than it did was that we don't have systematic evidence that civil liability, tort liability has had a severe effect upon a variety of goods- and service-producing industries already in the United States." Among other things, Crandall's comments suggest that private action may be sufficient to handle many issues raised by this set of concerns, although others continue to voice a need for policy monitoring if not intervention.

---

of business and professional organizations. Michael Greenbaum, apparently wary of government intervention, maintained that "informal standards serve the industry well by defining public expectations and setting clear objectives" and argued for "guidelines and self-regulating bodies that comprise the principal constituents."

Security, Reliability, and Architecture

Concerns about security lead to considerations of mechanisms that may also provide protections for the privacy of personal information, intellectual property, freedom from theft of service, integrity of information and systems, availability of service, and other vulnerable elements. Effective design and implementation of those mechanisms, plus associated policies and practices, have implications for the architecture of the information infrastructure. See Box 6.7.

Comments by Ed Hammond of Duke University Medical Center and others underscored the importance of engaging people with large-volume, specialized needs in areas of national importance, such as health care, both because of the wide-ranging consequences of decisions and because the issues may be nonobvious, counterintuitive, or contentious.[21] Quincy Rodgers argued that determinations of level of security and methods of implementation should be seen as business decisions, which in turn has implications for standardization, service provider decisions about whether specialized access devices (e.g., set-top boxes) may be available retail or leased, and the role of governments.

In many instances a common framework or architecture is preferable,

BOX 6.7
The Challenge of Meeting Different Needs Simultaneously

With respect to a uniform security mechanism in an NII, whose interests are being protected? I suggest that there will have to be a range of mechanisms provided by many different parties to protect network providers from one another and from their computer operators, content providers from theft of intellectual property, and consumers from detriment to their privacy interests. And so we shouldn't expect to have a secure network by simply getting some sort of oligopolistic control as we can say that our broadcast networks are secure because it's very rare that an outsider is able to broadcast an illicit television program.

—Allan Schiffman, Terisa Systems/CommerceNet

The ideal system permits us to have a system in which all who need data can have exactly what they need. It's complicated by the fact that there are 40 different types of people that probably have a legitimate need for access to health care information.

—Ed Hammond, Duke University Medical Center

both to achieve economies in developing and implementing a cross-cutting service and because to achieve interoperability some degree of standardization may be needed. Contributors raised a range of concerns, including issues associated with electronic signatures and cryptographic key and certificate management, which require supporting "infrastructures" (see the white paper by Robert Aiken and John Cavallini); the absence of corresponding cross-community or cross-sectoral processes, some of which require international interaction, on mechanisms for security and other protections;[22] and the need for yet other processes to ensure that a complex and multifaceted information infrastructure can, like the relatively simpler telephone network, meet national security and emergency preparedness needs (see the white paper by Lois Clark McCoy et al.). The rallying cry in the national security and emergency preparedness area is for an "emergency lane on the information superhighway," addressing inherent security and reliability issues plus support for the security needs of those managing public crises that require rapid recovery, disaster recovery, and mobilization.

Although forum discussions and white papers affirmed the value of a security architecture, progress toward implementing it seems hampered by the same factors that hamper progress toward implementing common architecture generally. For example, John McDonald of MBX Inc. listed in a white paper a number of trends that have led to a "concentration of network assets" that increases vulnerability to a single switch failure, line cut, or software system crash, notwithstanding the application of a variety of techniques that enhance network integrity. He noted that some of the trends are unintended side effects of strategies to ensure compliance with federal regulations and argued that integrity and robustness must be "considered from the ground up" and, presumably, in a coordinated manner.[23] Software is a huge expense for telecommunications equipment vendors because the fundamental technical approach they are taking to network control leads to systems that are inherently rigid and subject to failures, requiring heroic efforts to make them robust enough to operate in the real world. Newer and more flexible and robust approaches have been emerging; an issue for the technical and vendor communities is where, when, and how to advance and implement them.

This project does suggest that addressing security, reliability, recoverability, and associated protections may present one of the most constructive vehicles available for the government to influence overall architectural development in the evolving information infrastructure. Doing so will inevitably require resolving issues associated with cryptography policy, a topic well beyond the scope of this project but under consideration in another by CSTB.[24]

Government as User and Service Provider

Government public services will touch most citizens and many organizations in residences, places of business, and public spaces. Examples include law enforcement, health care information sharing and service delivery, research and education, environmental monitoring, national security, and more. Some will involve multiple levels of government, and some may blend government and commercial elements. For example, the relatively heterogeneous Intelligent Transportation System (ITS) fostered by the Department of Transportation reflects multilevel government interests in safety, efficiency, and capacity plus commercial applications. Jim Keller and Lewis Branscomb of Harvard University suggested that the ITS offers a model combining general-purpose information infrastructure with specific systems implemented in more closed fashion over or connected to the NII. Providing another example, the white paper by John Ziebarth et al. proposes a testbed for network-accessible information storage, access, and system management to better handle huge collections of regulatory information from multiple government institutions.[25]

National Institute of Standards and Technology Director Arati Prabhakar cast the opportunities for government use as part of the larger context of public-private interaction: "One of the great opportunities here is to abandon the traditional way that government agencies and departments often come at new capabilities. Agencies say, 'Let's go create this unique solution which will then be immune to all technological changes in the future.' Today we really have a chance to try to couple agencies and departments as they are doing their jobs, using these new technologies. We have a chance to link them to where the technology is going by linking them to the private sector activities." Emphasizing the cross-cutting nature of government applications, Aiken and Cavallini explain that the "[government services information infrastructure; GSII] is that portion of the NII used to link government and its services, enables 'virtual agency' concepts, protects privacy, and supports emergency preparedness needs."

Government databases provide a natural focus for government applications of information infrastructure, given the federal government's unique collections of data and information that are of broad interest and might be more broadly used in the future if made more accessible. The Government Information Locator Service is a cross-cutting information access initiative that could be used to explore various approaches and implementation issues; the National Spatial Data Clearinghouse is one of several more specialized information access programs that could also yield broader insights. Aiken and Cavallini note that government applications need not be viewed as "one size fits all," any more than private sector applications are. Diversity of service offings can still be compatible with interoperability. "[Start] with what the GSII will be used for ... and with those people who share common interests in both using and providing the GSII. The applications should determine what standards and technologies are required and will provide interoperability among their own constituency as well as with other groups, if properly coordinated." They cite government-supported scientific research as a domain in which the affinity group concept has been and should continue to be explored in terms of essential processes—requirements, coordination, interoperability, cross-sector exchange. As Mark Abbott of Oregon State University observed, experiences in the area of ocean and earth sciences research suggest that the record may be mixed: advances in information infrastructure prompt changes in the conduct of science, some carrying with them new distractions and costs. But this is the value of experiments: they show what works well, what does not, and where to direct future effort.

The above observations suggest that the federal government, in particular, may come full circle, from instigator of computer technology applications in the 1940s and 1950s to, on average, repository of obsolete technologies in the 1970s and 1980s, to a spearhead in the 1990s for innovative applications that may facilitate private sector activities and associated social and economic benefits. This vision, expressed primarily through white papers, does not imply monolithic construction projects. But it does imply farsighted procurement of commercial technology (goods and services) and equally farsighted applications-development decisions.[26] The history of the Internet shows that applications and experiments in certain user domains—and, increasingly important today, applications that are cross-domain in nature—may provide one of the most constructive vehicles available to the government for stimulating private action. As suggested by Aiken and Cavallini, information infrastructure can be part of a system for facilitating government-industry interactions.

Technology Development Through R&D

The present Internet provides evidence of the constructive role that government expenditures on R&D can often play. However, much research and development work remains to be done to develop the information infrastructure technology base, and as that base evolves it will reveal a stream of new challenges. That conclusion was apparent from many sources of evidence:

- Deployment plans for proven technologies, reflecting lack of readiness of the next generation of technology;
- Delay or moderation of deployment plans subject to various tests and trials,
- Difficulties using today's technologies that announced plans appear to ignore; and
- Expectations for greater if unspecified internetworking, and recognition that something more than conventional communications or passive entertainment would be required to drive significant advances.

Like regulation, R&D was not a focus of this project. Yet ideas for R&D work that emerged from the discussion suggest opportunities for constructive and (in contrast to regulation) relatively noncontroversial government involvement. As Allan Schiffman of Terisa Systems/ CommerceNet summed it up,

> I'm not one who thinks that the technology issues are completely settled yet. Certainly not in distributed computing, platforms, or common interfaces. Maybe the guys who are rolling the fiber optics out understand what's going on, but I'm not sure that the rest of the technology is in place. There is still room for a good deal more experimentation. The government has played a pretty useful role in that process up until now.

Many of those who suggested that issues are settled focused on the lower parts of the infrastructure. Activities are far less clear when it comes to the evolution of higher-level services. Accordingly, Randy Katz et al. assert in a white paper that "direct research and development is the most effective way to stimulate new service capabilities and associated commonalities."

One context for R&D that received considerable mention and support is the testbed—building on the history presented by the Internet and the more general recognition that understanding complex systems depends on building and testing them—and associated opportunities for collaborative exploration. Testbeds for R&D that supports applications (including interdisciplinary consideration of technical and nontechnical elements underlying successful applications in different domains) would be valuable. Under the testbed rubric, government can continue to promote the deployment of advanced information technologies in universities to stimulate the creation of applications that will make the core technology useful to society at large. Through these and other testbed efforts, government can foster greater transfer of ideas between universities and industry. Real partnerships between universities and industries are difficult to develop and maintain in a fast-moving industry and technical arena; this is a specific instance of the larger problem of facilitating large-systems research and industry-university collaboration (CSTB, 1994a).

Several areas of research were cited, directly or implicitly, in the course of the project. Four principal subject themes were architecture, for integrating a widening range of components and systems in a dynamic context; technology for information management; technology for greater security, privacy, and reliability; and technology for greater ease of use (both through better user interfaces[27] and better design generally).[28] See Box 6.8. These last two categories suggest a related need for research that addresses social processes relating to the adoption and use of information infrastructure. Katz et al. derive several topics for research by relating NII needs to directions established under the High Performance Computing and Communications Initiative, including the categories of information infrastructure services, system development and support environments, intelligent interfaces, and national challenge (major domain) problems. See Box 6.9 for elaboration on some of these topics.

Architecture and Networking

In the networking area, and associated with architecture, David Messerschmitt pointed to areas where little work is being done—quality of service, communications delay, and allocation of impairments across connected networks. Security complements these topics and also receives less attention than many believe is needed. Overall, as Messerschmitt noted, network signaling and control systems constitute an area in which considerable work is needed. Leonard Kleinrock of the University of California at Los Angeles and others outlined technology needs associated with extending the performance of wireless, untethered, and nomadic computing and communications systems, which translates into support for "ad hoc access to services." For example, Kleinrock enumerated several systems requirements and components (see Box 6.10), calling for a "reference model" for nomadicity to facilitate analysis and progress. He related support for nomadic access to basic network parameters—bandwidth, latency, reliability, error rate, delay, storage, processing power, interference, interoperability—in the context of very large scale, identified needs for middleware services, and noted that portable systems also require advances in size, weight, and battery power.

Another set of issues associated with networking and architecture and implicit in the discussions of deployment involves technology to lower the costs of achieving openness and symmetry. The lack of clarity regarding costs and benefits makes existing businesses reluctant to change dramatically, especially existing players that are starting from technology bases that have already been engineered to reduce costs as much as possible. This problem was stated elegantly and directly by Stewart Personick of Bell Communications Research:

> History has shown that lack of interoperability and openness can be a self-fulfilling prophecy . . . because without research on how to make network architectures and constructs that are conducive to interoperability, then what appears is not conducive to interoperability. It is not in the best interests of the largest participants in the industry to open anything up. It is politically correct to say that interoperability is good, but very few view it as the right thing to do from a business perspective. So how do you work out this conundrum? The largest participants are in the best position to fund R&D, but it is not in their interest to open up networks. Little guys can do certain things, but solving the interoperability problem is really tough. That is just one example, but a very important one in an area where somehow it is in the public's interest to promote interoperability and openness but the research has to be funded almost against the wishes of the biggest participants. That is an area where I believe government funding is absolutely essential.

As *Realizing the Information Future* (CSTB, 1994b) observed, more general and flexible technology looks more expensive than do the more specialized alternatives, and yet there may be little actual knowledge of relative costs or investigation of approaches that may add only modestly to costs.

BOX 6.8
Interface-related Research Needs

Human-Computer Interface Needs[1]

• *Human-computer dialogue.* Natural language, voice, and other modalities (pen, gestures, touch, and others) can be combined to produce the means for human-computer dialogue and interfacing dialogue techniques. Relevant research topics include speech recognition and synthesis; natural language processing and understanding (Cole and Garcia et al., 1995); semantics and prosody; lip-reading technologies in noisy environments (Garcia et al., 1994); and search, navigation (Shank, 1993), and retrieval from cyberspace using multimedia (Vin et al., 1991). Speaker identification techniques can be combined with secure passwords for use in control of computer access, and language identification may support improved multilingual interfaces (Wilpon et al., 1990).

• *Machine sensors for human-computer interface and general input/output to facilitate telepresence and teleoperation.* Such sensors as microphones in single and arrayed configurations, infrared and other means of scanning and computing distances, optical sensors at lightwave range including CCD [charge coupled device] cameras of small size, haptic interfaces, and other alternatives to click-and-point devices should be studied. Fusing sensor inputs to the computer with intelligent or learned action-response behavior would create a more realistic approach to machine learning and complex inferencing techniques, involving symbolic, fuzzy, and probabilistic approaches. A challenge is to fuse multiple sensor inputs to the computer in a cohesive and well-coordinated manner.

• *Large-volume storage (archival and nonarchival), database, and indexing technologies, including multiresolution and compression for different modalities.* Video and audio technologies (also indirectly related to speech and video synthesis) will require large compression factors and mechanisms for rapid encoding and decoding; they are difficult to index and access for retrieval and even then, mass storage database techniques will be required. Similarly, research on virtual environments requires efficient storage and compression technologies for input and output. Research on encoding should include both generation and perceptual factors (Flanagan, 1994). Additionally, multimedia databases require techniques for providing temporal modeling and delivery capabilities.

• *Virtual environments and their use in networking and wireless communication (tethered and untethered) networked environments, including applications in education (Kobb, 1993), telepresence, and telecommuting.* Wireless communication technology also includes requirements for geopositioning measures; local indoor infrared sensors for location; communications technologies at low, medium, and high bandwidth; and others. The technical challenges of wireless messaging are well known (Rattay, 1994). Durlach and Mavor (1995) make specific recommendations for federal investments in national research and development.

• *Applications of software engineering and CASE to the R&D of complex software systems and browsers to be used in human-computer interface (Andreessen, 1993).* Many modules of the software and interfaces for different modalities might be developed in a compact and reusable manner, taking advantage of existing and newly developed software techniques.

continues on next page

Intelligent Interfaces[2]

• *Human-computer interface.* Developments needed in this area include technologies for speech recognition and generation; graphical user interfaces that allow rapid browsing of large quantities of data; user-sensitive interfaces that customize and present information for particular levels of understanding; language corpora for experimental research; and human-machine interaction via touch, facial expression, gesture, and so on.

• *Heterogeneous database interfaces.* A capability is needed to enable a user to issue a query that is broadcast to the appropriate databases and to receive a timely response that is translated into the context of the user's query. Multiformatted data may range from ASCII text to numerical time series, to multidimensional measurements, to time series of digital imagery, and so on. Also of critical importance are the integration of metadata with the data and its accessibility across heterogeneous databases.

• *Image processing and computer vision.* Research areas include all aspects of theory, models, algorithms, architectures, and experimental systems from low-level image processing to high-level computer vision. Methodologies of pattern recognition should be further developed to allow automated extraction of digital image and other information from large databases.

• *User-centered design tools and systems.* User-friendly tools that combine data-driven and knowledge-based capabilities constitute one of the areas for new research.

---

[1]Adapted from "Statement on National Information Infrastructure Issues," a white paper contributed to the NII 2000 project by Oscar Garcia for the IEEE.
[2]Adapted from "The National Information Infrastructure: A High Performance Computing and Communications Perspective," a white paper contributed to the NII 2000 project by Randy H. Katz, William L. Scherlis, and Stephen L. Squires.

Information Management and Ease of Use

End users, especially those professionals in specialized domains of application, are usually concerned with problems of collecting, storing, finding, and manipulating information. They see communications as a means to an end. But until those domain-specific markets appear, communications providers focus on their communications facilities and basic services. This disjuncture appears to be slowing an important source of demand. Commented Lois McCoy, "What the user wants is the answer to his question. It doesn't make any difference what that question is."

The information management problem calls for R&D in many areas. One is how the user can find what is needed. Ross Glatzer, retired from Prodigy Services, remarked on how limited the state of the art is in today's on-line services arena: "Getting around on-line services today is like

BOX 6.9
R&D Needs for Information Infrastructure
Services and Systems Development

Information Infrastructure Services

• *Universal network services.* Techniques for improved ease of use, plug-and-play network interoperation, remote maintenance, exploitation of new "last-mile" technologies, management of hybrid and asymmetric network bandwidth, guaranteed quality of service for continuous media streams, and scale-up of network capabilities to dramatically larger numbers of users.

• *Integration and translation services.* Services for data format translation and interchange as well as tools to translate the access portions of existing programs. Techniques include wrappers that surround existing elements with new interfaces, integration frameworks that define application-specific common interfaces and data formats, and mediators that extend generic translation capabilities with domain knowledge-based computations, permitting abstraction and fusion of data.

• *System software services.* Operating system services to support the distribution of processing across processing nodes within the network, the partitioning of the application logic among heterogeneous nodes (based on specialized capabilities or asymmetric or limited bandwidth), guaranteed real-time response to applications for continuous media streams, and storage, retrieval, and input/output capabilities suitable for delivering large volumes of data to very large numbers of users. Techniques needed include persistent storage, programming language support, and file systems.

• *Data and knowledge management services.* Methods for tracking information transformation. Techniques include distributed databases, mechanisms for search, discovery, dissemination, and interchange, aggregating base data and programmed methods into objects, and support for persistent object stores incorporating data, rules, multimedia, and computation.

• *Information security services.* Techniques for privacy-enhanced mail, methods of encryption and key-escrow, and digital signatures. Also included are means for protecting the infrastructure, such as authorization mechanisms and firewalls, against intrusion and attack by worms, viruses, and trojan horses.

• *Reliable computing and communications services.* Techniques and mechanisms for restarting systems quickly, such as process shadowing, reliable distributed transaction commit protocols, and event- and data-redo-logging to keep data consistent and up to date in the face of system failures.

System Development and Support Environments

• *Rapid system prototyping.* Technologies for tools and languages that facilitate end-user specification, architecture design and analysis, component reuse, and prototyping; testing and on-line configuration management tools; and tools to support the integration and interoperation of heterogeneous software systems.

• *Distributed simulation and synthetic environments.* Methods for developing distributed simulation algorithms; geometric models and data structures; tools for scene description, creation, and animation; and integration of geometric and computational models of behavior into an integrated system description.

continues on next page

• *Problem solving and system design environments.* Examples of areas requiring research include efficient algorithms for searching huge planning spaces; more powerful and expressive representations of plans, operators, goals, and constraints; and the incorporation of efficient methods to facilitate scheduling and allocation of resources. The effects of uncertainty must be taken into account as well as the effects of goal interactions.

• *Software libraries and composition support.* Development of the underlying methodology, data structures, data distribution concepts, operating system interfaces, synchronization features, language extensions, and other technology to enable the construction of scalable library frameworks.

• *Collaboration and group software.* Methods for developing shared writing surfaces and live bulletin boards, version and configuration management, support for process and task management, capture of design history and rationale, electronic multimedia design notebooks, network-based video conferencing support, document exchange, and agents serving as intermediaries to repositories of relevant multimedia information.

SOURCE: Adapted from "The National Information Infrastructure: A High Performance Computing and Communications Perspective," a white paper contributed to the NII 2000 project by Randy H. Katz, William L. Scherlis, and Stephen L. Squires.

[trying to find] the guy who explains where he is [by] calling from . . . a phone booth at the corner of 'Walk and Don't Walk.' The leaders in on-line services will be those who can best integrate communications, information, and transactions." Andrew Lippman of the Massachusetts Institute of Technology expanded on the wish-list:

> You have to invent indices. You have to invent mechanisms and techniques by which you can accumulate, process, and reprocess the information. If you look at the Internet these days, you will find a tremendous amount of content-free information out on it that is purely in the form of index. There are music indices that do not play a note, but guide you through the world of music. That is the technical and architectural challenge that remains. Because the PC will predominate, it will foster symmetric industries. Probably entertainment will fall into line and at least merge inside of the computer, as will the signal processing. But the challenge that we have to face is how to build flexible databases.

Part of what is needed are advances in decision support systems, according to Gio Wiederhold of Stanford University, who derived inferences from his study of medical information needs. Wiederhold observed that "[m]aking choices is best supported by systems which provide a limited number of relevant choices (summaries, searching, selecting)." Similarly, Reagan Moore of the San Diego Supercomputer Center wrote of the need for techniques for data assimilation—mining and modeling—

BOX 6.10
Nomadicity Requirements and Components

Requirements

- Interoperation among many kinds of infrastructures (e.g., wireline and wireless)
- Ability to deal with unpredictability of user behavior, network capability, and computing platform
- Provision for graceful degradation
- Scale with respect to heterogeneity, address space, quality of service, bandwidth, geographical dimensions, number of users, and so on
- Integrated access to services
- Ad hoc access to services
- Maximum independence between the network and the applications from the user's viewpoint as well as from the development viewpoint
- Ability to match the nature of what is transmitted to the network bandwidth availability (i.e., compression, approximation, partial information, and so on)
- Cooperation among system elements such as sensors, actuators, devices, network, operating system, file system, middleware, services, and applications
- Ability to locate users, devices, services, and so on

Components That Can Help in Providing the Requirements

- An integrated software framework that presents a common virtual network layer
- Appropriate replication services at various levels
- File synchronization
- Predictive caching
- Consistency services
- Adaptive database management
- Location services (to find people and devices via tracking, forwarding, searching, and so on; an example of an emerging standard is Mobile IP)
- Discovery of resources
- Discovery of profile

SOURCE: Adapted from "Nomadic Computing and Communications," a white paper contributed to the NII 2000 Project by Leonard Kleinrock, University of California at Los Angeles.

especially for scientific research, while Richard Sharpe of the Hartford Foundation spoke of the technical and procedural challenges associated with collecting and aggregating data needed for innovative medical applications. Wiederhold also noted that otherwise reluctant people could be motivated to use the information infrastructure if it is seen as providing access to quality data (relevance, completeness, legitimacy). Related issues in standardizing data formats are discussed below.

One approach that attracted multiple comments was development of virtual environments, which were described as an approach to making cyberspace more intuitive and useful to a wider range of people, facilitating real-time, interactive human-computer communications. In the January workshop, Marty Tenenbaum of Enterprise Integration Technologies Corporation/CommerceNet observed that there was progress

> towards a more active collaboration where instead of clicking on something and getting a document, you are clicking on something and getting a three dimensional environment, a space on the Web where people can hang out and if other people are there at the same time, you are able to interact with them.

This concept was specifically advanced in the proposal for RegNet (see the white paper by Ziebarth et al.), which would involve three-dimensional volumetric regulatory information management (with cross-referenced databases). Donald Brutzman et al. go as far as to suggest in a white paper that virtual environments could be considered a superset of information infrastructure issues, in view of the concerns with scale, interactive three-dimensional graphics coordinating input devices with a single-screen display, and so on, with illustrations including a live three-dimensional sports stadium with instrumented players, a 100,000-player problem for a military war game, and virtual worlds as laboratories for robots and people in scientific research.

Standards

If consensus on system engineering and architecture issues for most of the NII network environment is to be implemented, that implementation will take the form of standards. The concepts of broad internetworking and open architecture presuppose standards. These standards may have the force of law when they are incorporated in regulatory processes. They may be formal, created through an approved consensus process, as has always been the case for the lower layers of telecommunications infrastructure. They may be informal or de facto industry standards created through a variety of institutions, including consortia of self-selected industry participants. Finally, they may be de facto standards made effective by the market power of the products embodying them.

The basic questions about what to standardize, where, when, and how are not new; the Technology Policy Working Group and others have considered them for some time.[29] Among participants in the NII 2000 project, there was general unease about a more active or direct government role supporting standards setting, except among those involved in broadcasting. As Quincy Rodgers summed it up,

What do you do? Do you standardize some? Do you standardize all? Do you standardize them through government action? Do you endure the delays that that approach can sometimes occasion? Have you dramatically improved the problem of bureaucratic standard setting by moving to some large private sector body? How does all of that fit at this stage of the development of these products?

Rodgers argued for de facto standards. Those familiar with telephony have noted that while centralized governmental decision making on standards can lead to unfortunate technology choices, the private sector process can perpetuate incompatibilities, as evidenced by divergent implementation of so-called "standard" integrated services digital network technology and technologies for video delivery.

Even in discussing government's internal needs, Aiken and Cavallini argued that "a modular, seamless integration and evolution of the multi-component GSII into the evolving NII will need to be based primarily on voluntary processes and proven interoperability solutions rather than on mandated standards." On the other hand, building on experience at ARPA, Randy Katz et al. suggest in their white paper that the "research [community] and government can take a leading role in establishing new commonalities that foreshadow industry standards." Also, although receiving little discussion, a government role for standards-related validation and dissemination could be valuable.

Thus the Internet standards are both de facto and consensus standards at one and the same time. One factor making that possible has been the important role that scientists and engineers, especially in universities, have played both as builders and users. This close-knit relationship between the "vendors" and "customers" is quite unique in standards making and is a powerful asset in obtaining both good standards and user acceptance of them.

The government's role in the development of the Internet standards was quite indirect. Nevertheless, government people, including experts in agencies such as ARPA, NSF, the Department of Energy, and the National Aeronautics and Space Administration, have made important personal intellectual contributions and, more importantly, have directed their research support to the most talented technical people in the national community. This use of R&D investment has constituted indirect support for standards making and is an excellent way to avoid the heavy hand that so many in industry fear, while creating options from which industry can choose.

International Issues

There was surprisingly little discussion of transnational issues from the industry experts. Although international issues were not a focus of this project, contributors generally assumed that international connectivity is a requirement, and experimentation with new services was reported to be taking place globally. The lack of concern expressed about incompatibilities in law and regulation, uncertainties about venues for legal accountability, and access to foreign markets perhaps reflected both the relative immaturity of information infrastructure developments overseas and the pragmatic, country-by-country approach of the international firms.

As a practical matter many of the most important commercial networks, such as the SWIFT system that supports international banking, have been in place internationally for some years. Among the more experimental developments, the Internet and the World Wide Web (Web) it supports are almost "the only game in town." Increasingly, commercial and recreational use of the GII can, technically, ignore national borders altogether, and that phenomenon warrants at least revisiting existing policies in such areas as export control, taxation, and enforcement of a wide range of rights and responsibilities.

As Maria Farnon of Tufts University notes in her white paper, "Bodies like the ITU [International Telecommunications Union] have grown increasingly irrelevant with the introduction of new services such as the Internet and have seen their turf eroded by new organizations that do not necessarily have official government sanction." These new services and organizations have been embraced or at least tolerated in almost every nation on earth, setting an important precedent for the value to each nation of reasonably unrestricted international access. See Box 6.11 for Farnon's observations on the Internet as an international phenomenon. Inputs to the NII 2000 project from satellite and smaller wireless system providers acknowledged the appeal of such technology for expanding global access in regions where wireline infrastructure is limited and the costs of building it are extremely high. Within individual countries, issues of open architecture, competition in telecommunications, and local equivalents of universal service are being debated; the G7 Ministerial Conference on the Information Society of February 1995[30] fostered cross-national discussion and experimentation; and the issue of international traffic settlements is one of many. Attorney Jonathan Band commented on the international attention now being devoted to system openness and harmonization of expectations for provisions in areas ranging from intellectual property protection to interoperability.

BOX 6.11
Politicoeconomic Implications of the Internet

Despite the clear intention of the industrialized world to foster the building of national backbones, and the gradual diffusion of connectivity in many developing countries, the traditional TO [state-owned telecommunications operator] structure, and the resulting legal and commercial models this fosters, remain serious obstacles to a truly international Internet. While technical difficulties can be overcome with resources from institutions such as the World Bank, NGOs [non-governmental organizations], and governments themselves, the traditional mind-set of control over the communications infrastructure and services is more difficult to displace. . . . [G]overnments have long justified their ownership of the telecommunications operator on the basis of national security reasons, and also derive significant political and revenue benefits from this ownership. Although this structure has been seriously undermined in the United States, the European Union, and parts of Asia, it remains strong elsewhere.

Ideally, an international network like the Internet should provide a protocol that is easily adapted to a wide variety of infrastructure development stages and should offer services that can be tailored to reflect the cultural, legal, and regulatory norms of every country. However, the model that the Internet has provided demonstrates that an international network will, by definition, still act to undermine many traditional structures that have evolved around the old TO system. Rather than seeking to impose old standards of behavior and control on the Internet, governments can best encourage the development of national information infrastructures by eliminating the inherent conflicts that exist between the new services and the domestic organization of telecommunications. This means introducing competition into all levels of service and allowing the market to drive pricing and standards.

SOURCE: Extracted from "How Do Traditional Legal, Commercial, Social, and Political Structures, When Confronted with a New Service, React and Interact?," a white paper contributed to the NII 2000 project by Maria Farnon.

Systems Data and Analysis for NII Assessment

Data issues are prosaic, mundane, and easily overlooked, but addressing them could be a simple and powerful way of improving private and public decision making. How can public or private entities aim to influence something without knowing the extent of an issue or the impact of a contemplated action? Again, the private sector has used market research data more or less effectively, but much of that information comes from proprietary and unpublished studies (yet another argument for public testbeds). Periodic assessments, using a mixture of public and private sector inputs as in the case of this project, may be a useful way for the government to gain information to be shared with all interested parties.

The AT&T divestiture has already detrimentally affected the availability of telephony statistics.[31]   Cable and wireless statistics are tracked largely by trade associations and market researchers (raising various concerns about the quality and completeness of data), and the decentralization and commercialization of the Internet are among the factors that make measuring its dimensions difficult. The white papers by Reagan Moore and by Hans-Werner Braun and Kimberly Claffy of the San Diego Supercomputer Center argue that "[t]he NII continues to drive funding into hardware, pipes, and multimedia-capable tools, with very little attention to any kind of underlying infrastructural sanity checks." The authors go on to relate deployment of new technology to measurement problems: "With the transition to ATM [asynchronous transfer mode] and high speed switches, it will no longer even be technically feasible to access IP [Internet Protocol] layer data in order to do traffic flow profiling, certainly not at switches within commercial ATM clouds." Meanwhile, the difficulty of gaining fresh insight into application domains suggests that there would be a benefit to more systematic study of how technology is selected and used in different settings.

Government as Convenor

Complementing and informing other government roles, convening—beyond that already provided by professional, trade, and private standards-setting organizations—appears to be helpful in encouraging better assimilation of information infrastructure by all users and providers. The good offices of state and federal government can break down some of the barriers to use of the information infrastructure for better health services, more effective education, distribution of government information and benefits, and so on. Private actions may not be sufficient for rapid progress and resolution in some critical arenas (e.g., education and health care) characterized by imperfect markets. In cases such as the interstate delivery of health care services, where legal barriers impede changes in professional practice, policy changes are needed to create efficient domain-specific information services. The issues, needs, opportunities, and handicaps in such areas have been surveyed many times over the past few years by the Information Infrastructure Task Force (IITF), Congress, trade and professional organizations, and independent analysts.[32]   The experience of this project, including a workshop and forum in which domain representatives expressed both frustration about difficulties in communicating with infrastructure providers and gratitude for the opportunity for learning and exchange, suggests that continued government support for convening different parties, bridging user and supplier communities, would have value.

Whatever the federal government does to foster convening should take into account the role of NII itself as an implicit, informal convening mechanism. As various contributors pointed out indirectly and directly, enhancements to the information infrastructure will allow people to coalesce both openly and privately, thereby changing the processes of government. Mixed expectations were voiced by one participant in connection with the use of information infrastructure to support electronic democracy. As Michael Greenbaum of Bell Atlantic Corporation speculated:

> At its best it will give voice and cohesion to the underrepresented. At its worst it will enable terrorists and hate groups to act under the cover of anonymity. This medium is better suited than most to building constituency, rather than just mass communications. It should be approached with caution as a means for formal and informal referendum, through which activist groups might unduly influence representatives and undermine the deliberative aspect of a representative democracy.

Although not everyone will use the technology, the deeper information infrastructure becomes embedded in U.S. society, the more some degree of access will become a part of what it means to be an informed voter.

CONCLUSIONS

The NII 2000 project suggests that most in industries that supply information infrastructure would support a variety of roles for government, roles that are complex, often subtle, sometimes active. But these roles are, like the work of private firms, intertwined with private roles and subject to a broad range of uncertainties about future possibilities and problems. The steering committee heard broad support for the government contributing as an enlightened customer and participant in building the NII. In particular, it heard an expression of the need for continued government support of innovation in the form of support for university-based research and development, both basic and applied. But there was also general (albeit not unanimous) enthusiasm for accelerated deregulation—not only to speed market entry but also to allow licensed carriers the freedom to use their assigned spectrum innovatively—implying a reduction in governmental authority to direct NII evolution unilaterally.

The concerns expressed about the lagging of many domain-specific areas of application, despite the prospect for important economic drivers from the application industries, suggest that this enabling role for governments reaches into many areas of government responsibility and is important at the state as well as the federal level. Thus responsibility for constructive government participation will be decentralized, raising questions about whether an overall systems view can or should be sustained in some continuing activity or organization.

The steering committee concluded that a consensus vision—however indistinct and subject to evolutionary modification—of the NII in the first decades of the 21st century should form its core but should not represent a constraint on all NII developments. Articulating and evolving national goals, and driving toward a national consensus, are important elements of the government role. It is a difficult role in which leadership—as opposed to unilaterial action or definitions—can help to overcome the confusion and misunderstanding that typically accompany technically complex phenomena. There is general agreement that government can play a role in bringing diverse interests together to seek out consensus on values and objectives for the national capability and on architectural principles supportive of those values. If it is done right, that consensus will govern many of the public and private sector actions. Leadership and articulation stand in contrast to regulation or judicial action: not everything can be defined by rules. People in organized societies do things because there are corresponding norms and understandings. But we have already seen in many industries, including telecommunications, that if government defines too many rules, eventually all people do is try to work around them.

Reconciling divergent positions and priorities within the government may be a critical first step, since the government itself is as diverse as other sectors of society. For example, it may be the case that entirely different priorities would emerge from the Department of Defense (DOD) and the Social Security Administration; within the DOD, the different services have had a hard time achieving interoperability. The IITF has been an experiment in cross-agency coordination. While it has helped to articulate and explore many key issues, the question remains as to which part of the decentralized government will articulate the goals and guide the architecture (CSTB, 1994b).

This project itself represents a step by the federal government, acting through the IITF, to explore the extent of the consensus on which federal policy making and leadership can rest. What is the proper mechanism for pursuing this exploration? The project did not discuss specific institutional structures. However, it seems evident that something more long range and more centered in private sector participation is needed than the IITF and the former NII Advisory Council. The essential requirement is that both the information service providers and the information creators and users in the private commercial and not-for-profit sectors must be fully involved, along with relevant government bodies.

Second, the primary economic drivers of the NII will be found, the steering committee believes, within the most important domains of the national life—health services, education, electronic commerce (including goods distribution, marketing, and retailing), and public safety and the like. (While an important factor, entertainment appears to be less of a driver than anticipated at this project's outset.) Because the ability of these domains to take full advantage of the NII is more limited by factors inherent within those domains than by shortcomings in the information network support, progress in creating these services will lie primarily in the hands of the professional groups and firms concerned. These responsibilities clearly fall primarily to public and private institutions outside the realm of telecommunications and high-performance computing, and they must be taken up by the relevant bodies in their own self-interest. However, the federal government and the states can, within their own operational missions, act to reduce the barriers to the creation of need-based demand for information infrastructure.

The NII 2000 project did not conclude (although it was hypothesized at the project's outset) that all information networks must be open and interoperable. Some mature and specialized applications can justify their unique application-specific architectures by the cost reduction they afford. But the powerful lesson to be learned from the Internet is the value of an open interface on which all kinds of new and mature services can be built, one that allows an experimental new service to look for users among the entire population with access to a digital network. Government should adopt policies intended to retain the power of a service like the Internet to be a testbed for innovations and a link among many resources for both information and its processing and distribution.

Both federal and state governments have the opportunity to increase their own efficiency and improve their services to the public through the development and use of the NII. A current initiative toward that end focuses on "reinventing government." These efforts should be undertaken under policy guidelines supporting the future evolution of the NII, as well as the best use of currently available facilities. In other words, the government should further the development of the core functions of the NII, using a "learn-and-change-by-doing" approach. This will place the government's purchasing power squarely behind the goal of national, consensus-based progress. In this endeavor, the federal and state governments must seek a concerted strategy, since each has the potential for strong influence in the evolution of the NII.

Perhaps the most important role government can play, especially at the federal level, is the continued vigorous support of advanced research into digital networking, with the objective of creating opportunities for the private sector to sustain the maximum amount of generality and flexibility at minimum cost. Much of this work can be carried out in support of government applications, and much can be carried out in collaboration with private industry; much is appropriate to the university environment. It should be noted that different parts of the information industry are structured quite differently with respect to available R&D resources. Historically, the regulated telephony industry has been quite research-intensive. The cable TV industry and, more importantly, the domain-specific application industries do not have this tradition of research, depending instead on the vendors that support them; they would benefit, in particular, from partnership projects with government agencies.

Finally, as noted above, there is much political debate about the effect deregulation, plus a blizzard of anticipated technological and market innovations, will have on the structure, profitability, and competitiveness of the many segments of the information industry. There is a continuous role to be played in evaluating and then acting (or not acting). At times, these actions are taken to remove impediments, and at other times, to encourage changes in direction. This is no different from what any corporate manager faces: the need to continuously evaluate and to correct the course accordingly.

But the government should not try to manage the evolution of industry structure, barring evidence of serious inequities or economic problems. It should keep its tools, such as the Federal Communications Commission and the National Telecommunications and Information Administration, available to deal with any situation that might arise in the future. Particularly important will be better data collection and analysis to reduce some of the guesswork and improve the bases for decision making in industry, government, and elsewhere on infrastructure development, selection, and use. In any case, the slower pace of deregulation and privatization in most other nations will require active engagement with those policies in the interest of achieving a vigorous and effective GII in which U.S. suppliers are not competitively disadvantaged.

NOTES

1. See CSTB (1994b,d). Also, the federal government has pursued a variety of initiatives that support the evolution of information infrastructure technology, including those relating to high-speed and optical networks, digital libraries, mobile computing, and so on.

2. Government-funded networking research and development can explore architectural alternatives that cut across existing implementations, creating options for new configurations of the great range of available technologies.

3. See CSTB (1995b) for additional discussion.

4. Antitrust law and regulation, frequently misunderstood in any event, received little direct attention from project participants. Although, if anything, antitrust policy seeks to promote entry where a competitive market is sustainable, its effects may be most evident in this context as a factor affecting the com-

position and conduct of consortia and alliances (such as those for joint personal communication service licenses), or in government investigations of major players such as Microsoft to look into the possibility of monopolization.

5.   One possible form of government involvement that was not suggested or discussed was targeted investment downstream in production, as through investment incentives. For commentary on the difficulties and ramifications of attempts to direct the allocation of private capital, see Beltz (1991):

> [T]he HDTV debate has amply illustrated the hazards of high-technology politics and industry-led targeting. Rather than one industry voice to guide policy makers, there are many. Just as multiple technologies are involved in HDTV and the related final product markets, so also are there multiple interest groups, each with its own policy agenda and report documenting its critical importance. The range of interested parties includes TV programmers, TV equipment suppliers, cable companies, satellite companies, over-the-air broadcasters, domestic and foreign TV manufacturers, U.S. semiconductor manufacturers, telecommunications companies, and computer manufacturers—the list seems endless. Which industry voice should be followed? Whose agenda for the development of high-resolution systems, standards, and components should be chosen? Who should decide?

6.   Public-private interaction in the context of railroad development is discussed in CNRI (1995a, p. 5), which observes, "Public sponsorship and joint public/private enterprise had characterized public works projects since construction started on the Erie Canal in 1817. Moreover, leaving aside the questions of the federal land grants for the moment, the rise of the railroads was accompanied by a relative decline in the value of federal investment."

7.   This point is discussed at length in *Realizing the Information Future: The Internet and Beyond* (CSTB, 1994b).

8.   See CSTB (1994b).

9.   Note that with respect to the issue of equitable access there is confusion over both mechanisms and objectives. Freer market entry and competition are mechanisms that can lower prices, which can in turn support a broader set of customers. However, they are generally not sufficient to address the needs of either the truly disenfranchised (whose means are too limited to support even low competitive prices) or those living in (e.g., rural) areas that are costly to serve. The white paper by the Organization for the Protection and Advancement of Small Telephone Companies notes, for example, that some areas are characterized by longer subscriber loops and other impediments to digital service.

Perhaps some cause for optimism can be read into recent analyses of AT&T, which, as noted in CNRI (1995b), suggest that consumer demand motivated the expansion of the scope of AT&T's service in conjunction with the technological and management factors addressed in more conventional analyses.

10.   For example, forum participant Allan Arlow noted that the market success of different advanced network access interfaces will create a de facto definition of an "info have" that law or regulation could make de jure.

According to an editorial in the *New York Times* of September 5, 1995, entitled "The Information 'Have Nots'":

> The basic promise of the information age—that books, facts and figures will be widely disseminated over the telephone lines—will come to nothing unless public access to computers and telecommunications technology is broadly expanded. The public libraries should be one source of easy access. They are struggling to offer the services but are faltering because of high telecommunication costs.
>
> A recent survey of what the Department of Commerce describes as the "information have nots" revealed that about 20 percent of America's poorest households do not have telephones. Only a fraction of those who do will be able to afford the computers and related equipment that grant access to the information society. The children of those households start out at an obvious disadvantage, as do adults who could benefit from on-line training or avail themselves of on-line jobs search materials and so on. States that house a disproportionate number of the country's poor will need to take special care to secure broad access to avoid an information underclass.

11.   Although inherently attractive to policy makers, the concept of making the national information infrastructure available via libraries and public access kiosks was roundly criticized in research conducted by U S West about a year ago. The research sampled hundreds of consumers in urban as well as rural settings—essentially all of them said they would be dissatisfied with public access. While public access seems workable for books (whereby consumers can buy their own favorites at a reasonable price) and database research (which few consumers do), respondents appeared to put access to the NII on a par with having television and telephones—they are not about to go to the local library to have it.

12.   These include the federal inter-agency Information Infrastructure Task Force and the former associated National Information Infrastructure Advisory Council, the American National Standards Institute and the associated Information Infrastructure Standards Panel, the Cross-Industry Working Team organized under the auspices of the Corporation for National Research Initiatives, the Council on Competitiveness, EDUCOM, the Coalition for Networked Information and its member organizations, and others.

13.   For example, David Messerschmitt commended the framework provided by the treatment of the industrial, scientific, and medical bands of spectrum, a zone where relatively little regulatory control is imposed on use as long as interference is minimized. During the January workshop, the Federal Communications Commission's Mike Marcus asked about the desirability of expedited approvals for testbeds and experiments analogous to those for fast-track Title III radio experiments, noting that the absence of such a process has been associated with delays for certain service trials.

14.   Or sometimes sharing in the cost of nodes and transport; see the white paper by the Organization for the Protection and Advancement of Small Telephone Companies.

15. Telecommunications reform legislation could substantially alter the framework for federal regulation (changing the enabling statute(s)) and also affect state regulation to the extent that it provides for federal preemption. The process of deregulation is clearly in motion; the uncertainties prior to and during the NII 2000 project have related to timing and application or emphasis.

One issue contemplated in legislative discussions is some kind of requirement to increase connectivity from schools. Thus, AT&T received considerable attention for announcing its own plans to offer "free Internet access and voice-messaging services to 110,000 public and private schools" at a cost of about $150 million over 5 years. Beginning in fall 1996, the package would include "free dial-up Internet access, browser software, and 100 free hours of use, with a 30 percent discount on service thereafter"; the voice messaging service would be free for the first 3 months. See Naik (1995b).

16. For example, a month before the spring forum, Bell Atlantic announced it was suspending two of its video dial-tone applications (also known as "214s") then pending before the Federal Communications Commission. The regional Bell holding company (RBOC), which had proposed using hybrid fiber coaxial cable and asymmetric digital subscriber line systems in different areas, stated that changes in technology necessitated changes in its applications. On May 25th, the day after the forum and nearly a year after Bell Atlantic had originally filed its applications, the RBOC withdrew its 214s altogether.

17. These actions suggest questions about the desirability of and business case for the technology paths outlined in the filings and about whether the process itself will continue to be a requirement, now that telecommunications reform legislation has been passed. In these and other cases, the presence, absence, or degree of regulation may be cited as justification for or against action, but other factors clearly affect the desirability of a particular course of action.

18. Such as project contributors Peter Huber of the Manhattan Institute, David Messerschmitt of the University of California at Berkeley, and James McKinney of the Advanced Television Systems Committee.

19. For fuller consideration see such other CSTB reports as *Realizing the Information Future* (1994b), *The Changing Nature of Telecommunications/Information Infrastructure* (1995b), and *Rights and Responsibilities of Participants in Networked Communities* (1994d).

20. The Aspen Institute has recently published a report on such a concept (see Firestone and Schement, 1995).

21. The Information Infrastructure Task Force, through its Committee on Applications and Technology, has put considerable emphasis on convening people in major application areas, such as health care and education.

22. This point was argued by Ken Klingenstein of the University of Colorado at Boulder during the forum.

23. Similarly, David Messerschmitt noted that "transcoders already introduced in cellular telephony preclude privacy by end-to-end encryption," pointing to insufficient attention historically to privacy in the development of cellular networks.

24. The report of CSTB's project on national cryptography policy, requested

by the Defense Authorization Act of 1994, is scheduled to be published in mid-1996.

25.   They relate their testbed to four modes of regulatory interaction: a one-to-one exchange between entities (e.g., a private entity requesting information from an agency); a one-to-two relationship (e.g., for dispute resolution); a one-to-many relationship; and a many-to-many configuration (e.g., negotiated rulemaking).

26.   The broad applicability of some government applications is consistent with a variety of ongoing initiatives—congressionally driven procurement reforms, the National Performance Review, and the Goverment Information Technology Systems working group, a sister to the Technology Policy Working Group (TPWG), under the Information Infrastructure Task Force, and efforts to harmonize technology development and exploration efforts, such as those led by the TPWG, with efforts focused on applying information infrastructure.

27.   See the white paper by Oscar Garcia on behalf of the IEEE.

28.   The concern with design was noted at the forum by Walter Wiebe of the National Science Foundation.

29.   See Kahin and Abbate (1995) for an overview. See also Besen and Farrell (1994) and Farrell and Shapiro (1992).

30.   More information is available on-line at http://www.ispo.cec.be (EC Information Society Project Office Webserver) under *G7 Information Society Conference.*

31.   The basic problem is that activity devolved to multiple entities, only some of which were required to report key statistics to the government. Another problem is the broadening of the scope of concern from telephony to a larger mix of services within the NII. The need to resort to subjective or speculative market research estimates for a variety of communications and information services in the Department of Commerce's *Industrial Outlook* volumes is but one indicator.

32.   Several such efforts are referenced in the bibliography.

Bibliography

Alex. Brown & Sons Inc. 1995. *Planet Web: Browsing for Dollars, Investment Opportunities in the Internet and Online World.* Alex. Brown & Sons Inc., Baltimore, Md., September.

Anderson, Robert H., Tora K. Bikson, Sally Ann Law, and Bridger M. Mitchell. 1995. *Universal Access to E-Mail: Feasibility and Societal Implications.* Center for Information Revolution Analyses, RAND Corporation, Santa Monica, Calif.

Andreessen, M. 1993. "NCSA Mosaic Technical Summary," National Center for Supercomputing Applications, Software Development Group, University of Illinois, Urbana, Ill.

Andrews, Edmund L. 1995a. "F.C.C. Will Not Force Rate Increase for Digital Phone Lines," *New York Times*, May 31, p. D4.

Andrews, Edmund L. 1995b. "New TV System Endorsed Amid Doubt on Future," *New York Times*, November 29, pp. D1 and D4.

Anthes, Gary H. 1995a. "Companies Usher in Internet Security Products," *Computerworld*, June 26, p. 56.

Anthes, Gary H. 1995b. "Small Firms Get Low-Cost On-Line Access," *Computerworld*, April 3, p. 28.

Apple Computer Corporation. 1995. "Petition for Rulemaking: 'NII Band,'" *In the Matter of Allocation of Spectrum in the 5 GHz Band to Establish a Wireless Component of the National Information Infrastructure.* Presented before the Federal Communications Commission, Washington, D.C., May 24.

Areeda, Phillip. 1990. "Essential Facilities: An Epithet in Need of Limiting Principles," *Antitrust Law Journal*, Vol. 58, pp. 841-894.

Arlen, Gary H. 1995a. "As IVDS Deadline Looms, Licenses Plan Limited Service," *Information & Interactive Services Report*, February 15, pp. 8-11.

Arlen, Gary H. 1995b. "Online Audience at 9.8 Million Users in Wake of MSN, AOL Marketing," *Information & Interactive Services Report*, October 20, pp. 1-2 and 15-16.

Arlen, Gary H. 1995c. "OnLine Audience Tops 8.5 Million, with 95% Served by 'Big Six': Marketing Binge Accelerates as Operators Await Microsoft Network Arrival," *Information & Interactive Services Report*, July 14, pp. 1-2, 14-19.

Arlen, Gary H. 1996. "Consumer On-line Audience Tops 11.3 Million Users, Up 79% During 1995," *Information & Interactive Services Report*, January 12, p. 1.

Arnst, Catherine, with Kevin Kelly, and Peter Burrows. 1995. "Phone Frenzy: Is There Anyone Who Doesn't Want to be a Telecom Player?," *Business Week*, February 20, pp. 92-97.

Asker, James R. (ed.) 1995. "In Orbit," *Aviation Week & Space Technology*, May 29, p. 74.

Associated Press. 1995. "AT&T School Offer: Free Internet Access," *New York Times*, November 1, p. D5.

Bangemann, Martin (Chair) and the High-Level Group on the Information Society. 1994. *Europe and the Global Information Society: Recommendations to the European Council*. European Council, Brussels, Belgium, May 26.

Barboza, David. 1995. "The Media Business: Advertising," *New York Times*, August 22, p. D6.

Baumol, William J., and J. Gregory Sidak. 1994a. "The Pricing on Inputs Sold to Competitors," *Yale Journal on Regulation*, Vol. 11, pp. 171-202.

Baumol, William J., and J. Gregory Sidak. 1994b. *Toward Competition in Local Telephony*. Massachusetts Institute of Technology and the American Enterprise Institute for Public Policy Research, Cambridge, Mass.

Beltz, Cynthia A. 1991. *High-Tech Maneuvers: Industrial Policy Lessons of HDTV*. AEI Press (publisher of the American Enterprise Institute), Washington, D.C.

Berners-Lee, Tim, Robert Cailliau, Ari Luotonen, Henrik Frystyk Nielsen, and Arthur Secret. 1994. "The World-Wide Web," *Communications of the ACM* 37(8):76-82.

Besen, Stanley M., and Joseph Farrell. 1994. "Choosing How to Compete: Strategies and Tactics in Standardization," *Journal of Economic Perspectives* 8(2):117-131.

Betts, Mitch. 1995. "Internet Renews Tax Battles," *Computerworld*, June 19, p. 64.

Betts, Mitch, and Gary H. Anthes. 1995. "On-line Boundaries Unclear," *Computerworld*, June 5, pp. 1 and 16.

Blodgett, Mindy. 1995. "Middleware Spurs Growth in Wireless Data Market," *Computerworld*, June 26, pp. 55, 57.

Bloomberg Business News. 1995. "A Video Phone for the Wrist," *New York Times*, August 3, p. D8.

Booker, Ellis. 1995a. "Agent-less Travel Planning Surges On-line," *Computerworld*, May 15, p. 20.

Booker, Ellis. 1995b. "Netscape Offers One-Stop Internet Sign-up," *Computerworld*, June 5, p. 14.

Booker, Ellis. 1995c. "The Web vs. Notes vs. Microsoft Exchange," *Computerworld*, May 29, p. 26.

Bray, Nicholas, and Paul B. Carroll. 1995. "Banks Go to the Source to Cut Phone Bills," *Wall Street Journal*, October 6, p. A10.

Brightman, Joan. 1994. "Hybrid Fiber/coax: Front Runner In the Broadband Transmission Race," *Telephony*, November 28, pp. 42-50.

Brock, Gerald W. 1995. *The Economics of Interconnection*. Teleport Communications Group, Staten Island, New York, April.

Brodsky, Ira. 1995. "Wireless World," *Internet World*, July. Available on line from http://pubs.iworld.com.

Burgess, John. 1995. "Apple's $500 Answer to Simplicity," *Washington Post*, September 11, pp. 17 and 20 of the business weekly insert.

Business Week. 1995. September 25, p. 110.

Cable Regulation Digest. 1995. "Thompson (sic) Lands $1 Billion Tele-TV Contract," September 25, available on-line from http://www.vortex.com/pn/cable1.html.

Cauley, Leslie. 1995a. "Bell Atlantic Asks the FCC to Suspend Two Applications for Video Networks," *Wall Street Journal*, April 26, p. B6.

Cauley, Leslie. 1995b. "Bell Curves: Phone Giants Find Interactive Path Full of Obstacles," *Wall Street Journal*, July 24, p. A1.

Cauley, Leslie. 1995c. "PacTel Puts Off Interactive Video Plans, Concentrating Instead on Wireless Cable," *Wall Street Journal*, September 28, p. A3.

Chandrasekaran, Rajiv. 1994. "On-line Highway a Costly Toll Road for Rural Users," *Washington Post*, November 7, pp. A1 and A14.

Chrisman, Nicholas. 1994. "A Vision of Digital Libraries for Geographic Information or How I Stopped Trying to Find the On-Ramps to the Information Superhighway," *GeoInfoSystems*, April, pp. 21-24.

Clark, Don. 1995a. "Microsoft Says It Has New Partners Lined Up for Its Planned On-Line Service," *Wall Street Journal*, May 11, p. B4.

Clark, Don. 1995b. "Netscape's Balloon Could Be Popped by Developments at Microsoft," *Wall Street Journal*, August 10, p. B3.

Clark, Don. 1995c. "Sign-Ups for Microsoft Network Show Strength but Trail Some Expectations," *Wall Street Journal*, November 21, p. B10.

Clark, Don, and Joan E. Rigdon. 1995. "Stripped-Down PCs Will Be Talk of Comdex," *Wall Street Journal*, November 10, pp. B1 and B7.

Clay Whitehead Associates. 1994. *Business Opportunities and Risks for Electric Utilities in the National Information Infrastructure: Executive Summary*. EPRI TR-104539. Prepared for the Electric Power Research Institute by Clay Whitehead Associates, McLean, Va., October.

Code of Federal Regulations (CFR). 1994. Telecommuncation: 47, parts 20 to 39, a codification of documents published as a special edition of the *Federal Register*, Office of the Federal Register, National Archives and Records Administration, U.S. Government Printing Office, Washington, D.C., revised as of October 1.

Cole, Jeff. 1995. "In New Space Race, Companies Are Seeking Dollars from Heaven," *Wall Street Journal*, October 10, pp. A1 and A8.

Cole, R., O.N. Garcia, et al. 1995. "The Challenge of Spoken Language Systems: Research Directions for the Nineties," *IEEE Transactions on Speech and Audio Processing*, January.

Committee on Applications and Technology (CAT), Information Infrastructure Task Force Committee. 1994a. *Putting the Information Infrastructure to Work*. Information Infrastructure Task Force, U.S. Department of Commerce, Washington, D.C.

Committee on Applications and Technology (CAT), Information Infrastructure Task Force. 1994b. *The Information Infrastructure: Reaching Society's Goals*. U.S. Government Printing Office, Washington, D.C., September.

Committee on Information and Communications (CIC). 1995. *High Performance Computing and Communications: Foundation for America's Information Future*. National Science and Technology Council, Washington, D.C.

Communications Daily. 1995a. "Bright Future Seen for Broadcast, Telcos and Cable by 10 CEOs," September 29, p. 5.

Communications Daily. 1995b. "Comm. Daily Notebook," September 1, p. 5.

Communications Daily. 1995c. "Manufacturers Unveil Cable Modems; CableLabs to Work on Protocols," December 1, pp. 2-3.

Communications Daily. 1995d. "Sales of Digital Satellite Receivers," August 2, p. 11.

Communications Daily. 1995e. "Telecom Reform Delay Causing 'Smart Procrastination' by Buyers, Cable Says," November 2, p. 3.

Computer Science and Telecommunications Board (CSTB), National Research Council. 1993a. *Information Technology in the Service Society: A Twenty-first Century Lever*. National Academy Press, Washington, D.C.

Computer Science and Telecommunications Board (CSTB), National Research Council. 1993b. *National Collaboratories: Applying Information Technology for Scientific Research.* National Academy Press, Washington, D.C.

Computer Science and Telecommunications Board (CSTB), National Research Council. 1994a. *Academic Careers for Experimental Computer Scientists and Engineers.* National Academy Press, Washington, D.C.

Computer Science and Telecommunications Board (CSTB), National Research Council. 1994b. *Realizing the Information Future: The Internet and Beyond.* National Academy Press, Washington, D.C.

Computer Science and Telecommunications Board (CSTB), National Research Council. 1994c. *Research Recommendations to Facilitate Distributed Work.* National Academy Press, Washington, D.C.

Computer Science and Telecommunications Board (CSTB), National Research Council. 1994d. *Rights and Responsibilities of Participants in Networked Communities.* National Academy Press, Washington, D.C.

Computer Science and Telecommunications Board (CSTB), National Research Council. 1995a. *Information Technology for Manufacturing: A Research Agenda.* National Academy Press, Washington, D.C.

Computer Science and Telecommunications Board (CSTB), National Research Council. 1995b. *The Changing Nature of Telecommunications/Information Infrastructure.* National Academy Press, Washington, D.C.

Computer Science and Telecommunications Board (CSTB), National Research Council. 1995c. *Keeping the U.S. Computer and Communications Industry Competitive: Convergence of Computing, Communications, and Entertainment.* National Academy Press, Washington, D.C.

Computer Science and Telecommunications Board (CSTB), National Research Council. 1995d. *Evolving the High Performance Computing and Communications Initiative to Support the Nation's Information Infrastructure.* National Academy Press, Washington, D.C.

Computer Systems Policy Project (CSPP). 1993. *Perspectives on the National Information Infrastructure: CSPP's Vision and Recommendations for Action.* Computer Systems Policy Project, Washington, D.C.

Computer Systems Policy Project (CSPP). 1994. *Perspectives on the National Information Infrastructure: Ensuring Interoperability.* Computer Systems Policy Project, Washington, D.C., February.

Computerworld. 1995. "Video Nets Stall; Data Nets Rev Up," June 12, p. 12.

Corcoran, Elizabeth. 1995a. "Banks Gear Up to Offer Host of On-Line Services: Competition May Provide Wealth of Choices," *Washington Post,* July 18, pp. D1 and D5.

Corcoran, Elizabeth. 1995b. "Room with a Different View: Computer Makers Find a Way to Scale Back Fears of the Microsoft Network," *Washington Post,* August 5, p. D1.

Corporation for National Research Initiatives (CNRI), Amy Frielander. 1995a. *Emerging Infrastructure: The Growth of Railroads.* Corporation for National Research Initiatives, Reston, Va.

Corporation for National Research Initiatives (CNRI), Amy Frielander. 1995b. *Natural Monopoly and Universal Service: Telephones and Telegraphs in the U.S. Communications Infrastructure, 1837-1940.* Corporation for National Research Initiatives, Reston, Va.

Council on Competitiveness (COC). 1993a. *Competition Policy: Unlocking the National Information Infrastructure.* Council on Competitiveness, Washington, D.C., December.

Council on Competitiveness (COC). 1993b. *Vision for a 21st Century Information Infrastructure.* Council on Competitiveness, Washington, D.C., May.

Council on Competitiveness (COC). 1994. *Breaking the Barriers to the National Information Infrastructure.* Council on Competitiveness, Washington, D.C., December.

Cowen & Company. 1995. *Industry Strategies, Data Networking Industry: Internet Mania.* Cowen & Company, September 5.

Cox, Donald C. 1995. "Wireless Personal Communications: What Is It?," *IEEE Personal Communications,* April, pp. 20-35.

Cross-Industry Working Team. 1994a. *An Architectural Framework for the National Information Infrastructure.* Cross-Industry Working Team, Corporation for National Research Initiatives, Reston, Va., September.

Cross-Industry Working Team. 1994b. *Electronic Cash, Tokens and Payments in the National Information Infrastructure.* Cross-Industry Working Team, Corporation for National Research Initiatives, September.

Csenger, Michael. 1995. "Fore Leads ATM Monitoring Charge," *Network World,* June 12, p. 6.

Darby Associates. 1995. "Regulation and Shareholder Value: An Organizing Framework," *Communications Business & Finance,* May 12, p. 14.

Durlach, N.I., and A.S. Mavor, eds. 1995. *Virtual Reality: Scientific and Technological Challenges.* National Academy Press, Washington, D.C.

Economides, Nicholas. 1994. "The Economics of Networks." EC-94-24. A white paper available from the Leonard N. Stern School of Business, New York University.

Economides, Nicholas, and Charles Himmelberg. 1995. "Critical Mass and Network Size with Application to the U.S. FAX Market," a white paper available from the Leonard N. Stern School of Business, New York University, New York.

Economides, Nicholas, and Lawrence J. White. 1994. "One-Way Networks, Two-Way Networks, Compatibility, and Public Policy," A white paper available from the Leonard N. Stern School of Business, New York University.

The Economist. 1993. "A Survey of Telecommunications: The End of the Line," October 23.

The Economist. 1995. "A Survey of the Internet: The Accidental Superhighway," July 1.

EDGE: Workgroup Computing Report, April 3, 1995, p. 21.

Electronic Government Report. 1995. "Do You Know Your D-U-N-S? Dun & Bradstreet Systems Gains Prominence for Electronic Commerce," April 28, p. 11.

Electronic Industries Association and Telecommunications Industry Association. 1994. *EIA and TIA White Paper on National Information Infrastructure.* Electronic Industries Association and Telecommunications Industry Association, Washington, D.C.

Electronic Mail & Messaging Systems. 1995. "EMMS Quarterly Mailbox Census," July 24, pp. 3-5.

Electronic Marketplace Report. 1995. "Physicians Online Service Prospers," August 22, p. 6.

Elliott, Stuart. 1995a. "A Study by Four Agencies Paints a Surprising Portrait of Interactive Computer Users," *New York Times,* September 25, p. D9.

Elliott, Stuart. 1995b. "Hotwired Gets Nielsen to Rate Its Cyberspace Auditing to Help Advertisers Feel Comfortable," *New York Times,* June 19, p. D8.

Elliott, Stuart. 1995c. "The Internet Is Being Used Because, as an Executive Says, Everyone Wants a Connection to What's New," *New York Times,* April 24, p. D10.

Eriksson, Hans. 1994. "MBone: The Multicast Backbone," *Communications of the ACM* 37(8):54-60.

Farhi, Paul. 1993. "Blockbuster, Bell Atlantic Discussing 'Video-on-Demand' Deal," *Washington Post,* January 20, p. G1.

Farhi, Paul. 1995. "Dishing Up the Business Gets Tougher," *Washington Post,* September 6, pp. G1 and G3.

Farrell, Joseph, and Carl Shapiro. 1992. "Standard Setting in High Definition Television," *Brookings Papers on Economic Activity: Microeconomics,* Martin Neil Baily and Clifford Winston (eds.). Brookings Institution, Washington, D.C.

Federal Communications Commission (FCC). 1994. *Statistics of Communications Common Carriers, 1993/1994* edition. U.S. Government Printing Office, Washington, D.C.

Feinmore, Charles, Bruce Field, Howard Frank, Elden Georg, Michael Papillo, Glenn Reitmeier, Will Stackhouse, and Craig Van Degrift (Workshop Program Committee). 1994. *Report on the Workshop on Advanced Digital Video in the National Information Infrastructure.* NISTR 5457. National Institute of Standards and Technology, U.S. Department of Commerce, Washington, D.C.

Feller, Gordon. 1995. "Management Strategies: Users and Vendors to Split Cost of Multimedia Apps Development," *Network World,* May 15, p. 45.

Firestone, Charles M., and Jorge Reina Schement (eds.). 1995. *Toward an Information Bill of Rights & Responsibilities.* Aspen Institute, Washington, D.C.

Fitzgerald, Michael. 1995. "FCC Inks ISDN Price-cut Plan," *Computerworld,* June 5, p. 15.

Flanagan, J.L. 1994. "Speech Communication—An Overview," in *Voice Communication Between Humans and Machines,* D.V. Roe and J. Wilpon (eds.). National Academy Press, Washington, D.C.

Flynn, Laurie. 1995. "Intuit Gets 19 Contracts for Home-Banking Software," *New York Times,* July 15, p. 39.

Freedman, David H. 1994. "A Romance Blossoms Between Gray Matter and Silicon," *Science,* Vol. 265, August 12, pp. 889-890.

Friedman, Clifford H. 1994. *New Age Media II.* Bear Stearns, New York, November.

Frost & Sullivan. 1995. *U.S. Fiber-in-the-loop Markets.* Frost & Sullivan, April.

Garcia, O.N., with A.J. Goldschen and E. Petajan. 1994. "Continuous Optical Automatic Speech Recognition by Lipreading," in *Proceedings of the Twenty-Eighth Annual Asilomar Conference on Signals, Systems, and Computers,* October 31-November 2, Pacific Grove, Calif.

Gebase, Len, and Steve Trus. 1994. *Analyzing Electronic Commerce.* National Institute of Standards and Technology Special Publication 500-218. U.S. Government Printing Office, Washington, D.C.

General Accounting Office. 1987. *Telephone Communications: Controlling Cross-Subsidy Between Regulated and Competitive Services.* GAO/RCED-88-34. General Accounting Office, Washington, D.C., October.

General Accounting Office. 1994. *Information Superhighway: Issues Affecting Development.* GAO/RCED-94-285. General Accounting Office, Washington, D.C., September 30.

Gilder, George. 1994. "Telecosm: The Bandwidth Tidal Wave," *Forbes ASAP,* December 5, pp. 163-177.

Gillin, Paul. 1995. "Best of Browser Breed Bows," *Computerworld,* June 26, p. 56.

Global Telecommunications Infrastructure Research Project. 1994. *Building the National Information Infrastructure in K-12 Education: A Comprehensive Survey of Attitudes Towards Linking Both Sides of the Desk.* Center for Telecommunications Management, University of Southern California, Los Angeles, Calif, April.

Goff, Leslie. 1995. "Internet Options Everywhere," *Computerworld,* July 24, p. 96.

Goldman, Kevin. 1995. "Advertising: Now Marketers Can Buy a Service to Track Internet Customer Usage," *Wall Street Journal,* April 5, p. B5.

Greif, Irene (ed.). 1988. *Computer-Supported Cooperative Work: A Book of Readings.* Morgan Kaufmann, San Mateo, Calif.

Halper, Mark. 1995. "Another IRS Insanity," *Forbes ASAP,* August 28, pp. 26-28.

Hamlin, Suzanne. 1995. "Time Flies, But Where Does It Go?" *New York Times,* September 6, pp. C1 and C6.

Hamm, Steve. 1995. "Apple's Spindler Lifts Veil on Pippin Technology," *PC Week Online,* December 4, accessible via http://www.zdnet.com/~pcweek/news/1204/o4ham.html.

Hansell, Saul. 1994. "Banks Go Interactive to Beat the Rush of Services," *New York Times,* October 19, pp. D1 and D4.

Hansell, Saul. 1995a. "Citibank Will End Most Fees on Electronic Transactions," *New York Times,* May 24, pp. D1-D2.

Hansell, Saul. 1995b. "Credit Cards on Internet Given a Lift," *New York Times,* June 24, p. 35.

Hardy, Eric S. 1995. "Technobubble," *Forbes,* September 25, pp. 206-208.

Hart, Oliver, and Jean Tirole. 1990. "Vertical Integration and Market Foreclosure," *Brookings Papers on Economic Activity: Microeconomics, 1990,* Martin Neil Baily and Clifford Winston (eds.). Brookings Institution, Washington, D.C., pp. 205-287.

Hayes, Mary. 1995. "CompuServe Tests ISDN: Adoption May be Slow, Even if Users Clamor," *InformationWeek,* October 9, p. 98.

Henderson, John. 1995. "Economic Multi-format Decoding in the Home Receiver," an unpublished white paper prepared for Hitachi America, August 29.

Hertz, Frank. 1995. "High-speed Connections: Faster Speeds, New Modem Standards Keep Your Customers On-line," *VARbusiness,* April 1, p. 119.

Higgins, Kelly Jackson. 1995a. "TCP/IP Becoming Standard Equipment in NOSes, OSes: Various Levels of Support Are Available Today, but the Trend Is to Integrate the Protocol Stack at the Factory," *Network World,* May 29, p. L11-L16.

Higgins, Steve. 1995b. "Is Sell Now, Profit Later Right Internet Strategy?," *Investor's Daily,* October 24, p. A8.

Hodge, Winston William. 1994. *Interactive Television: A Comprehensive Guide for Multimedia Technologists.* McGraw-Hill Visual Technology Series, McGraw-Hill Inc., New York.

Hodge, Winston, and Chuck Milligan. 1994. "True Video on Demand vs. Near Video on Demand: Statistical Modeling, Cost, and Performance Trade-offs," *1994 NCTA Technical Papers.* National Cable Television Association, Washington, D.C.

Hoffman, Thomas, and Mitch Betts. 1994. "Bank Law to Spur IS Revamps," *Computerworld,* September 19, pp. 1 and 127.

Infonetics Research Inc. 1994. *The Emerging Remote Access Market.* Infonetics Research Inc, San Jose, Calif., June.

Information & Interactive Services Report. 1995a. "NCSA Sets New Standard for Browser Power: Latest Beta a Revolutionary Change," May 5, pp. 5-6.

Information & Interactive Services Report. 1995b. "SPRY Names 24 Partners for Internet Direct Program," May 5, pp. 6-7.

Information & Interactive Services Report. 1995c. "TCI Takes Aim at Internet Service for Residences and Business: New Venture With Venture Capital Firm Uses Hybrid System for Home Access," May 19, pp. 3-5.

Information Infrastructure Task Force (IITF). 1993. *The National Information Infrastructure: Agenda for Action.* Information Infrastructure Task Force, U.S. Department of Commerce, Washington, D.C., September 15.

Information Infrastructure Task Force (IITF). 1994. *National Information Infrastructure— Progress Report: September 1993 –September 1994.* Information Infrastructure Task Force, U.S. Department of Commerce, Washington, D.C., September 13.

Information Infrastructure Task Force (IITF). 1995. *Global Information Infrastructure: Agenda for Cooperation.* Information Infrastructure Task Force, U.S. Department of Commerce, Washington, D.C., February.

Interactive Multimedia Association (IMA). 1994. *IMA Inter-Industry Set-top Summit.* Report of a workshop held April 21 in Arlington, Va. Interactive Multimedia Association, Annapolis, Md., May 23.

Intercast. 1995. "Leaders in PC, Broadcast, and Cable Industries Announce Formation of Industry Group to Promote New Digital Medium for the Home PC," press release dated October 16, available from http://www.intercast.org.

International Data Corporation (IDC). 1995a. "IS Priorities: As the Information Highway Era Begins," a white paper and special advertising supplement appearing in *Computerworld,* May 22.

International Data Corporation (IDC). 1995b. *LAN Penetration and Implementation Plans: 1995 Global IT Survey Results.* International Data Corporation, Framingham, Mass.

International Data Corporation (IDC). 1995c. *Modem Market Forecast, 1994-1999,* press release dated October 5, 1995 available on-line from http://www.idcresearch.com.

International Data Corporation (IDC). 1995d. *PC NIC Market Forecast, 1994-1995.* International Data Corporation, Framingham, Mass.

International Data Corporation (IDC). 1995e. *Portable LAN Connectivity Market Forecast, 1994-1999.* International Data Corporation, Framingham, Mass.

International Data Corporation (IDC). 1995f. *Preliminary LAN Hub Market Forecast, 1995-1999.* International Data Corporation, Framingham, Mass.

Jackson, William. 1995. "SSA Begins Kiosk Info Pilot; Transactions Will Come," *Government Computer News,* July 17, p. 9.

Kahin, Brian (ed.). 1994. *Information Infrastructure Sourcebook: Version 4.0.* Center for Science and International Affairs, John F. Kennedy School of Government, Harvard University, Cambridge, Mass.

Kahin, Brian, and Janet Abbate (eds.). 1995. *Standards Policy for Information Infrastructure.* Harvard Information Infrastructure Project, MIT Press, Cambridge, Mass.

Kahn, Alfred E., and William E. Taylor. 1994. "The Pricing of Inputs Sold to Competitors: A Comment," *Yale Journal on Regulation,* Vol. 11, pp. 225-240.

Katz, Michael L., and Carl Shapiro. 1994. "Systems Competition and Network Effects," *Journal of Economic Perspectives* 8(2):93-115.

Katz, Randy H. 1995. "Adaptation and Mobility in Wireless Information Systems," an unpublished white paper available from http://daedalus.cs.berkeley.edu, version dated August 18.

Keegan, Paul. 1995. "The Digerati!," *New York Times Magazine,* May 21, pp. 38-45 and 86-88.

Kessler, Andrew J. 1995. "Out at the Top, II," *Forbes,* September 25, p. 200.

Kirkpatrick, David. 1994. "How PCs Will Take Over Your Home," *Fortune,* February 21, pp. 100-104.

Kobb, B.Z. 1993. "Personal Wireless," *IEEE Spectrum,* June, p. 25.

Krause, Reinhardt. 1995. "Improved ADSL Compression Lures Semiconductor Firms," *Electronic News,* April 10, p. 8.

Kraushaar, Jonathan M. 1995a. *Fiber Deployment Update: End of Year 1994.* Federal Communications Commission, Washington, D.C., July.

Kraushaar, Jonathan M. 1995b. *Infrastructure of the Local Operating Companies Aggregated to the Holding Company Level.* Federal Communications Commission, Washington, D.C., April.

Kraut, R., W. Scherlis, T. Mukhopadhyay, J. Manning, and S. Kiesler. 1996. "Homenet: A Field Trial of Residential Internet Services," *Proceedings of CHI '96.* Association of Computing Machinery, New York, forthcoming.

KRT Graphics. 1995. "PCs and Income," *Washington Post,* April 20, p. B13.

Landler, Mark. 1995. "The Dishes Are Coming: Satellites Go Suburban," *New York Times,* May 29, pp. 37 and 40.

Lefkin, Peter. 1995. "IISP—Brief Summary of IISP Identified NII/GII Standards Needs," e-mail message to IISP mailing list dated November 27.

Lewis, Peter. 1995. "On the Net: Another Survey of Internet Users Is Out, and This One Has Statistical Credibility," *New York Times,* October 30, p. D5.

Libicki, Martin C. 1994. *Standards: The Rough Road to the Common Byte.* Program on Information Resources Policy (Center for Information Policy Research and Harvard University), Cambridge, Mass., October.

Liebowitz, S.J., and Stephen E. Margolis. 1994. "Network Externality: An Uncommon Tragedy," *Journal of Economic Perspectives* 8(2):133-150.

Lindstrom, Annie. 1995a. "Bell Atlantic Puts Video Architecture Plans On Hold," *Telephony,* May 1, p. 6.

Lindstrom, Annie. 1995b. "New Cable Modems Ready for Blast-off," *Telephony,* May 22, p. 20.

Lindstrom, Annie. 1995c. "US West Decides to Put Video Dial-tone Plans on Ice," *Telephony,* June 5, p. 6.

Lippman, John. 1995. "Pacific Telesis and Times Mirror End On-line Venture Due to Market Changes," *Wall Street Journal,* October 23, p. B9.

Lucky, Robert W. 1995. "Reflections: Where Did the Web Come From?," *IEEE Spectrum,* July, p. 15.

MacKie-Mason, Jeffrey K., and Hal Varian. 1995. "Economic FAQs About the Internet," a white paper available from http://www.sims.berkeley.edu/resources/infoecon/faqs.

Maresca, Thomas. 1995. "Jupiter's Home PC Projections," *Interactive Home,* April, available via http://www.jup.com/edroom/newsletters/cia/cia4-5.htm.

Markoff, John. 1994. "A Rough Start for Digital TV," *New York Times,* September 21, pp. D1, D5.

Markoff, John. 1995. "AT&T Plan Links Internet and Satellites," *New York Times,* October 4, pp. D1 and D4.

McCarthy, Shira. 1995. "Ameritech Switches Network Plans," *Telephony,* July 3, p. 6.

McConnell, Chris. 1995. "Telcos Pushing FCC for VDT Changes," *Broadcasting & Cable,* July 31, p. 39.

McConville, Jim. 1995. "Calling All Cash Cows: Searching for New Revenue Streams," *Broadcasting & Cable,* May 15, p. 22.

McWilliams, Brian. 1995. "Financial Insecurity," *ComputerWorld,* June 26, pp. 79-80 and 84.

McWilliams, Gary, with Peter Burrows, Kathy Rebello, and Larry Armstrong. 1995. "PCS: The Battle for the Homefront," *Business Week,* September 25, pp. 110-114.

Mehta, Stephanie N. 1994. "IndustryNet Puts Businesses in Fast Lane," *Wall Street Journal,* October 11, p. B2.

Messmer, Ellen. 1995a. "Banks Set Up Net for Electronic Payments," *Network World,* May 8, pp. 6 and 78.

Messmer, Ellen. 1995b. "NaviSoft Offers Server, Authoring Tool for Web," *Network World,* June 26, p. 31.

Messmer, Ellen. 1995c. "UUNET Encryptor Offers Users Secure Internet Communications," *Network World,* May 29, p. 45.

Mills, Mike. 1995a. "Bell Atlantic Metering Plan Falls Flat," *Washington Post,* October 16, pp. 15 and 20 of the Business Section.

Mills, Mike. 1995b. "Interactive TV: The Leap Looks a Long Way Off," *Washington Post,* July 2, pp. H1 and H4.

Mills, Mike. 1995c. "Video on Demand: Still on Hold," *Washington Post,* December 9, pp. A1 and A14.

Mills, Mike, and Paul Farhi. 1995. "Bell Atlantic to Shift to 'Wireless Cable' TV," *Washington Post,* May 17, pp. F1-F2.

Morris, Charles R., and Charles H. Ferguson. 1993. "How Architecture Wins Technology Wars," *Harvard Business Review* 71(2):86-96.

Mossberg, Walter S. 1995. "Personal Technology," *Wall Street Journal*, July 27, p. B1.

Naik, Gautam. 1995a. "A Lot of Little Hassles Slow Spread of Wireless Network," *Wall Street Journal*, May 11, pp. B1-B4.

Naik, Gautam. 1995b. "AT&T to Give 110,000 Schools Free Services," *Wall Street Journal*, November 1, pp. A3 and A8.

National Cable Television Association (NCTA). 1993. *Cable Television and America's Telecommunications Infrastructure*. National Cable Television Association, Washington, D.C., April.

National Institute of Standards and Technology (NIST). 1994a. *Framework for National Information Infrastructure Services (Draft)*. National Institute of Standards and Technology, U.S. Department of Commerce, Gaithersburg, Md., July.

National Institute of Standards and Technology (NIST). 1994b. *Networking, Telecommunications and Information Technology: The Requirements of U.S. Industry*. Proceedings of the Advanced Technology Program workshop held August 30-31, Gaithersburg, Md., U.S. Department of Commerce, Washington, D.C.

National Institute of Standards and Technology (NIST). 1994c. *Report on the Workshop on Advanced Digital Video in the National Information Infrastructure*. U.S. Department of Commerce, Washington, D.C.

National Research Council. 1995. *Standards, Conformity Assessment, and Trade*. National Academy Press, Washington D.C.

National Telecommunications and Information Administration (NTIA). 1991. *The NTIA Infrastructure Report: Telecommunications in the Age of Information*. U.S. Department of Commerce, Washington, D.C., October.

National Telecommunications and Information Administration. 1994. *20/20 Vision: The Development of a National Information Infrastructure*. U.S. Department of Commerce, Washington, D.C., March.

Network Security Standards Oversight Group, President's National Security Telecommunications Advisory Committee. 1994. *Network Security Standards for the Public Switched Network: Issues and Recommendations*. President's National Security Telecommunications Advisory Committee, Washington, D.C., October.

New York Times. 1995. "Chase Introducing New Electronic-Banking Account," *New York Times*, June 13, p. D23.

New York Times. 1995. "The Information 'Have Nots,'" September 5, p. A16.

North American Telecommunications Association (NATA). 1995. *1995 Telecommunications Market Review and Forecast*. NATA, Washington, D.C.

O'Brien, Timothy L. 1995. "Home Banking: Will It Take Off This Time?" *Wall Street Journal*, June 8, pp. B1 and B7.

Office of the Vice President. 1993. *Creating a Government That Works Better & Costs Less: Reengineering Through Information Technology (Accompanying Report of the National Performance Review)*. U.S. Government Printing Office, Washington, D.C., September.

Office of Technology Assessment (OTA). 1995. *Wireless Technologies and the National Information Infrastructure*. U.S. Government Printing Office, Washington, D.C., July.

Olsen, J.S., S. Card, T. Landauer, G.M. Olsen, T. Malone, and J. Leggett. 1993. "Computer-supported Cooperative Work: Research Issues for the 90s," *Behavior and Information Technology* 12, 115-129.

Peyton, David. 1994. *The National Information Infrastructure—Overcoming the Obstacles: Financial, Regulatory, and Technical*. Information Technology Association of America, Arlington, Va., September.

Plantec, Peter. 1995. "MPEG-2: The New World Standard for High-quality Digital Video," an advertisement supplement in *InformationWeek*, September 25, between pp. 85 and 86.

Poppel, Harvey, and Craig Marino. 1995. "The Wireless Melting Pot," *Telephony*, July 24, pp. 30-35.

Rattay, K. 1994. "Wireless Messaging," *AT&T Technical Journal*, May/June.

Reed, David P. 1995. "The Transition to Digital Television Distribution Systems: A Technological View of Expected Interoperability," a white paper presented at *1995 Telecommunications Policy Research Conference*, Solomons, Md., October 1.

Report on Electronic Commerce. 1995a. "Interactive Advertising," July 11, p. 13.

Report on Electronic Commerce. 1995b. "Intuit Unleashes Fall Lineup: Command of Market With Quicken Spurs Microsoft into Giving Money Away," July 25, pp. 1-2, 12-14.

Report on Electronic Commerce. 1995c. "The Taxman Cometh OnLine," June 13, pp. 1-2, 7, and 14-16.

Rigdon, Joan E. 1995a. "Blame Retailers for Web's Slow Start as a Mall," *Wall Street Journal*, August 16, pp. B1 and B5.

Rigdon, Joan E. 1995b. "Netscape Must Turn Business Strategy Upside Down to Sustain Enthusiasm," *Wall Street Journal*, August 11, p. A3.

Robichaux, Mark. 1995a. "Cable-TV Firms Wonder If It's Time to Get Hooked Up," *Wall Street Journal*, August 3, p. B4.

Robichaux, Mark. 1995b. "On-line Push Being Readied by Cable Firms," *Wall Street Journal*, November 29, pp. A3-A4.

Rohde, David. 1995a. "Desktop Computer-telephone Integration: Fact or Fiction?" *Technology Update*, May 15, p. 35.

Rohde, David. 1995b. "Once out of Reach, T-3 Lines Zoom as Local Access Option," *NetworkWorld*, May 15, pp. 1, 8.

Samuels, Gary. 1995. "Crowded Skies," *Forbes*, May 22, pp. 98-100.

Sandberg, Jared. 1995a. "AT&T Is Still Missing Its Internet Voice: Phone Giant Hasn't Divulged Strategy for New Market," *Wall Street Journal*, June 16, p. B7.

Sandberg, Jared. 1995b. "Netscape Has Technical Whiz in Andreessen," *Wall Street Journal*, August 11, pp. B1-B2.

Sandberg, Jared. 1995c. "On-Line Services' User Counts Often Aren't What They Seem" *Wall Street Journal*, October 6, pp. B1 and B6.

Sandberg, Jared. 1995d. "On-Line Population Reaches 24 Million in North America," *Wall Street Journal*, October 30, p. B3.

Schwartz, Evan I. 1995. "People Are Supposed to Pay for This Stuff?" *Wired*, July, pp. 148-153, 187, 190-191.

Shaffer, Richard A. 1995. "Speed Freaks: Try ISDN Now," *Forbes*, November 6, p. 348.

Shank, Gary. 1993. "Abductive Multiloguing: The Semiotic Dynamics of Navigating the Net," *Electronic Journal on Virtual Culture* 1(1).

Shapiro, Eben. 1995. "Time Warner Wins Cellular Customers in Rochester, N.Y.," *Wall Street Journal*, July 3, p. B8.

Shapiro, Eben, and Mark Robichaux. 1995. "Time Warner to Put a Town On-Line in Test of Service," *Wall Street Journal*, July 18, p. B5.

Shenon, Philip. 1995. "2-Edged Sword: Asian Regimes on the Internet," *New York Times*, May 29, pp. 1 and 40.

SIMBA Information Inc. 1995. *Online Services: 1994 Review Trends & Forecast Update*. SIMBA Information Inc., Wilton, Conn.

Simnett, Richard, Thomas R. Spacek, and Padmanabhan Srinagesh. 1995. "An Economic Analysis of the Claimed Applicability of the Bill and Keep Interconnection Arrangement to Local Telecommunications Competition," an unpublished white paper available from Bell Communications Research, Morristown, New Jersey.

Singletary, Michelle. 1995. "Now Home May Be Where the Bank Is," *Washington Post*, January 16, business section, p. 1.

Skrzycki, Cindy. 1993. "Data Highway Plan Costs May Decline: Cheaper Systems May Edge Out Fiber-Optics," *Washington Post,* January 20, p. G1.

Sullivan-Trainor, Michael L. 1995. "The Internet Page: Serving up the Web: Financial, Technical, and Security Barriers Limit In-house Management," *Computerworld,* May 15, p. 62.

Swisher, Kara. 1995. "Internet's Reach in Society Grows, Survey Finds," *Washington Post,* October 31, pp. A1 and A6.

Taubes, Gary. 1994a. "Do Immunologists Dream of Electric Mice?," *Science,* Vol. 265, August 12, pp. 886-888.

Taubes, Gary. 1994b. "Taking the Data in Hand 'Literally' with Virtual Reality," *Science,* Vol. 265, August 12, pp. 884-886.

Technology Policy Working Group (TPWG), Information Infrastructure Task Force. 1994. "Services and the National Information Infrastructure," draft for public comment. Technology Policy Working Group, Washington, D.C., December 2.

Technology Policy Working Group (TPWG), Information Infrastructure Task Force. 1995a. "A Process for Government Selection of Standards for Its National Information Infrastructure (NII) Activities," draft for public comment. Technology Policy Working Group, Washington, D.C., December 14.

Technology Policy Working Group (TPWG), Information Infrastructure Task Force. 1995b. "Advanced Digital Video and the National Information Infrastructure," draft for public comment. Technology Policy Working Group, Washington, D.C., February 15.

Telco Competition Reports. 1994a. "LECs, Competitors Debate Interconnection, Compensation Plans at Washington Conference," December 8, pp. 2-5.

Telco Competition Reports. 1994b. "State Update: Michigan PSC Orders Interconnection Trials, Denies Request to Mandate Interim Arrangements," December 8, p. 5.

Telecommunications Reports. 1994. "U S West Revises Its Video Dial-Tone Assumptions," June 6, pp. 19-21.

Telecommunications Reports. 1995a. "ANTEC Gets Service Contract with Pacific Telesis," July 24, p. 7.

Telecommunications Reports. 1995b. "Bell Atlantic to Expand Virginia Video Dial-Tone Trial," May 29, p. 31.

Telecommunications Reports. 1995c. "Bell Atlantic Won't Resubmit VDT Plans Soon," May 29, pp. 30-31.

Telecommunications Reports. 1995d. "BellSouth Proposes Integrated Phone/Video Network," July 24, p. 7.

Telecommunications Reports. 1995e. "Bill Would Overhaul Info Technology Procurement," June 26, p. 25.

Telecommunications Reports. 1995f. "Broadcasters Differ over Digital TV Standards," July 10, pp. 22-23.

Telecommunications Reports. 1995g. "Coalition Issues Draft Worldwide Digital Standard," June 26, p. 25.

Telecommunications Reports. 1995h. "Companies Plan to Offer TV Services over PCs," July 24, p. 4.

Telecommunications Reports. 1995i. "Local Exchange Competition Is Decade Away, Report Says," June 19, p. 37.

Telecommunications Reports. 1995j. "NTIA Urges FCC to Act on Wireless Data Petitions," November 6, pp. 40-41.

Telecommunications Reports. 1995k. "Pacific Bell to Offer 'First' Integrated FSN Network," July 24, pp. 3-4.

Telecommunications Reports. 1995l. "Parties View Redacted VDT Tariff as Insufficient," May 29, p. 31.

Telecommunications Reports. 1995m. "Restrictive FCC Rules Could Be Death Knell for VDT Service, Broad Coalition Warns," July 24, pp. 5-6.

Telecommunications Reports. 1995n. "Video Inquiry Highlights Telcos' Apprehension About VDT Service, Dispute over Program Access," July 10, pp. 18-21.

Templin, Neal. 1995. "Santa Brought Many Gizmos for the Internet," *Wall Street Journal,* December 26, pp. B1 and B3.

Texas Education Network. 1995. *Networks for Goals 2000 Reform: Bringing the Internet to K-12 Schools.* Southwest Educational Development Library, Austin, Tex.

Timmins, Annmarie. 1995. "Messaging Vendors Back 'Net Security Standards," *Network World,* July 24, p. 14.

Trachtenberg, Jeffrey A., and Mark Robichaux. 1995. "Bell Alliance to Buy Over $1 Billion of Set-Top Boxes to Offer Wireless TV," *Wall Street Journal,* September 22, p. B3.

Tye, William B. 1994. "The Pricing of Inputs Sold to Competitors: A Response," *Yale Journal on Regulation,* Vol. 11, pp. 203-224.

U.S. Bureau of the Census, Current Business Reports. 1995. *Annual Survey of Communication Services: 1993.* U.S. Government Printing Office, Washington, D.C.

Vernon, Mary K., Edward D. Lazowska, and Steward D. Personick (eds.). 1994. *R&D for the NII: Technical Challenges.* EDUCOM, Washington, D.C.

Veronis, Suhler & Associates. 1994. *Communications Industry Forecast: 1994-1998.* Veronis, Suhler & Associates, New York, July.

Veronis, Suhler & Associates. 1995. *Communications Industry Forecast: 1995-1999.* Veronis, Suhler & Associates, New York, July.

Vin, Harrick M., et al. 1991. "Hierarchical Conferencing Architectures for Inter-Group Multimedia Collaboration," in *Proceedings of the ACM Conference on Organizational Computing Systems,* November, Atlanta, Ga.

Waldrop, M. Mitchell. 1994a. "Culture Shock on the Networks," *Science,* Vol. 265, pp. 879-881.

Waldrop, M. Mitchell. 1994a. "Software Agents Prepare to Sift the Riches of Cyberspace," *Science,* Vol. 265, pp. 882-883.

Wallace, Bob. 1992. "Study Raises Concerns About National ISDN," *Global Services,* June 29, pp. 27-28.

Wallace, Bob. 1995. "AT&T, Sprint to Offer Nationwide T-1 ATM," *Infoworld,* February 27, p. 1.

Wall Street Journal. 1995a. "FutureShop: No Cash Accepted; Microchip-Card Purchases Only," July 13.

Wall Street Journal. 1995b. "Microchip Cash Card May Replace Coins, Bank Notes, and Credit Cards," July 13, p. B7.

Wall Street Journal. 1995c. "Oracle Plans to Sell Network Computer," October 6, p. B7.

Wall Street Journal. 1995d. "SNET Is Seeking to Offer Video, Interactive Services," April 28, p. B5.

Warner, Fara. 1995. "On-Line Services Try to Define Their Identities," *Wall Street Journal,* July 12, p. B1.

Watt, Peggy. 1995. "Nomadic Users Have Growing Field of Choices," *Network World,* July 10, p. L4.

Wexler, Joanie. 1995a. "Carriers Build Nets for Electronic Commerce," *Network World,* May 15, p. 15.

Wexler, Joanie. 1995b. "PCS Players Mull Network Compatibility Issues," *Network World,* June 12, p. 6.

Wildstrom, Stephen. 1995. "Phone Circuits to the Fast Lane," *Business Week,* February 27, p. 28.

Wilpon, J., L. Rabiner, C.-H. Lee, and E. Goldman. 1990. "Automatic Recognition of Keywords in Unconstrained Speech Using Hidden Markov Models," *IEEE Transactions on Acoustics, Speech, and Signal Processing,* ASSP-38, November, pp. 1870-1878.

Winslow, Ron. 1994. "A Trip to the Mayo Clinic Via Information Highway," *Wall Street Journal,* October 17, 1994, pp. B1 and B7.

Wirbel, Loring. 1995. "WANs Focus on Home and Small Office Market," *Electronic Engineering Times,* March 27, p. 40.

Wireless Information Networks Forum (WINForum). 1995. "Petition for Rulemaking," *In the Matter of Allocation of Spectrum in the 5.1 to 5.35 GHz Band and Adopt Service Rules for a Shared Unlicensed Personal Radio Network.* Presented before the Federal Communications Commission, Washington, D.C., May 24.

Wireless Messaging Report. 1994. "Survey Predicts Boom in Sales of Wireless LANs: School, Industry, Health Markets Eyed," November 8, p. 15.

Wireless Messaging Report. 1995a. "FCC Proposes 900 MHz SMR Auction Rules, Divides Spectrum," May 9, p. 11.

Wireless Messaging Report. 1995b. "New Spectrum Rules Adopted in FCC's 'Refarming' Proceeding," July 4, p. 9.

Wireless Messaging Report. 1995c. "Paging Industry Adds 7.5 Million Customers in 1994," July 4, p. 5.

Wireless Messaging Report. 1995d. "PCS Licenses: Carriers Pay a High Price for Their PCS Licenses," May 9, pp. 6-11.

Wireless Messaging Report. 1995e. "Wireless Data Predicted to Have Mass Marketing Turnaround," July 4, pp. 3-4, 15.

Yankee Group. 1995a. *Honing the Competitive Edge: The Public Network Access Market and Integrated Access Devices.* Yankee Group Data Communications Service, Bolton, Mass., April.

Yankee Group. 1995b. *Out in the RAIN: The Remote Area Internetworking Market.* Yankee Group Data Communications Service, Bolton, Mass., February.

Zelnick, Nate. 1994. "Microsoft Takes the OnLine Plunge; How Big Will the Splash Be?," *Information & Interactive Services Report,* November 18, pp. 1-2 and 14-20.

Ziegler, Bart. 1995a. "IBM to Make Low-Cost PC for Networks," *Wall Street Journal,* November 14, p. B19.

Ziegler, Bart. 1995b. "Publishers Scramble into On-Line Services, But Payoff Is Unclear," *Wall Street Journal,* April 26, pp. A1 and A6.

Ziegler, Bart. 1995c. "Staid Phone Giants Try Marriage to Hollywood," *Wall Street Journal,* May 24, pp. B1 and B10.

Zuckerman, Laurence. 1995. "With Internet Cachet, Not Profit, A New Stock Amazes Wall Street," *New York Times,* August 10, pp. A1 and B1.

Appendixes

A

Workshop Participants and Agenda

PARTICIPANTS

Duane Adams, Advanced Research Projects Agency
Robert J. Aiken, Department of Energy/Lawrence Livermore National
   Laboratory
Robert C. Atkinson, Teleport Communications Group
David J. Barram, Department of Commerce
Tora K. Bikson, RAND Corporation
Alan R. Blatecky, MCNC
Robert J. Bonometti, Office of Science and Technology Policy
Cynthia H. Braddon, The McGraw Hill Companies
Lewis M. Branscomb, Harvard University
Vito Brugliera, Zenith Electronics Corporation
James H. Burrows, National Institute of Standards and Technology
James A. Chiddix, Time Warner Cable
Yi-Tzuu Chien, National Science Foundation
Melvyn Ciment, National Science Foundation
David D. Clark, Massachusetts Institute of Technology
Mark Corbitt, Federal Communications Commission
Michael Corrigan, General Services Administration
George Cotter, National Security Agency
D. Joseph Donahue, Thomson Consumer Electronics
H. Allen Ecker, Scientific-Atlanta Incorporated
Joseph A. Flaherty, CBS Incorporated

Howard Frank, Advanced Research Projects Agency
Bernard R. Gifford, Academic Systems Corporation
Paul E. Green, Jr., IBM T.J. Watson Research Center
Richard R. Green, Cable Television Laboratories Incorporated
Michael D. Greenbaum, Bell Atlantic Corporation
Allen S. Hammond, New York Law School
Daniel Hitchcock, Department of Energy
Sally E. Howe, National Coordination Office for High Performance
    Computing and Communications
Paul E. Hunter, National Aeronautics and Space Administration
Laura M. Jennings, Microsoft Corporation
Brian Kahin, J.F. Kennedy School of Government, Harvard University
Richard T. Liebhaber, MCI Communications Corporation
Robert W. Lucky, Bell Communications Research
Marina M. Mann, Electric Power Research Institute
Eric K. Marcus, Commerce Clearing House Incorporated
Michael J. Marcus, Federal Communications Commission
Clement J. McDonald, Regenstrief Institute for Health Center
James C. McKinney, Advanced Television Systems Committee
David G. Messerschmitt, University of California at Berkeley
Avram C. Miller, Intel Corporation
Graham Mobley, Scientific-Atlanta Incorporated
Mahal Mohan, AT&T Corporation
Lloyd N. Morrisett, John and Mary Markle Foundation
Michael R. Nelson, Office of Science and Technology Policy
Richard E. Ottinger (retired), Georgia Public Telecommunications
    Commission
Michael A. Papillo, Houston Associates Incorporated
Stewart D. Personick, Bell Communications Research
Anthony M. Rutkowski, Internet Society
Lawrence Seidman, Hughes Telecommunications and Space Sector
Richard S. Sharpe, John A. Hartford Foundation
Donald W. Simborg, KnowMed Systems
J. Marty Tenenbaum, Enterprise Integration Technologies Corporation
    (EIT)/CommerceNet
Shukri Wakid, National Institute of Standards and Technology
Marvin I. Weinberger, Infonautics Corporation
Stephen S. Wolff, Cisco Systems Incorporated

AGENDA

Monday, January 16, 1995

5:30 p.m.   Reception with Project Liaisons

6:00   Dinner

6:45   Welcome: *Lewis Branscomb*, Workshop Chair

Tuesday, January 17, 1995

Participants-at-large (all discussion panels):
Tora Bikson, RAND Corporation
Michael Greenbaum, Bell Atlantic Corporation
Allen Hammond, New York Law School
Brian Kahin, Harvard University
David Messerschmitt, University of California at Berkeley

9:00   Introduction and Charge to Workshop: *Lewis Branscomb*

9:15   TPWG and Its Sponsorship of the NII Technology
              Deployment Project:
              Howard Frank, Advanced Research Projects Agency

9:30   Technology Deployment Scenarios
              Discussion Leader: *Robert Lucky*, Bell Communications
              Research
              Steering Committee Participants:
              James Chiddix, Time Warner Cable
              Joseph Flaherty, CBS Incorporated
              Richard Liebhaber, MCI Communications Corporation
              Invited Participants:
              Robert Atkinson, Teleport Communications Group
              Marina Mann, Electric Power Research Institute
              James McKinney, Advanced Television Systems Committee
              Mahal Mohan, AT&T Corporation
              Richard Ottinger, Georgia Public Telecommunications
                 Commission (retired)
              Stewart Personick, Bell Communications Research
              Lawrence Seidman, Hughes Telecommunications and
                 Space Sector

1:00 p.m.   End-user Hardware/Software Issues
             Discussion Leader: *James Chiddix*, Time Warner Cable
             Invited Participants:
                 Vito Brugliera, Zenith Electronics Corporation
                 Joseph Donahue, Thomson Consumer Electronics
                 Allen Ecker, Scientific-Atlanta Incorporated
                 Richard Green, Cable Television Laboratories Inc.
                 Laura Jennings, Microsoft Corporation
                 Avram Miller, Intel Corporation

3:00   Domain-Specific Applications: Specialized vs.
                 Common Conditions
             Discussion Leaders: *Cynthia Braddon*, The McGraw-Hill
                 Companies, and *Donald Simborg*, KnowMed Systems
             Invited Participants:
                 Education
                     Alan Blatecky, MCNC
                     Bernard Gifford, Academic Systems Corporation
                     Marvin Weinberger, Infonautics Corporation
                 Health care
                     Clement McDonald, Regenstrief Institute
                     Richard Sharpe, John A. Hartford Foundation
                 Publishing
                     Eric Marcus, Commerce Clearing House Inc.

5:00   Day One Concludes

5:15   Reception

6:30   Dinner

7:30   Remarks: *Lewis Branscomb*, Workshop Chair
             Speech: *David Barram*, Deputy Secretary,
                 Department of Commerce

Wednesday, January 18, 1995

9:00   The Internet as an NII Model
            Discussion Leader: *Richard Liebhaber,* MCI Communications
            Steering Committee Participant:
            David Clark, Massachusetts Institute of Technology
            Invited Participants:
            Anthony Rutkowski, Internet Society
            Marty Tenenbaum, EIT/CommerceNet
            Stephen Wolff, Cisco Systems Incorporated

10:45   Dueling Definitions
            Discussion Leader: *David Clark,* Massachusetts Institute of
            Technology
1:00 p.m.   Capstone—NII Technology Deployment:
            Barriers and Drivers
            Discussion Leader: *Joseph Flaherty,* CBS Incorporated

            Members of the Steering Committee and
            Designated Participants

2:45   Springing Forward: Next Steps, White Papers, and the
            May 23-24 Forum

            Members of the Steering Committee
            Plenary Discussion

4:30   Adjourn

B

Forum Participants and Agenda

PARTICIPANTS

Alden Abbott, Department of Commerce

Mike Abel, NEC America

Duane A. Adams, Advanced Research Projects Agency

Robert J. Aiken, Department of Energy/Lawrence Livermore National
Laboratory

Paul Allison, North Communications

Allan J. Arlow, Attorney at Law, Washington, D.C.

Eric M. Aupperle, Merit Network Incorporated

Donald M. Austin, National Coordination Office for High Performance
Computing and Communications

Henriette D. Avram, Library of Congress (retired)

Wendell B. Bailey, National Cable Television Association

Jonathan Band, Morrison and Foerster

John Baras, University of Maryland

Carol Barnes, National Institute of Standards and Technology

Bruce Barrow, Defense Information Systems Agency

Richard Barth, Motorola Incorporated

Herbert Becker, Library of Congress

Scott Behnke, DynCorp

Louis Berger, BBN Systems and Technologies

Henry Bertoni, Polytechnic University, Brooklyn

Kul Bhasin, NASA Lewis Research Center

Charles Billingsley, Information Technology Association of America
Alan R. Blatecky, MCNC
Robert T. Blau, BellSouth Corporation
Robert Bonometti, Office of Science and Technology Policy
Jane Bortnick Griffith, Library of Congress
Heather Boyles, FARNET Incorporated
Cynthia H. Braddon, The McGraw-Hill Companies
George Brandenburg, Harvard University
Anne Wells Branscomb, Harvard University
Lewis M. Branscomb, Harvard University
Tim Brennan, UMBC/Resources for the Future
Charles Brownstein, Corporation for National Research Initiatives/
    Cross-Industry Working Team
Donald P. Brutzman, Naval Postgraduate School
James H. Burrows, National Institute of Standards and Technology
Daniel F. Burton, Council on Competitiveness
Aubrey M. Bush, National Science Foundation
Ty Carter, American Bankers Association
Deborah Castleman, Department of Defense
Lynn Chapman, Raychem Corporation
Nim Cheung, Bell Communications Research
James A. Chiddix, Time Warner Cable
Yi-Tzuu Chien, National Science Foundation
Eliot J. Christian, U.S. Geological Survey
David D. Clark, Massachusetts Institute of Technology
Whit Clay, Capitoline/MS&L
Tim Clifford, DynCorp
Guy Copeland, Computer Sciences Corporation
Mark Corbitt, Federal Communications Commission
Robert R. Cordell, Bell Communications Commission
Michael L. Corrigan, EDS
George Cotter, National Security Agency
Robert W. Crandall, Brookings Institution
John C. Davis, Department of Defense
John Deferrari, U.S. General Accounting Office
Paul Detering, Raychem Corporation
Gilbert Devey, National Science Foundation
D. Joseph Donahue, Thomson Consumer Electronics Incorporated
Norman Douglas, National Communications System
Don Dulchinos, Cable Television Laboratories Incorporated
Lammot du Pont, National Institute of Standards and Technology
H. Allen Ecker, Scientific-Atlanta Incorporated
Dennis W. Elliott, ALOHA Networks Incorporated

Joel Engel, Ameritech
Erik Fair, Apple Computer Incorporated
Maria Farnon, Tufts University
Gerald Faulhaber, University of Pennsylvania
David Feldmeier, Bell Communications Research
Francis Dummer Fisher, University of Texas
Joseph A. Flaherty, CBS Incorporated
Howard Frank, Advanced Research Projects Agency
Barbara Y. Fraser, CERT Coordination Center
Richard B. Friedman, University of Wisconsin Medical School
Cita Furlani, National Institute of Standards and Technology
Donald Fye, GTE Personal Communications Services
Bernard R. Gifford, Academic Systems Corporation
Warren Gifford, Bell Communications Research
John Gilsenan, Department of State
Joseph Gitlin, John Hopkins Medical Institutions
Ross S. Glatzer, Prodigy Services Company (retired)
Norman Glick, National Security Agency
Gayle F. Gordon, Department of the Interior
Diana Gowen, MCI
Paul E. Green, Jr., IBM T.J. Watson Research Center
Richard R. Green, Cable Television Laboratories Incorporated
Michael D. Greenbaum, Bell Atlantic Corporation
Marjorie Greene, First Washington Associates
Irene Greif, Lotus Development Corporation
David Gross, AirTouch Communications Incorporated
Daniel Grulke, Department of Defense
W. Ed Hammond, Duke University Medical Center
Kathryn Hanson, Silicon Graphics
John Harrald, George Washington University
Frank Hartel, National Institutes of Health
Ted Hartson, Post Newsweek Cable
Stephen Haynes, WESTLAW
John Hestenes, National Science Foundation
Jenifer Hill, Capitoline/MS&L
Terence Hill, International Monetary Fund
Lincoln Hoewing, Bell Atlantic
Lee Holcomb, National Aeronautics and Space Administration
Eric S. Hood, NorthwestNet
Edward Horowitz, Viacom Incorporated
Ellis Horowitz, University of Southern California
Sally E. Howe, National Coordination Office for High Performance
    Computing and Communications

Kathleen Huber, Bay Networks
Peter W. Huber, Manhattan Institute for Policy Research
Paul E. Hunter, National Aeronautics and Space Administration
Lionel S. Johns, Office of Science and Technology Policy
David Johnson, CTA Incorporated
Elizabeth Johnston, General Accounting Office
Anita K. Jones, Department of Defense
Charles N. Judice, Bell Atlantic
Brian Kahin, Harvard University
Kevin Kahn, Intel Corporation
Ellen S. Kappel, Joint Oceanographic Institutions Incorporated
James H. Keller, Harvard University
Leonard Kleinrock, University of California at Los Angeles
Ken Klingenstein, University of Colorado at Boulder
Marilyn Kraus, Defense Information Systems Agency
Richard Kuhn, National Institute of Standards and Technology
Henry Lai, General Services Administration
Larry Landweber, University of Wisconsin
Carl E. Landwehr, Naval Research Laboratory
Barry M. Leiner, Advanced Research Projects Agency
Ted Leventhal, Business Research Publications
Martin Libicki, Institute for National Strategic Studies
Richard T. Liebhaber, MCI Communications Corporation
Andrew Lippman, Massachusetts Institute of Technology
Fred Scoresby Long, National Weather Service
Jonathan Low, Department of Labor
Robert W. Lucky, Bell Communications Research
Daniel Lynch, Interop Company and Cybercash Incorporated
David Lytel, Office of Science and Technology Policy
Mary Madigan, Personal Communications Industry Association
John Major, Motorola Incorporated
Marina M. Mann, Electric Power Research Institute
Robert Mason, Case Western Reserve University
Alan McAdams, Cornell University
Lois Clark McCoy, National Institute for Urban Search and Rescue
Jack McDonald, MBX Incorporated
Bernadette McGuire-Rivera, National Telecommunications and
    Information Administration
James McKinney, Advanced Television Systems Committee
Milo Medin, @Home
Michael Melas, IBM Research Division
David G. Messerschmitt, University of California at Berkeley

Jennifer Miller, International Communications Industry Association
Gary J. Minden, Advanced Research Projects Agency
Graham Mobley, Scientific-Atlanta Incorporated
Mahal Mohan, AT&T Corporation
Tracie E. Monk, DynCorp
Frank R. Moore, Institute for Electrical and Electronics Engineers
Lloyd N. Morrisett, John and Mary Markle Foundation
Sushil G. Munshi, Sprint Corporation
Michelle Muth, U.S. Office of Consumer Affairs
Tassos Nakassis, National Institute of Standards and Technology
Paul Narula, AG Communication Systems
Michael North, North Communications
Ann Okerson, Association of Research Libraries
Michael A. Papillo, Houston Associates Incorporated
Gregory L. Parham, Department of Agriculture
Stewart D. Personick, Bell Communications Research
Lawrence P. Petak, Federal Communications Commission
Eugene T. Phillip, National Communications Agency
Ronald W. Piasecki, General Services Administration
Robert S. Powers, MCI Telecommunications Incorporated
Arati Prabhakar, National Institute of Standards and Technology
April Ramey, Department of Treasury
Gordon Ray, NEC America Incorporated
John C. Redmond, GTE Laboratories
Ira Richer, MITRE Corporation
John Philip Riganati, David Sarnoff Research Center
Carl Ripa, Bell Communications Research
Linda G. Roberts, Department of Education
Michael M. Roberts, EDUCOM
Robert Roche, Cellular Telecommunications Industry Association
Thomas C. Rochow, McDonnell Douglas Corporation
Quincy Rodgers, General Instrument Corporation
Jeffrey H. Rohlfs, Strategic Policy Research
Tom Rowbotham, Technology Strategy, BT Centre, London
Jashojit Roy, National Institute of Standards and Technology
Deborah Rudolph, Institute for Electrical and Electronics Engineers
John Ryan, Institute for Electrical and Electronics Engineers
Nora H. Sabelli, National Science Foundation
Damian Saccocio, America Online
Pamela Samuelson, University of Pittsburgh School of Law
Allan M. Schiffman, Terisa Systems/CommerceNet
Gail Garfield Schwartz, Teleport Communications Group

Mary Anne Scott, Department of Energy
Molly Shaffer, Department of Commerce
Richard S. Sharpe, John A. Hartford Foundation
Robert Shepherd, Defense Information Systems Agency
M. Wayne Shiveley, MITRE Corporation
Edward H. Shortliffe, Stanford University School of Medicine
Curtis A. Siller, Jr., AT&T Bell Laboratories
Donald W. Simborg, KnowMed Systems
Karen Sollins, Massachusetts Institute of Technology
Thomas Spacek, Bell Communications Research
Padmanabhan Srinagesh, Bell Communications Research
Gilbert Staffend, Allied Signal Automotive
Mark Stahlman, New Media Associates Incorporated
Ross Stapleton-Gray, D.C. Charter, Internet Society
Robert Steele, Boeing Information Services
Rupert Stow, Rupert Stow Associates
Edmond Thomas, NYNEX Science and Technology Incorporated
Jack Thompson, Gnostech Incorporated
Suzanne P. Tichenor, Council on Competitiveness
Frank Tong, IBM T.J. Watson Research Center
John C. Toole, National Coordinating Office for High Performance
    Computing and Communications
William Turnbull, National Coordinating Office for High Performance
    Computing and Communications/National Oceanographic and
    Atmospheric Administration
Leslie L. Vadasz, Intel Corporation
Hal Varian, University of California at Berkeley
Shukri Wakid, National Institute of Standards and Technology
Stuart Wecker, Symmetrix Incorporated
Stephen B. Weinstein, NEC USA Incorporated
Allan H. Weis, Advanced Network and Services Incorporated
Thomas E. Wheeler, Cellular Telecommunications Industry Association
Walter Wiebe, Federal Networking Council
Steven S. Wildman, Northwestern University
Roxanne Williams, Department of Agriculture
Michael Winter, Department of Transportation
Hank Wolf, IEEE-USA Committee on Communications and Information
    Policy
Stephen S. Wolff, Cisco Systems Incorporated
Ronald Zellner, Texas A&M University
Stephen Zilles, Adobe Systems Incorporated

FORUM AGENDA

Monday, May 22, 1995

6:00 p.m.   Reception

7:00 p.m.   Dinner Speech: *Mark Stahlman*, New Media Associates

Tuesday, May 23, 1995

8:30 a.m.   Welcoming Remarks: *Suzanne Woolsey*,
              National Research Council
            Overview: *Lewis M. Branscomb*, Forum Chair
            Keynote Address: *Arati Prabhakar*, Director,
              National Institute of Standards and Technology

9:00 a.m.   NII 2000: Is the Future Now?
            Moderator: *Robert W. Lucky*, Bell Communications
            Research
            Participants:
              Edward D. Horowitz, Viacom Incorporated
              Peter W. Huber, Manhattan Institute for Policy Research
              David G. Messerschmitt, University of California at Berkeley
              Quincy Rodgers, General Instrument Corporation

10:40 a.m. Reaching the End User
            Moderator: *Leslie L. Vadasz*, Intel Corporation
            Participants:
              Paul E. Green, Jr., IBM T.J. Watson Research Center
              Irene Greif, Lotus Development Corporation
              Leonard Kleinrock, University of California at Los Angeles
              J. Graham Mobley, Scientific-Atlanta Incorporated
              Michael North, North Communications
              Hal Varian, University of California at Berkeley

1:00 p.m.   Technology Deployment: Investment and Experimentation

            Wireline Communications
            Moderator: *James A. Chiddix*, Time Warner Cable
            Participants:
              Wendell B. Bailey, National Cable Television Association
              Tim Clifford, DynCorp (formerly with Sprint Corporation)
              Joel Engel, Ameritech
              Richard R. Green, Cable Television Laboratories
                Incorporated
              Mahal Mohan, AT&T Corporation

> *Stewart D. Personick*, Bell Communications Research
> *Robert S. Powers*, MCI Telecommunications Corporation
> *John C. Redmond*, GTE Laboratories
> *Gail Garfield Schwartz*, Teleport Communications Group
> *Edmond Thomas*, NYNEX Science and Technology
>   Incorporated

2:45 p.m.   Wireless Communications
> Moderator: *Joseph A. Flaherty*, CBS Incorporated
> Participants:
> *D. Joseph Donahue*, Thomson Consumer Electronics
>   Incorporated
> *Mary Madigan*, Personal Communications Industry
>   Association
> *John Major*, Motorola Incorporated
> *James C. McKinney*, Advanced Television Systems
>   Committee
> *Robert Roche*, Cellular Telecommunications Industry
>   Association

4:00 p.m.   Emerging Architecture
> Moderator: *David D. Clark*, Massachusetts Institute of
> Technology
> Participants:
> *Jonathan Band*, Morrison and Foerster
> *Robert T. Blau*, BellSouth Corporation
> *Kevin Kahn*, Intel Corporation
> *Andrew Lippman*, Massachusetts Institute of Technology
> *Padmanabhan Srinagesh*, Bell Communications Research

Wednesday, May 24, 1995

8:30 a.m.   Recap of Tuesday Session: *Lewis M. Branscomb*,
>   Forum Chair
> Perspectives from the TPWG: *Duane A. Adams*,
>   Technology Policy Working Group

9:00 a.m.   Doing Business on the NII

> Technical Requirements (Application-Related Standards
>   and Beyond)
> Moderator: *Donald W. Simborg*, KnowMed Systems

Participants:
W. Ed Hammond, Duke University Medical Center
James H. Keller, Harvard University
Lois Clark McCoy, National Institute for Urban Search
   and Rescue
Linda G. Roberts, Department of Education
Thomas C. Rochow, McDonnell Douglas Corporation

Business and Protection Issues
Moderator: *Cynthia H. Braddon,* The McGraw-Hill
   Companies
Participants:
Robert W. Crandall, Brookings Institution
Michael D. Greenbaum, Bell Atlantic Corporation
Allan M. Schiffman, Terisa Systems/CommerceNet
Donald W. Simborg, KnowMed Systems
Steven S. Wildman, Northwestern University

1:00 p.m.   The Internet: A Model
             Moderator: *Richard T. Liebhaber,* MCI Communications
                Corporation
             Participants:
             Ross S. Glatzer, Prodigy Services Company (retired)
             Daniel C. Lynch, Interop Company and Cybercash
                Incorporated
             Milo Medin, @Home
             Allan H. Weis, Advanced Network and Services
                Incorporated
             Stephen S. Wolff, Cisco Systems Incorporated

2:30 p.m.   Forks in the Road: Private Sector Uncertainties/
             Public Policy Realities
             Moderator: *Irene Greif,* Lotus Development Corporation
             Questions From the Audience: Q & A Finale
                • Where are the inconsistencies?
                • Where is the best business case?
                • Is all the technology here yet?
                • What more would you like to hear?

4:30 p.m.   Adjournment with Request for Additional White Papers
             and Comments

C

Call for White Papers (Abridged)

The NII 2000 Steering Committee—a group of high-level executives and distinguished academicians—seeks white papers from academia, businesses, foundations, industry, interest groups, trade associations, and other interested parties on topics relevant to NII technology deployment. The steering committee is charged by the Technology Policy Working Group (TPWG) of the federal Information Infrastructure Task Force with a year-long course of activities to develop a baseline understanding regarding what technologies are to be deployed when, where, and by whom. The project is being coordinated by the Computer Science and Telecommunications Board (CSTB) and is drawing upon inputs from multiple industries, sectors, organizations, and individual experts. A list of NII 2000 Steering Committee members is attached.

All white papers will be made available to federal NII decision makers and be considered for discussion at a Spring Forum in Washington, D.C., May 23–24, 1995. White paper authors will have the opportunity to revise their papers after the Spring Forum. All papers—regardless of whether they are selected for discussion at the Spring Forum—will be presented to the government and will contribute to the Steering Committee's final NII 2000 report to the TPWG and the public.

RESPONDING TO THE CALL

In keeping with its charge, the NII 2000 Steering Committee seeks properly documented discussions with quantitative evidence/analysis on technical, financial, and economic aspects of technology deployment issues and prospects for the next 5 to 7 years. Issues of particular interest to the steering committee include the following:

1. Architecture and Facilities

- Bandwidth capacity available to and from government (all levels), corporations (domestic and international), small businesses, and residences; also mobile users of portable platforms
- Interoperability and openness: dimensions, barriers, and facilitators
- Interactivity and symmetry (i.e., relative support for two-way communication)
- Internetworking and interconnection regarding different kinds of networks and services
- Public networks, private networks, virtual private networks

2. Enabling Technologies (e.g., end-user devices, interfaces, and protocols)

3. Recovery of Carrier Costs (facilities and/or services) in an Open-network Environment

4. Middleware Technologies/Capabilities: (e.g., mechanisms such as digital signatures, encryption or search agents that protect intellectual property, privacy, security; directory services)

5. Applications

- Expected capabilities for digital libraries, distributed collaboration, software agents, "smart cards," telecommuting, video delivery (on-demand and near-on-demand), multimedia services
- Expected attributes and implementation of electronic kiosks/public access facilities
- Technology deployment issues affecting a particular domain (e.g., education, finance, manufacturing, transportation), which may have implications for other domains (e.g., establishing standards in health care)
- Critical hardware and/or software interface features, requirements, and standards

6. Equitable Access and Public Service Obligations (relative costs and implementation rates)

7. Research and Development (i.e., critical areas for future projects in device, software, and systems research; also private sector trends and priority areas for government-funded research)

FORMAT REQUIREMENTS SUMMARY

• Papers should begin with a brief statement of a problem and concentrate on analysis and forecast (5- to 7-year horizon) of deployment issues and key factors, including sources of uncertainty, contingencies, barriers, and facilitators. Conclusions should concisely state the business case for a given deployment effort and any implications for public policy.

• Submissions should be double-spaced and should not exceed 6,250 words (approx. 25 pages).

• All papers must be signed by a principal and accompanied by a signed NRC copyright release agreement.

• Statistics must be referenced; cites should be formatted as endnotes.

COMPUTER SCIENCE AND TELECOMMUNICATIONS BOARD

Established by the National Academy of Sciences in 1916, the National Research Council (NRC) is the federal government's principal advisor on science and technology issues. The NRC conducts its work primarily by convening experts (serving pro bono) on a given issue. Within the NRC, the CSTB oversees technology and policy projects related to information infrastructure and similar topics.

WHITE PAPER CRITERIA AND FORMAT

Criteria

To the degree relevant, each paper should:

• Distinctly frame a problem/issue related to NII technology deployment;

• Make a projection regarding that problem/issue over the next 5 to 7 years;

• Provide a comprehensive baseline and status report of key developments related to that problem or issue;

• Assess the interaction between technical and nontechnical (legal/regulatory, economic, social) factors;

• Identify contingencies and uncertainties related to investment and deployment of new technologies;

• Identify key applications, enabling technologies, and capabilities;

- Identify classes of users to be served, noting (a) which users may be served most easily or quickly, (b) which users are more difficult to serve (and why), and (c) market ramp-up expectations and determinants;
- When using terms such as "interactive," "open," "scalable," provide a short definition or context for understanding how those terms are being used; and
- Identify possible public, private, or public/private sector responses.

Format

A. Statement of the Problem

Each paper should provide a 1 to 2 paragraph statement of the particular technology deployment issue.

B. Background (approximately 4 to 5 pages)

This section should provide a baseline understanding of the technology, service, industry, domain, or issue in question, and define terms. A picture of the current "state-of-play" should emerge from the section.

C. Analysis and Forecast (approximately 12 to 15 pages)

This third section is the heart of the paper and as such, should look at some of the broad factors (economic, legal/regulatory, social, technical) influencing deployment decisions. In particular, authors should (to the extent relevant) (a) identify contingencies and uncertainties affecting investment decisions, (b) discuss factors used by the industry/domain in making the business case for a new technology, and (c) make projections regarding the next 5 to 7 years. This section should also include a discussion of barriers to resolving any outstanding problems/issues.

D. Recommendations (approximately 3 to 4 pages)

In this final section, authors should state whether and how the problem(s) identified can best be addressed by the private sector, the public sector, or by a cooperative effort between the two.

E. Additional Resources (optional)

A listing of relevant documents, analyses, forecasts is welcome. Authors may attach these source materials as appendices.

D

White Papers Received

Mark R. Abbott (Oregon State University), "The National Information Infrastructure and the Earth Sciences: Possibilities and Challenges"

Robert J. Aiken and John S. Cavallini (U.S. Department of Energy), "Government Services Information Infrastructure Management"

Allan J. Arlow (telecommunications consultant, Annapolis, Md.), "Cutting the Gordian Knot: Providing the American Public with Advanced Universal Access in a Fully Competitive Marketplace at the Lowest Possible Cost"

Wendell Bailey (National Cable Television Association) and James Chiddix (Time Warner Cable), "The Role of Cable Television in the NII"

Jonathan Band (Morrison and Foerster, Washington, D.C.), "Competing Definitions of 'Openness' on the GII"

Richard C. Barth (Motorola Incorporated), "Communications for People on the Move: A Look into the Future"

Robert T. Blau (BellSouth Corporation), "Building the NII: Will the Shareholders Come (And If They Don't, Will Anyone Really Care?)"

Gregory Bothun (University of Oregon), Jim Elias (U S West Communications), Randolph G. Foldvik (U S West Communications), and Oliver McBryan (University of Colorado), "The Electronic Universe: Network Delivery of Data, Science, and Discovery"

Jill Boyce, John Henderson, and Larry Pearlstein (Hitachi America Ltd.), "An SDTV Decoder with HDTV Capability: An All-Format ATV Decoder"

Lewis M. Branscomb and Jim Keller (Harvard University), "NII and Intelligent Transportation Systems"

Hans-Werner Braun and Kimberly Claffy (San Diego Supercomputer Center), "Post-NSFNET Statistics Collection"

Charles N. Brownstein (Cross-Industry Working Team), "NII Roadmap: Residential Broadband"

Vito Brugliera (Zenith Electronics), James A. Chiddix (Time Warner Cable), D. Joseph Donahue (Thomson Consumer Electronics), Joseph A. Flaherty (CBS Inc.), Richard R. Green (Cable Television Laboratories), James C. McKinney (ATSC), Richard E. Ottinger (PBS), and Rupert Stow (Rupert Stow Associates), "The NII in the Home: A Consumer Service"

Donald P. Brutzman, Michael R. Macedonia, and Michael J. Zyda (Naval Postgraduate School), "Internetwork Infrastructure Requirements for Virtual Environments"

John S. Cavallini and Mary Anne Scott (U.S. Department of Energy) and Robert J. Aiken (U.S. Department of Energy/Lawrence Livermore National Laboratory), "Electric Utilities and the NII—Issues and Opportunities"

David D. Clark (Massachusetts Institute of Technology), "Interoperation, Open Interfaces, and Protocol Architecture"

Tim Clifford (DynCorp), "Service Provider Interoperability and the National Information Infrastsructure"

Robert W. Crandall (Brookings Institution), "Funding the National Information Infrastructure: Advertising, Subscription, and Usage Charges"

D. Joseph Donahue (Thomson Consumer Electronics), "NII in the Home"

H. Allen Ecker and J. Graham Mobley (Scientific-Atlanta Inc.), "The Evolution of the Analog Set-Top Terminal to a Digital Interactive Home Communications Terminal"

Dennis W. Elliott and Norman Abramson (ALOHA Networks Inc.), "Spread Aloha Wireless Multiple Access: The Low-Cost Way for Ubiquitous, Tetherless Access to the Information Infrastructure"

Joel S. Engel (Ameritech), "Plans for Ubiquitous Broadband Access to the National Information Infrastructure in the Ameritech Region"

Maria Farnon (Tufts University), "How Do Traditional Legal, Commercial, Social, and Political Structures, When Confronted with a New Service, React and Interact?"

Charles H. Ferguson (Vermeer Technologies Inc.), "The Internet, the World Wide Web, and Open Information Services: How to Build the Global Information Infrastructure"

Francis Dummer Fisher (University of Texas at Austin), "Organizing the Issues"

Richard Friedman and Sean Thomas (University of Wisconsin), "The Argument for Universal Access to the Health Care Information Infrastructure: The Particular Needs of Rural Areas, the Poor, and the Underserved"

David A. Garbin (MITRE Corporation), "Toward a National Data Network: Architectural Issues and the Role of Government"

Oscar Garcia (submitted for the IEEE Computer Society), "Statement on National Information Infrastructure Issues"

Joseph Gitlin (Johns Hopkins University), "Proposal for an Evaluation of Health Care Applications on the NII"

Ross Glatzer (Prodigy Services, retired), "The Internet: A Model: Thoughts on the Five-Year Outlook"

Jiong Gong and Padmanabhan Srinagesh (Bell Communications Research), "The Economics of Layered Networks"

Marjorie Green (First Washington Associates), "As We May Work: An Approach Toward Collaboration on the NII"

Paul E. Green, Jr. (IBM T.J. Watson Research Center), "Making Fiber Optic Bandwidth Available to End Users"

Richard R. Green (Cable Television Laboratories Inc.), "Cable Television Technology Deployment"

Michael D. Greenbaum (Bell Atlantic) and David Ticoll (Alliance for Emerging Technologies), "Privacy, Access and Equity, Democracy, and Networked Interactive Media"

W. Ed Hammond (Duke University Medical Center), "The Use of the Social Security Number as the Basis for the National Citizen Identifier"

Peter W. Huber (Manhattan Institute), Boban Mathew (Yale University), and John Thorne (Bell Atlantic), "Estimating the Costs of Telecommunications Regulation"

Kevin C. Kahn (Intel Corporation), "Residential PC Access: Issues with Bandwidth Availability"

Randy H. Katz (University of California at Berkeley), William L. Scherlis (Carnegie Mellon University), and Stephen L. Squires (Advanced Research Projects Agency), "The National Information Infrastructure: A High Performance Computing and Communications Perspective"

Leonard Kleinrock (University of California at Los Angeles), "Nomadic Computing and Communications"

Mary Madigan (Personal Communications Industry Association), "NII 2000: The Wireless Perspective"

Robert M. Mason, Chester Bowling, and Robert J. Niemi (Case Western Reserve University), "Small Manufacturing Enterprises and the National Information Infrastructure"

Lois Clark McCoy and Douglas Gillies (National Institute for Urban Search and Rescue) and John Harrald (NIUSR and George Washington University), "Architecture for an Emergency Lane on the NII: Crisis Information Management"

John C. McDonald (MBX Inc.), "Aspects of Integrity in the NII"

David G. Messerschmitt (University of California at Berkeley), "What the NII Could Be: A User Perspective"

Avram Miller and Ogden Perry (Intel Corporation), "Role of the PC in Emerging Information Infrastructures"

Mahal Mohan (AT&T Corporation), "NII Evolution—Technology Deployment Plans, Challenges, and Opportunities: AT&T Perspective"

Reagan W. Moore (San Diego Supercomputer Center), "Enabling Petabyte Computing"

Organization for the Protection and Advancement of Small Telephone Companies (OPASTCO), "Private Investment and Federal National Information Infrastructure (NII) Policy"

Tom Perrine (San Diego Supercomputing Center), "Thoughts on Security and the NII"

Stewart D. Personick (Bell Communications Research), "Trends in Deployments of New Telecommunications Services by Local Exchange Carriers in Support of an Advanced National Information Infrastructure"

Robert S. Powers (MCI Telecommunications Inc.), Tim Clifford (DynCorp), and James M. Smith (Competitive Telecommunications Association), "The Future NII/GII—Views of Interexchange Carriers"

J.C. Redmond, C.D. Decker, and W.G. Griffin (GTE Laboratories Inc.), "Technology in the Local Network"

Robert F. Roche (Cellular Telecommunications Industry Association), "Recognizing What the NII Is, What It Needs, and How to Get It"

Thomas C. Rochow, George E. Scarborough, and Frank David Utterback (McDonnell Douglas Corporation), "Electronic Integrated Product Development as Enabled by a Global Information Environment: A Requirement for Success in the Twenty-First Century"

Quincy Rodgers (General Instrument Corporation), "Interoperability, Standards, and Security: Will the NII Be Based on Market Principles?"

Russell I. Rothstein and Lee McKnight (Massachusetts Institute of Technology), "Technology and Cost Models of Connecting K-12 Schools to the National Information Infrastructure"

David Schell, Lance McKee, and Kurt Buehler (Open GIS Consortium), "Geodata Interoperability—A Key NII Requirement"

Daniel Schutzer (Citibank), "Electronic Commerce"

Gail Garfield Schwartz and Paul E. Cain (Teleport Communications Group), "Prospects and Prerequisites for Local Telecommunications Competition: Public Policy Issues for the NII"

John W. Thompson, Jr. (GNOSTECH Incorporated), "The Awakening 3.0: PCs, TSBs, or DTMF-TV: Which Telecomputer Architecture Is Right for the Next Generations' Public Network?"

Gio Wiederhold (Stanford University), "Effective Information Transfer for Health Care: Quality versus Quantity"

Ronald D. Zellner, Jon Denton, and Luana Zellner (Texas A&M University), "Integrating Technology with Practice: A Technology-enhanced Field-based Teacher Preparation Program"

Ziebarth, John P. (National Center for Supercomputing Applications), W. Neil Thompson (U.S. Nuclear Regulatory Commission), J.D. Nyhart (Massachussetts Institute of Technology), Kenneth Kaplan (Massachusetts Institute of Technology), Bill Ribarsky (Georgia Institute of Technology), Gio Wiederhold (Stanford University), Michael R. Genesereth (Stanford University), Kenneth Gilpatric (consultant to National Performance Review NetResults.Regnet; formerly with Administrative Conference of the United States), Tim E. Roxey (National Performance Review RegNet.Industry, Baltimore Gas and Electric, and Council for Excellence in Government), William J. Olmstead (U.S. Nuclear Regulatory Commission), Ben Slone (Finite Matters Ltd.), Jim Acklin (Regulatory Information Alliance), "REGNET: An NPR Regulatory Reform Initiative Towards NII/GII Collaboratories"

Stephen N. Zilles and Richard Cohn (Adobe Systems Incorporated), "Electronic Document Interchange and Distribution Based on the Portable Document Format, an Open Interchange Format"

E

NII 2000 Liaisons

Andrew Blau, Benton Foundation
Michael Borrus, Berkeley Roundtable on the International Economy
Fiona Branton, Computer Systems Policy Project
Charles N. Brownstein, Corporation for National Research Initiatives/
    Cross-Industry Working Team
Daniel F. Burton, Council on Competitiveness
Ty Carter, American Bankers Association
Ed Fouhy, Pew Center for Civic Journalism
Paul Hart, United States Telephone Association
Ted Heydinger, Information Technology Industry Council
Lincoln Hoewing, Bell Atlantic
Suzanna Hoppszallern, American Hospital Association
Laurie Itkin, National Conference of State Legislatures
Mary Gardiner Jones, Alliance for Public Technology
Jeffrey Joseph, U.S. Chamber of Commerce
Robert Kahn, Corporation for National Research Initiatives
Linda Laskowski, U S West Communications
Doug Miller, Software Publishers Association
Jennifer Miller, International Communications Industry Association
William Morin, National Association of Manufacturers
Paul Evan Peters, Coalition for Networked Information
David Peyton, Information Technology Association of America
Carol Risher, Association of American Publishers

Michael M. Roberts, EDUCOM
Deborah Rudolph, Institute for Electrical and Electronics Engineers
Ellen Schned, Viacom International
Robert Smith, Jr., Interactive Services Association
Roger Smith, American Electronics Association
Casmir Skrzypczak, NYNEX Corporation
Suzanne P. Tichenor, Council on Competitiveness
Frederick Weingarten, The Computer Research Association
Eric Wolferman, Newspaper Association of America
Mark Zalewski, X.9 Financial Services

F

Letter from Vice President Albert Gore
March 6, 1995

Dear Dr. Branscomb:

On behalf of the Administration, I want to thank you for the work that you and your colleagues are doing in connection with the National Research Council's "NII 2000" Committee.

There is one issue that the Administration is particularly interested in that I hope the Committee can shed some light on. Although the Administration's NII policy is technology neutral, we would like to see an NII that allows individuals to be producers as well as consumers of information, that enables "many to many" communication, and that provides a "general purpose" infrastructure capable of supporting a wide range of services.

The NRC's previous report on the NII, *Realizing the Information Future,* concluded that some U.S. companies may invest in an infrastructure that is capable of providing one-way video delivery but not a broader range of services. For this reason, it would be very helpful to have an objective assessment of the capabilities of different residential broadband architectures (e.g., hybrid fiber-coax, fiber-to-the-curb, wireless alternatives) being deployed by the private sector. The NRC could select a representative sample of applications and services (videoconferencing, high-speed access to the Internet or other on-line services, telecommuting, distance learning, grassroots electronic publishing) and determine whether the broadband architectures under consideration will be capable of supporting these applications.

Clearly, market considerations will drive the technology and architectural decisions of U.S. telecommunications providers. Futhermore, a network that may originally support a limited range of services can be incrementally upgraded in response to consumer demand. The Administration has absolutely no interest in mandating a particular technology. This would be completely contrary to the Administration's NII philosophy.

However, we are interested in working cooperatively with industry and academia to promote a shared vision of a versatile, general purpose infrastructure with a "Jeffersonian" architecture. We would welcome any concrete suggestions the Committee may have for advancing these goals.

Thank you again for your work on this important NRC Committee.

Sincerely,

(signed)

Al Gore

G

Acronyms and Abbreviations Used

ACS	access control and security
ADSL	asymmetric digital subscriber line
ARDIS	Advanced Radio Data Information Service
ARPA	Advanced Research Projects Agency
ATIS	Alliance for Telecommunications Industry Solutions
ATM	asynchronous transfer mode
ATV	Advanced Television
BDSL	broadband digital subscriber line
BTA	basic trading area
CAT	Committee on Applications and Technology
CDMA	code-division multiple access
CDPD	cellular digital packet data
CIC	Committee on Information and Communications
CNRI	Corporation for National Research Initiatives
COC	Council on Competitiveness
COMPLEC	competitive local exchange carrier
CPU	central processing unit
CSPP	Computer Systems Policy Project
CSTB	Computer Science and Telecommunications Board
CTIA	Cellular Telecommunications Industry Association

DBS	direct broadcast satellite
DET	digital entertainment terminal
DOD	Department of Defense
DOE	Department of Energy
DOS	Disk Operating System
EDI	electronic data interchange
EIA	Electronic Industries Association
FCC	Federal Communications Commission
FTTC	fiber to the curb
Gbps	gigabits per second
GII	global information infrastructure
GILS	Government Information Locator Service
GSM	Global System for Mobile Communications
GSSI	government services information infrastructure
GUI	graphical user interface
HCT	home communications terminal
HDSL	high-bit-rate digital subscriber line
HDTV	high-definition television
HFC	hybrid fiber coaxial cable
HPCCI	High Performance Computing and Communications Initiative
HTML	Hypertext Mark-up Language
IC	integrated circuit
IEEE	Institute for Electrical and Electronics Engineers
IETF	Internet Engineering Task Force
IISP	Information Infrastructure Standards Panel
IITF	Information Infrastructure Task Force
IMA	Interactive Multimedia Association
IP	Internet Protocol
IS	information systems
ISDN	Integrated Services Digital Network
ISP	Internet service provider
ITS	Intelligent Transportation System
ITU	International Telecommunications Union
IXC	interexchange carrier
kbps	kilobits per second

LAN	local area network
LATA	local access and transport area
LEC	local exchange carrier
LEO	low earth orbit
LMDS	local multipoint distribution service

MAN	metropolitan area network
Mbps	megabits per second
MIS	management information systems
MMDS	multichannel multipoint distribution service
MPEG	Motion Picture Experts Group
MSO	Multiple System Operator
MTA	major trading area

NAP	network access point
NASA	National Aeronautics and Space Administration
NATA	North American Telecommunications Association
NCTA	National Cable Television Association
NII	national information infrastructure
NIM	network interface module
NIST	National Institute of Standards and Technology
NSF	National Science Foundation
NTIA	National Telecommunications and Information Administration
NTSC	National Television System Committee

| ODN | Open Data Network |
| OTA | Office of Technology Assessment (U.S. Congress; closed 1995) |

PAL	phase alternation by line
PC	personal computer
PCIA	Personal Communications Industry Association
PCS	personal communication service
PDA	personal digital assistant
POP	point of presence
POTS	"plain old" telephone service

| QAM | quadrature amplitude modulation |
| QOS | quality of service |

| R&D | research and development |
| RBHC | regional Bell holding company |

RBOC	regional Bell operating company
RTIF	*Realizing the Information Future* (CSTB, 1994b)
SDTV	standard definition television
SECAM	sequential *couleur avec memoire*
SMDS	switched multimegabit data service
SME	small manufacturing enterprise
SONET	Synchronous Optical NETwork
SQL	Structured Query Language
STB	set-top box
STT	set-top terminal
TCP	Transmission Control Protocol
TDMA	time-division multiple access
TPWG	Technology Policy Working Group
TV	television
URL	universal resource locator
VAN	value-added network
VBI	vertical blanking interval
VPN	virtual private network
VSAT	very small aperture terminal
VSB	vestigial side band
WAN	wide area network
WINF	WINForum; Wireless Information Networks Forum
WWW, Web	World Wide Web